TIME'S UP!

A Memoir of the American Century

BY

Robert Cabot

INTRODUCTION BY
ROBERT W. FULLER

McPherson & Company
KINGSTON, NEW YORK
2019

Published by McPherson & Company, Publishers
Post Office Box, 1126, Kingston, New York 12402.
WWW.MCPHERSONCO.COM
Designed by Bruce R. McPherson
Typeset in Minion Pro
First edition 2019
1 3 5 7 9 10 8 6 4 2

Library of Congress Publishing-in-Publication Data

Names: Cabot, Robert, author. | Fuller, Robert W. (Robert Works), 1936–
writer of introduction.
Title: Time's up! : a memoir of the American century / by Robert Cabot ;
introduction by Robert W. Fuller.
Other titles: Memoir of the American century
Description: First edition. | Kingston, New York : McPherson & Company, [2019]
Identifiers: LCCN 2018046589 | ISBN 9781620540367 (alk. paper)
Subjects: LCSH: Cabot, Robert. | Authors, American--20th century--Biography |
United States--Civilization--20th century--Anecdotes. | Upper
class--Massachusetts--Boston--Biography. | Cabot family. |
Diplomats--United States--Biography | Counterculture--United
States--Biography. | Cabot, Robert--Travel. | United States. Army. Signal
Corps--Biography. | World War, 1939-1945--Personal narratives, American.
Classification: LCC PS3553.A28 A3Z46 2019 | DDC 813/.54 [B] --dc23
LC record available at https://lccn.loc.gov/2018046589

NOTE: Some of the passages regarding my experiences of World
War Two are revisions of passages from my quasi-autobiographical
novel, *The Isle of Khería*.

Frontispiece: At Maxwelton Lagoon, Whidbey Island, 2014,
photograph by Penny Cabot.

To :

My Family

My Friends

Contents

Introduction

I FOUND out what Robert Cabot was made of at 16,000 feet on the Karakoram Highway from Pakistan to China. The driver with whom we'd hitched a ride had stopped for the night near a dilapidated hut. Hoping to find bunks, I went in to discover nothing but a dirt floor. When I complained, Robert—then in his sixties—responded by stretching out under the stars on one of several old wooden benches near the hut, and suggesting that I do likewise.

I attributed Robert's unflappability to his having known the worst. When he turned eighteen, with reluctant parental permission he enlisted in the Army and was assigned to the Signal Corps. Throughout World War II—in London for MI training, then Africa, Corsica, the Southern France landing, the Battle of the Bulge, occupied Germany—he served in an independent, highly mobile company intercepting and deciphering enemy radio communications. This dangerous but critical mission meant spending much of the war close to the front in austere conditions. In comparison, a bench at high altitude alongside the Karakoram Highway was a piece of cake. Robert's stoic practicality reminded me of how soft my life had been when compared to those who, like him, had come of age in wartime and experienced its horrors first hand.

A biography of the great Italian-American physicist Enrico Fermi bears the title *The Last Man Who Knew Everything*. It's perhaps no more hyperbolic to describe Robert Cabot as "The Last Man to *Do* Everything."

By birth, Robert was an insider; by choice, he was an outsider. Within the Cabot Clan, he was seen as the "black sheep." Mid-career, still in his early thirties, he jettisoned his State Department job with the Marshall Plan—and subsequent economic aid programs in Italy, France, Thailand, and Ceylon—in favor of the chancy life of a writer. Time and again, he took risks uncommon among those born to privilege. In his first published book, *The Joshua Tree*, he gave voice to the incipient environmental movement. His travels, which include sailing solo across the Atlantic, are mirrored by a lifelong inward odyssey that has kept him young and fruitful.

In his tenth decade, Cabot paused to look at the arc of his life and to explore the relationship between his personal journey and the vicissitudes of twentieth-century America. I found the parallels illuminating and profound. Despite the existential threats that he recounts, the deep resonance between his story and America's gives reason to hope.

Robert W. Fuller
July 28, 2018

TIME'S UP!

Prologue

Why Now?

REMEMBERING A CENTURY—MINE AND MY COUNTRY'S.
America's hundred years in the sun—her brief global
predominance—fit loosely into the twentieth century. From
the vast expansion of the American Empire as the Victorian
century faded, to the beginning years of the twenty-first
century—America's ascendancy seems largely finished. Her
self-righteous, arrogant imperialism is fading. Her image of
leadership in seeking the ideal of true democracy, of social
justice, of universal human rights, of capitalism—the image
is tarnished. Her assumed role as benefactor and policeman of the world is increasingly illusory. Her destructive
consumerism and reckless greed for the planet's dwindling
resources are now facing their consequences and limits.
Her productive genius, her supremacy in the sciences and
technology are now met by effective competition. Her military might seems increasingly inappropriate when dealing
with the new realities of international, intranational, and
ideological conflicts, with insurgencies, terrorism, rogue
nuclear threats, nuclear warfare, and overshadowing all, the
approaching nightmare of global warming.

America's dollar as the global reserve currency is under

assault. Her role as keeper of the global purse has been exposed as gravely mismanaged. With an increasingly dysfunctional government, and the democratic process seriously weakened, the real control is evermore in the hands of unregulated multinational corporations, lobbyists, wealthy individuals given free rein by the Supreme Court to influence what is left of the democratic process, and extreme politicians across the spectrum. All too familiar signposts on a road to fascism. Is it only her language that is ever more dominant, the global lingua franca?

It was my century too. I return to it, to my memories of my world and a large part of my life, the swirls of attitudes and events and people around a long, privileged, and wildly varied American life. A memoir, though not a history, not an autobiography. As the American century, the 1900s, began to wind down, my life moved from active responses to events to an inner mode. These last decades—centered on family and friends, old and new, on writing several novels and this memoir—are referred to here, but in an autobiography they would be paramount, extolling the rich rewards of my life. And a caveat—memories happen in the present.

∽1∽

Puritan Remnants

I ENTERED America's century in 1924. World War I was over, Europe lay devastated, millions killed—a hundred thousand of them Americans. America had emerged vastly enriched, capitalism sanctified, and with a huge, growing, and largely unacknowledged empire.

Me just born, gums soon sucking on a silver spoon. Slaves, rum, opium, piracy, ruthlessness, hard work, entrepreneurial talent, astute marriages, luck, and thrift—that's where the spoon came from. The first Cabot to immigrate to America arrived from England in 1700, settling in Salem, by then a thriving port in the Massachusetts Bay Colony. This John Cabot soon became a prosperous merchant. His descendants continued as seafaring merchants and branched out into the very profitable businesses of legalized piracy, the slave trade, the rum trade, the Chinese opium trade, and well-chosen marriages. To wealth, to respectability—money, position, power—generations of it.

They left the sea, continued largely as entrepreneurs, though there were some notable doctors, a politician or two. It was dominantly a male ethos with dutiful women. Marriages were careful—no racial mixing, no Catholics, no southern Europeans, no Jews, no non-whites. No prodigals, no spendthrifts, no failures—that I know of—for more than a century. Nor, with some exceptions, did these Cabots fit the stereotype of the Boston Brahmin—the highly educated intellectuals, the humanists, men and women of arts and letters, with permissible leisure—albeit a leisure enabled by the sweat and sufferings of the masses of immigrants, slaves, and the rape of the native populations. No, the Cabots were largely Philistines and political conservatives. My father, his father, others in the line, were industrialists, players in the immense creation of American wealth. These men's wives were generally supportive but suppressed.

Another piece of the genes of this family was cult-like Puritan morality and a powerful work ethic. My father, his father—brilliant scientific minds, phenomenal memories— they were driven men, working, traveling, adventuring virtually until they died—my grandfather at one hundred and one, my father at ninety-eight.

The moral extremist was my paternal grandfather. His was a principal voice in Boston's Watch and Ward Society, a small group of self-appointed censors who previewed books and films—salaciously, one would guess—and banned many, much to the delight of the rest of the world, for to be banned-in-Boston was a great sales boost. He was an excessive disciplinarian, unbending as a father and grandfather, self-righteous, tactless to the point of cruelty, rigidly abstemious. The novelist and journalist John Gunther, in reviewing a biography of him, wrote:

> Godfrey Cabot was a man who was all at once a demon, a monster, and a worthy citizen typical of his age and milieu…a revelation of the Puritan mentality…Thank goodness the species is extinct.

My father was not that extreme, but he too was racist to

My paternal grandparents: Godfrey Lowell Cabot and Maria Moors Cabot,
in the 1940s.

a degree, intolerant, with narrow measures of success. He
was quite ready to use his powers abusively on "lesser" folk.
Though he could be charming, even to those "lesser" people,
humiliation was his stock-in-trade.

My mother's family shared some of the work ethic, but
not the razor-sharp mind, the abuse of power, the disdain
of others' dignities. Her father and his brother started life
as destitute orphans. Both made good. Banking for one, the
other in manufacturing—shoes, including, we grandchildren were told, the copper-toed crush-proof boots for the
police force, allegedly giving us "cops." The two brothers
married two sisters, a pattern that was remarkably common
among their forebears. They retired comfortably at early
ages, the two families living together in the same home. Two
loving, non-judgmental families, unconcerned with making
their marks on the world—a world they seemed to largely
ignore—once they'd achieved genteel comfort.

My maternal grandparents, Louise and Louis Wellington, c. 1945.

My mother's family name was Wellington. It has a distinguished ring to it, but her parents were modest farmers, descendants of immigrants from an obscure English village, Wellington. Field Marshal Arthur Wellesley, hero of the Napoleonic wars, when awarded a title, chose to be the Duke of Wellington, where his Irish family owned some property, though he apparently visited the village only once in his life.

Winters, they lived in a graceful Bullfinch brick rowhouse on Beacon Hill, the house where I was born. Summers, the two families would move out of the city to their lovely historic house on a traditional farm with an old-time farming family to run it. Riding and carriage horses, a onehorse sleigh, bells and all—to the delight of my mother and her sisters. Two great Percheron workhorses, Sun and Moon. Cows in a hay barn under an enormous loft with mountains of hay to the rafters—to the delight of us grandchildren.

In sharp contrast to my father's side, the two families in which my mother grew up had considerable artistic taste. Her Uncle Arthur and his wife Tanta, childless until quite late in life, traveled widely in Europe, accumulating an impressive collection of antique furniture. They were all excellent pianists. My perhaps errant memory sees them sitting at two grand pianos playing eight-handed pieces.

My mother deeply but rather indiscriminately loved music. Not so my father. Music and most of art for him seemed to be inconsequential, even frivolous, bordering on immoral. Mother was a rudimentary pianist, but she loved to play and sing sentimental songs from popular musicals, and have sing-alongs with us of sweet tunes for children. "Leary the Lamplighter" and others are still sung at family reunions

My love for reading came from her. She read everything that came her way—again, it seems to me now, without much discrimination. She subscribed to the Book-of-the-Month Club for years and was a devoted member of a neighborhood ladies book-reading group, their Shakespeare Club. She would read aloud hour after hour to us children— winter evenings in front of the fire, our collie Lucky lying beside us, our father sitting at the other end of the living room reading Fortune magazine. She usually knitted while reading with her book on a music stand. She rarely looked at her flying fingers, though she used the awkward German method—which I can still manage. Dickens, Kipling, novel after novel, story after story. And she excelled at role-playing in her reading.

That role-playing and the novelists she chose to read were no doubt unconscious expressions of her distress at the inequalities and injustices that she observed everywhere. She had a deep reservoir of compassion, though her feelings were usually thwarted or suppressed as a result of the repressive Puritanism of her misogynous environment, and though the emotions she was able to express sometimes lapsed into awkward sentimentality. She bore a profound unease with privilege, even with the thought that privilege should be earnable.

Privilege. An obstacle or a gift? Branded by it or offered opportunity—effete or effective—cosseted or challenged. Dualities I would be dealing with throughout my life.

~2~

The Big Stick

M**Y COUNTRY** entered its century of ascendancy as a privileged adolescent with extraordinary human and natural resources. The immigrants who wrested the land from the Native Americans were ambitious, motivated, ready to take extreme risks to achieve freedom from the oppressions of their origins. Pragmatic, fiercely individualistic, self-reliant, often lawless, brutal, hyper-greedy. Yet they were largely gifted with highly educated leaders, many of them well-to-do land-owners and slave-owners, who pulled together a union—from colonies to federal states.

A union isolated by vast oceans from the debilitating dissensions of its European origins. A union that flourished. A union, though, that slaughtered the native populations and destroyed their civilizations, that enslaved vast numbers of Africans.

Estimates are that by 1853 when the trans-Atlantic slave trade was officially banished by international agreement, about 4,000,000 Africans who had been captured by slave traders died in captivity before being herded onto ships. Another 2,200,000 died on the Atlantic crossing. About 12,000,000 Africans arrived in the Americas. Of these, 650,000 arrived in what became the United States. Within the United States, active slave trading continued until emancipation in 1863. By then, 650,000 had become 4,000,000.

The estimates of pre-Columbian native populations in the areas that became the United States vary wildly. At the low end, there were perhaps a million. At least ninety percent of them succumbed at the hands of European colonizers— disease, wars, deliberate extermination, genocide. The last "Wild Man," Ishi, the sole survivor of his slaughtered tribe, turned himself in in 1911 to a rancher near Sacramento. Ishi ended up in a San Francisco museum showing school children how to shape arrow heads. In short order, he was killed by a white-man's disease. We had ethnically cleansed ourselves of Indians, herding survivors of the genocide into reservations, denying them automatic citizenship until 1924, but nevertheless drafting them to fight in our wars, with or without citizenship.

From the beginning, we were a union which flourished in its exploitation of seemingly limitless space, natural resources, and subjugated peoples. The original land area of the United States, land that had been brutally stolen from the often-welcoming Indians, and torn from European empires, in 1803 was more than doubled by the Louisiana Purchase. We bought the entire heartland of the continental United States from France for three cents an acre. When the agreement was made, Napoleon said:

> I have given England a maritime rival who sooner or later will humble her pride.

Most of the remaining third of what is now the contiguous forty-eight states—the West and Southwest—we stole from the Mexicans in a disgraceful cooked-up war in 1846. We had held off the British feint at her former American colonies in the War of 1812 and gave a further twist to the lion's tail of the British Empire in our brazen Pig War on San Juan Island in the Pacific Northwest.

In 1867, we bought Alaska from the economically stressed Russians—owners by declaration and occupation. With lies, cynical diplomacy, and a show of military might, we deposed the Queen and annexed Hawaii—after many of the original inhabitants had died of white-man's diseases. At the end of the nineteenth century, five of today's fifty states were still territories or colonial possessions, and the American empire was reaching further out across the oceans—while chastising European nations for their colonial expansions.

We grabbed Puerto Rico, Cuba, Guam, and the Philippines from Spain in another cooked-up war at the turn of that century. We colonized the Samoan Islands with Britain and Germany, and in 1900, made a deal with our co-colonizers, taking territorial possession of American Samoa. In 1903, we made a deal with Panama, setting up the American Panama Canal Zone. In 1917, we bought from the Danes what became the American Virgin Islands. After World War II, we took over the Marshall Islands under a United Nations mandate.

We sent the Marines into Central and South America dozens of times—and still do—enabling and protecting American corporations in the acquisition and exploitation of immense tracts of agricultural land primarily for growing bananas, coffee, and sugar cane for export.

From 1800 to 2000, the United States engaged in more than two hundred foreign military excursions. The twenty-first century is already adding rapidly to the total. By the end of the twentieth century, we owned or leased upwards of one thousand military bases in more than one hundred countries other than the U.S.—though it seems that even the Pentagon has difficulty with the arithmetic, and it attempts to keep many bases secret.

⌖

Manifest Destiny, Teddy Rossevelt's Big Stick, Go West Young Man, The Less Red Indians the Better—those were the slogans I learned early on. The globe of the world that I grew up with was predominantly pink—the British Empire—and much of the rest was splotched with the colors of the many European, Asian, and African empires. America's reach overseas seemed relatively minor, and to even refer to an American Empire was considered scandalous and un-American until quite recently. But minor our empire was not, even near the beginning of my hundred years, even before looking at our burgeoning economic, political, and cultural hegemony over most of the world.

An important aspect of the American hold on the world was our economic socio-cultural influence. Coca Cola was invented in 1886. Hollywood opened its first film studio in 1911. Henry Ford started producing cars in 1903, his first production-line Model T—the Tin Lizzie—came out in 1908. The first powered flight was in 1903 in North Carolina. Americans were to carry their products and culture worldwide, bringing their often rebellious origins, their frontiersman's energy, excitement, and success across oceans—and often their evangelistic, self-righteous, zeal—over-riding cultures and creating expectations and markets as they went.

They also carried with them their political idealism and achievements in governance. The success of the American colonies' revolt against Britain and the circumstance of the extraordinary wisdom of the Founding Fathers created a

"The Rough Riders" by Udo Keppler, from *Puck*, July 27, 1898.

system of government under a constitution that became the envy of, and a model for, much of the rest of the world. That Constitution, through most of my life, and I believe for most Americans throughout these hundred years, was as holy as the Bible. When my special American hero of that century, Franklin Delano Roosevelt, misguidedly attempted to monkey with its careful balance of powers with a plan to enlarge the Supreme Court and pack it with justices sharing his sympathies, Americans were deeply shocked and quickly killed the scheme. That there was not a similarly quick, effective response to the startling abuse of the Constitution in the first years of the twenty-first century, particularly with Bush v. Gore, is a sad coda to the American Century.

History moves on, and the dwindling of the American Empire and its overwhelming power may well be quite appropriate. But the corruption and loss of the American political and humanitarian ideal during the eight years of the George W. Bush presidency, with some hiatus under Obama, and a return to destruction under Trump as he sets out on the road to fascism? This is not the country we had hoped for. The subsequent growing dysfunction of our federal government, the deepening divisions of our body politic, and our failure to respond effectively and in a timely manner to global warming promise little for an American resurgence.

～3～

Coal-Gas Lights, Party-Line Phones, Thunder Mugs Under Our Beds

THOUGH I was not born until the third decade of the twentieth century, those first decades seem lodged in my memory too. Both my parents shared their earlier lives with us in great detail—photos, stories, places they still regularly revisited with us. And we were firmly Boston-based. America—and my family—was not on the move the way it is now.

The First World War was of enormous importance to us even as small children. I have no idea what role my mother's family played in that or in any of our twentieth century wars, but my paternal grandfather, though he was in his fifties, got himself a U.S. Navy commission and managed to assign himself to patrol for German submarines off Boston Harbor, piloting his own plane. He found none.

Throughout the war, my father was an Army Air Force biplane pilot teaching flying at Kelly Field, Texas. He was full of stories. I still see him demonstrating an Immelmann loop with his hands. He once showed us one of the pranks of the flying instructors. He had us freeze into an ice cube the ends of two pieces of string. We tied one string to a kite, the other to a little parachute we made to which was tied a teddy bear. It worked—a windy day, a half hour up in the sun, we taking turns on the line, and down floated Teddy. The pilot instructors had used a live cat.

He would say, defensively, that he was not sent to France because he was too good a pilot, too valuable as an instructor to be shot down "over there." Several parents of our schoolmates had vivid trench-warfare and prisoner-of-war stories to tell us. When I was eight or nine, my father took my brothers and me to a jittery sepia documentary movie being shown at a neighbor's house that emphasized the hypocrisy and brutality of the propaganda from both sides and the horrors of that "War-to-End-All-Wars." It made a deep impression on me. I still see the monstrous Hun chewing on a girl wrapped in an American flag, blood dripping down his chin, the British Tommy in death's throes, pierced through on a bayonet carried triumphantly by the spike-helmeted Kaiser.

There were profound transitions underway in those first two decades of the century, and there was much evidence in my early years of the contrasts. The town houses still had gas light fixtures as well as electricity. Telephones were novelties, often with cranks to ring through to an operator to whom you would announce the number you wished her to call for you, often on party lines which you shared with other subscribers, a source of much entertaining eavesdropping. Telegraphy was widely used, and we three brothers all learned Morse code, conversing around the world in dots and dashes on shortwave radios we cobbled together.

My father's mother drove—or was she driven?—in an electric car. A dying breed by then, it looked as if it really should be horse-drawn. My brothers and I fiddled with old Ford Model Ts and As, a decrepit Dodge, a decaying Pack-

A painting of my father, Lt. Thomas Dudley Cabot, 1918.

ard doomed to die in our inquisitive and careless hands. Electric streetcars, replacing the horsecars of the nineteenth century, ran hundreds of miles over much of New England. My father lifted me into the open cockpit of a float plane for a flight over a New Hampshire lake when I was five or six. During the thirties, there were still a few almost derelict sailing schooners plying the coast of New England, trading in coal and lumber, and much later in Boy Scouts.

Servants in the affluent quarters of the cities lived up back stairs in attics and worked in basement kitchens and in laundry and furnace rooms. Fifty-pound blocks of ice were carried in with tongs over an iceman's shoulder protected with an oily canvas. Coal for new-fangled central heating poured from horse-drawn wagons down metal shoots into ominous bins, clouds of coal dust seeping up through the houses.

For my first seven years, we lived in a rambling frame house—maybe it was a farm house once—in an inconspicuous suburb of Boston. I can still more or less draw the floor plan of that house. There was a good bit of land—a field, a copse of white oaks. A back laundry yard surrounded by a dark green lattice fence was a favorite place to climb for us three brothers, our collie Lucky tugging at our shoe strings. We weren't far from the Boston & Albany railroad track, commuter trains and freight trains sounding their lonely steam whistles at a nearby crossing. My first memory is of being wheeled in a baby carriage by our all-purpose Mary, my two older brothers trotting ahead. We later called Mary the Powerful Katrinka, a popular comic-strip character. Our cook was her sister Bella—two rough country girls from Scotland. Mary bossed our sweet and vulnerable mother mercilessly.

Bella was a meat-and-potatoes cook. Sundays, we three brothers would make toffee with her, pulling and doubling and re-pulling the warm goo many times, dusting it often with powdered sugar sprinkled thick on the kitchen table. When it got to the right stiffness, thick as a finger, in long strings that each of us was holding in arms outstretched, we'd cut it off with scissors into neat pieces onto a cookie tin to harden.

We would play house under that table, the leaves down, boxes to make walls and doors, cushions for beds. Alexa, Bella's daughter, a few years older than Louis, the oldest of us, looking on disdainfully or doing her homework in the corner.

Louis, Tommy, and Robby, one a year, then a five year pause and Mother gathered us around the piano in the living room of that first house and announced that we would soon have a little sister. An intrusion for the three of us, and sister Linda became the object of relentless brotherly tormenting from an early age.

My memory is that my older brothers would often leave me out of their doings. Yet even then I was quite comfortable with being left alone—early evidence of my enjoyment throughout my life of being often by myself.

In those years, we spent a part of every summer on a tiny primitive island on Lake Winnipesaukee in New Hampshire. A long day's drive in our Buick touring car, roof up in a rainstorm, cracked yellowing isinglass windows safety-pinned where the leaks were worst, the whole top flapping so we could hardly hear our father telling us, perhaps, the chemical processes of how steel is made. Two go-to-the-bathroom stops, and sandwiches, apples, cookies, lemonade. Off the main roads to cart paths, gates to open and close, cows looking on, out into fields. Stop at the big farmhouse for the keys, milk. On down to The Lake.

The Island was available through a friendship with the owner developed by my mother's parents and her uncle and aunt. The owner—as a child I often studied a framed photo of him in the living room of the large farmhouse that had once been his lakeside mansion—tall, dignified, in riding breeches, bushy gray sideburns. He was always referred to as Colonel Cummins. He had been a lieutenant colonel in a Vermont regiment that fought at Gettysburg. He owned a large estate, including the operating farm on the mainland, Spindle Point reaching far out into the lake, and Oak Island, later to be renamed Noël Island by sentimental Wellingtons. The mainland property had once been an elaborate Victorian spread—his sprawling home, guest cottages, enormous barns, carriage horses, Percherons, saddle horses. Fields leading down to the shore, a boat house that once sheltered a large steam yacht, a dock, a cobwebbed bowling alley which we still used once or twice a summer, a ridiculous stone fake lighthouse on the tip of Spindle Point—a plaque read something like, "For his Daughters, 1893, Chas. H. Cummins." Perhaps as a romantic retreat, on The Island he built a small house, two rooms only, the living room and the kitchen, and three small bedroom cottages.

By our time, the Cummins estate was considerably run down, no longer a Gay Nineties house-partying spot. Cracked and flaking orange trim on graying buildings, an empty boathouse but for one large rowboat. Still many cows, though, and the workhorses. I'm told that the whole place has disappeared—now houses everywhere, a bridge to our island, water skiers, golf courses, tennis, barbeques.

It took two trips in the rowboat to get us all and our

gear to The Island. Our parents would settle into one of the single-bedroom cottages, maybe a guest in the other. We children would sleep under mosquito nets on the porch of the two-room main house. A privy off in the woods with a Sears & Roebuck catalog for toilet paper, daddy-long-legs spiders by the dozen—or the handy thunder-mugs under our beds.. Lake water hand-pumped—drinking it without a thought—kerosene lanterns, ice that had been cut with huge one-man saws from the lake and stored through the summer under mounds of sawdust in the icehouse. Early morning rows for us three brothers—thwarts wet with dew, one of us steering with a canoe paddle, rowing back to the mainland farm to get fresh milk and cream and butter, maybe mail and a newspaper. Skinny diving off rocks into the Deep Hole, a tiny bit of sandy beach, reading in hammocks in the pine woods. It was a ten-minute walk from one side of that round island to the other.

Back: mother, Linda, father. Front: Tommy, myself, Louis. 1935

Camping on Spindle Point, canoeing. The SS Mount Washington, a paddle-wheeler, announcing itself with a faint blast of its horn from far across the lake as it passed the Spindle Point Lighthouse, its wake lapping our rocks many minutes later. Sleeping on our porch, the lake whispering on the ledge beneath us, a loon calling to the moon, "Indian Love Song" on Mother's crank-up gramophone, my loving parents drifting in their canoe under that moon.

Those were happy times for me, those summer weeks in my pre-teen years. Perhaps much of that was due to being in my mother's environment. Old-fashioned gentleness, kindness, lightness. But the loving side of my father was also more present. And that, in turn, might have stemmed from his slow recovery from many months spent on the edge of death. Delirious, lying in the dark in our suburban stone home—his screams, the doctors and nurses, Mother distraught but trying not to show it, we forever tip-toeing about. Some infection they couldn't locate or cure—long before sulfa drugs and antibiotics—until as a last resort they decided on exploratory surgery. They cut and cut into his abdomen, horizontally two thirds of the way around his entire body. They finally found and removed a massive leaking cyst.

Much of his recovery, they insisted, and he accepted, was to use his hands rather than his head. There on The Island, he would weave elaborate wicker baskets hour after hour. He would carve geometric creations out of long blocks of wood. Without cutting apart and gluing anything, he would transform them magically into links of a chain, which when finished would stretch out the block to three times its length. He would add a free-turning ball in its cage, a swivel joint, cork-screw spirals.

Where is all that now?

For those summer weeks, he became more accepting. He introduced us to the game of scouting. Opposing teams—we often had schoolmates or cousins visiting—creeping through the bushes trying to spy the enemy first. Call him out dead, and he'd have to slink off to the Graveyard. Creep on toward the enemy's fort, have I passed the Goal-Guard? Rise up, dash to…Goal! Goal! Goal! All in! It was more like a survival game than war. And I was good at it, better than my father, which he warmly acknowledged—to my grateful, embarrassed, and insincere denial.

Long walks, canoeing to Sally's Gut for a picnic. Camping, sleeping with our heads under the overturned canoe after an embarrassing and mystifying sex-ed talk, a morning jump into the lake, breakfast bacon burning as he filmed us drying by the campfire.

He taught us chess and knots—it was Mother who taught us card games and played board games with us. He would get us into spelling and geography games that were actually fun. He took over dish washing from Mother, but he never could manage to join in on one of Mother's sing-alongs.

The other half of our summers was quite a different matter. In Cohasset, on Massachusetts Bay an hour south of Boston, my father's favorite maternal uncle, John Moors, and Aunt Ethel moved every spring from posh, suburban Brookline to their enormous stone castle of a house back from and high above a rocky point where the seas would break spectacularly after a nor'easter. He was bedridden permanently with tuberculosis of the spine, they said. A wise, kind man, a thoughtful, conservative Republican, with a feisty redhead Socialist-inclining wife, the two forever arguing heatedly from opposite political points of view. When he died after World War II, she married an Englishman, Reverend Charles

Raven, Canon of Salisbury Cathedral and a controversial pacifist. She died on their honeymoon, age eighty-two—a gallant way to go. She bequeathed four million dollars to her black goddaughter. I found the Ethel Raven gravestone many years later in the Lyme Regis Cemetery.

Uncle John built a house for us on the far side of his extensive vegetable gardens and cow pastures. He admired my father's brilliant analytical mind and liked to have him around. During our summer weeks there, Father would commute by train to his Boston office. But he was an ardent sailor and had bought himself a second-hand Manchester Seventeen, Marconi-rigged racing sloop, joining the fleet of a dozen or so others in serious bi-weekly afternoon races. Wednesdays, when he would come home early from the office, and Saturdays. Uncle John spent hours every day wheeled out onto the balcony of his bedroom high on the sea side of his stone mansion. He would study the wind patterns and phone predictions to our father. And he followed the races closely with a telescope, the two of them joining for post-mortems after each race. The problem for me was that Father insisted that I join with my brothers in crewing for him. And he was a relentless, domineering skipper bent on winning. I was often terrified of him.

On the other hand, out from under his tyranny, I enjoyed sailing, still do. By the time I was eight, we three brothers each had a tiny seven foot sailing dinghy—Og, Gog, and mine was Magog. We joined the fleet of maybe a dozen of these Rookies, racing twice a week in and out of the yachts moored close together in Cohasset harbor, officiated over by the Captain of the Yacht Club, a cranky old-timer left over from the days of sailing ships. And just before we returned to our gloomy new stone house and school, we had a Chowder Race for the Rookie fleet when the tide was high enough to cover the miles of mudflats on the sides of the long dredged channel accessing the harbor. That race permitted us to add whatever rigs and sails we wished to our Rookies—bowsprits to carry jibs, spinnakers, one or two even tried square-s'ls on mini yardarms. We were closely followed by the Yacht Club's power boat, for there were many fun disasters.

The adults had their Chowder Race too, a handicap race for anything with sails, way out and down the coast, an anything-goes race too. And of course, a fish chowder feast at the Yacht Club when the last of us made it back.

We also spent a couple of weeks each summer on chartered sailing yachts—and later on a yawl my father had built in Maine—Depression cheap. We'd cruise to Maine, Nova Scotia, Cape Breton Island, and again he was often an unforgiving tyrant once we put to sea. We all were subjected to his tyranny, Mother most of all, though she got some protection by her seasick spells and her frequent headaches.

There were good times too. When we'd anchor and explore an island, take a plunge into icy Maine waters, the games of scouting on a rocky shore, charades after supper on board—The Game we called it. And we three often played three-handed bridge or hearts even while under sail—to the consternation of The Old Man, as we began to call him behind his back. He came down on me particularly, it seemed, because I would so often want to stay below to read during longer passages while the rest were on deck.

Good times too on the non-racing days in Cohasset. Nap-time after lunch, reading in a hammock. A walk through the pastures and vegetable gardens—stop for a few mouthfuls of red currants—and flower gardens for pinochle with Aunt Ethel. Games of badminton or croquet. The three of us building a small house as a dark-room for Louis's photography. Red Sox baseball games or big-band swing blasting on the car radio as we tooled about in our convertible Ford, drinking Coca Cola spiked with vanilla syrup, Alexa supposedly teaching Louis to drive, with Tommy and me bouncing in the rumble seat. Whatever became of rumble seats? On a convertible coupe, where the trunk would be now, was a sort of hatch door, which, when you pulled it open, became the back of a seat with room enough for two.

And all this summering went on during the height of the Depression. A large new stone house, a yacht, a European Grand Tour en famille, private schooling, two live-in servants (three with Bella's daughter Alexa), horses and fox-hunting, parents forever traveling and adventuring. Depression?—go figure. Privilege? Was I aware?—well, yes, but...

⌁

Our parents were determined and experienced outdoorsmen. Riding in the East, members of the fox-hunt club, pack tripping in the Rockies and Arizona's Superstition Mountains, rapid water canoeing, skiing, serious mountain climbing in the Alps, the Rockies. Not long before the Nazis invaded Poland and war began again, our father mounted an expedition with a team of scientists and mountaineers to make a first ascent of a 19,000 foot peak in Colombia's Sierra Nevada de Santa Marta, only to find, when they arrived in Colombia, that a Nazi expedition had arrived there just ahead of them. The Old Man's team made the ascent anyhow.

Our father and mother did a lot of conventional traveling too, often tying it in with business trips. There were murmurs among Mother's family, later reported to us, that we were left far too much in the charge of Mary and Bella and young Alexa.

Then there was Father's expedition on a chartered sailboat just after World War II to follow the directions of a detailed and apparently authentic map to a treasure buried on a mere sand bar of an island in the Caribbean. Mine detectors and all, but they said they found nothing but shells from U.S. Navy target practice.

My parents traveled often in Latin America. So far as I know, they never stayed at resorts. They, or at least he, were driven to less conventional recreations and adventure. Once they un-discovered an alleged mountain in Haiti. Some cartographer had estimated a major peak by extrapolating opposing slopes that, however, disappeared into a permanent cloud cover. It was on all the maps, but no, it wasn't there.

Another summer, again in the bottom of the Depression, we three brothers, our much younger sister, and a cousin were bundled with our parents into a seven-seater Dodge with a massive roof rack loaded with the necessaries. We boarded a Cunard liner, car and all, for Europe. Hiking in the Austrian Alps from hut to hut, kayaking on the Inn and the Enns, we three brothers copying the Heil Hitler of everyone who passed the Munich Beer Hall, bicycling in the Hague, glacier-skiing in the Italian Alps, grouse and rabbit shooting in Scotland. My one shot missed—the only time I've ever shot at a living creature.

I don't remember any museums or cathedrals or cultural events—well, maybe the Eiffel Tower and the Tower of London. The Grand Tour, but done their way, or at least his Cabotian way.

Thanksgivings and Christmases were huge family re-unions, first on the maternal side, and then the paternal, in large houses in Boston. Dozens of cousins, family games, turkeys, pies, a magician, charades, all the trappings. For me, except for the exciting drive into the city on a Common-wealth Avenue decorated with elaborate Christmas lights and decorations, these events were highly uncomfortable. I was low in self-esteem, shy, awkward among a sea of largely unfamiliar faces. And the contrasts of us haves to the mil-lions of suffering have-nots were deeply disturbing.

A pre-Christmas family ritual was my father's opening of the Christmas cards. He would have his secretary send out several hundred, some of which he would minimally personalize. Mother had no say in it that I could see. And a flood of mail would build up for weeks in a great cop-per bowl in our front hall. A few days before Christmas, he would gather us around a card table, Mother beside him. He would open each Christmas card and announce to us who it came from, why he—rarely she—was or was not impor-tant, how related to us, if at all—and that got complicated. Often Mother would not remember where or how they had met so-and-so. He would taunt and humiliate her for not remembering, particularly if it were an "important person", and she would cringe and belittle herself before us. Later, though, she would go through the cards and scissor off the fronts of the few she really liked, keeping them to send out to her own family and a few close friends the next year.

Radios were just coming in. My first, when I was maybe eight or nine, was a crystal set. I bought the parts with my ten-cents-a-week allowance. An antenna wire strung around my bedroom molding, well-hidden from parents, more wire coiled around a paper cup, a galena crystal lodged in a metal button, you'd clean it with Carbona—carbon tetrachloride, a deadly carcinogenic, it turned out much later. You'd poke a wire "cat's whisker" on a little arm into cracks of the crystal, fiddle with the coil, finding two or three different stations, if you were lucky, in your earphones. No house current, no batteries, just the power of the radio waves.

"The Lone Ranger," "The Shadow," "Little Orphan Annie," "Grand Central Station"—fifteen minute adventure serials flogging Ralston Cereal, Ovaltine, that kind of thing. And later Major Bowes's "Wheel of Fortune" ("...and where it stops no one knows"), Benny Goodman, Glen Miller. TV didn't show up in any substantial way till mid-century. I don't remember owning one until about 1967, long after it became enormously popular, I having resisted it for idiosyncratically lame reasons.

~4~

Alphabet Soup

I WAS BORN into the 'twenties—flapper days, the Charleston, Great Gatsby days, the economy on a roll. Republican presidents—Harding, Coolidge, and Hoover. A decade blind to the signs of looming economic disaster. During the 1928 presidential race, I was disciplined in kindergarten—while we shook milk in jars to make butter—for mindlessly shouting a Democratic slogan for Al Smith in a Republican Hoover-for-president-pure stronghold. Forewarnings, perhaps, of my many familial rebellions that even now persist.

Our father had largely supplanted his father in running their principal business, the manufacture of carbon black. Carbon black—pure carbon linked in colloidal form, soot, we'd call it—had been a minor product, used in ink and carbon paper, when my grandfather first started producing some in a shed in West Virginia, burning natural gas from nearby wells he had begun buying up. During World War I, it was discovered that if carbon black were added to rubber in large quantities, it would vastly improve rubber's durability. This opened an enormous and mushrooming market—tires. And it was relatively cheap and easy, in the early days, to make it. Natural gas, which was at first free in the Texas Panhandle, being flared off at oil wells to get rid of it, was simply burned in myriad small flames, starved of oxygen, under miles of moving metal sheets sliding over scrapers dropping the carbon black onto screw conveyers. A byproduct was blackish milk from local cows and permanent eye shadow for all the neighbors. The business flourished, keeping ahead of competition and eventually spreading around the globe—and into the Forbes Five Hundred.

Feeling flush, ignoring the signs of a dangerous economic bubble, our father bought eleven acres in a more exclusive suburb nearby. Construction of our imposing stone home actually began well after the 1929 crash—with cheap Italian laborers and masons, landscaped by a war-hero neighbor. How did he finance it in the midst of the Great Depression? A mystery.

We moved in shortly before the run on the banks that resulted in going off the gold standard. The gold bars that sat in Fort Knox, where are they now? Bank deposits were lost, the stock market tanked. Bankruptcies, foreclosures, suicides.

However, we, my family, somehow we did not go under.

As children, we were largely not directly affected by the Great Depression. The weekly handing to Mother of a tiny twenty-dollar gold coin for her household expenses stopped. Our parents tightened their belts. We children were protected in a safe family capsule.

But the impact of the Depression on the world around us was inescapable. The dole, the soup kitchens, the homeless, the begging, pitiful families knocking at our door for help, starvation, misery, Okies escaping the Dust Bowl. The Grapes of Wrath. The appeal of communism, the chicken-in-every-pot socialist movement, labor unions finally on the rise, the strikes.

Early in the Depression years, I became aware, even in

my insulated life, of extreme racism. Racially segregated schools, Jim Crow laws, Whites Only, poll taxes. The Ku Klux Klan, the burning crosses, the burning homes and churches, the many thousands of lynchings. Until 1967, interracial marriage was illegal in sixteen states.

Anti-Semitism was everywhere in our White-Anglo-Saxon-Protestant world. Jews, even the most famous, were not permitted in the best hotels and clubs. It crept into my own family. My father would speak of Jew-boys, and almost in the next breath would self-righteously declare that some of his best friends were Jews.

Shortly before I was born, the 18th Amendment to the U.S. Constitution was ratified prohibiting the sale and importation of "intoxicating liquors." The bigotry, hypocrisy, and futility of Prohibition—the speakeasy culture of illegal bars for those who could afford it, the bath-tub gin for others, the all-pervasive cynical disregard of law—were glaringly evident. Organized crime—Lucky Luciano, John Dillinger, Al Capone, the godfathers—was given an enormous boost from the made-to-order folly of Prohibition. In 1933, the American electorate had the good sense to repeal the Amendment. Yet four years later, in 1937, the possession or transfer of cannabis was criminalized by federal law.

The decade of the thirties was dominated by Franklin Delano Roosevelt. He had swept Hoover and the Republicans away in 1932 and stayed in the White House until he died in 1945, a few months into his fourth term. He brought together the ideas and the people to lead us on our way out of the Depression—and into and through World War II. His leadership acumen was evidenced from the beginning. He turned to an elite group of advisors, the Brain Trust—the Happy Hotdogs, named for one of its stars, Felix

Frankfurter. Frankfurter later became, surprisingly, a rather conservative Supreme Court justice. He rented our Cohasset, Massachusetts summer house once, visiting our Uncle John often in his stone castle. Thomas Corcoran, Tommy the Cork, another of the Happy Hotdogs, eighteen years later, by then a top-drawer lobbyist in Washington, guided a callow Yale Law School graduate, me, into a career with the government.

FDR's key adviser throughout the Depression and World War II was the immensely effective recovery czar Harry Hopkins. FDR's wife, Eleanor, was a key independent force throughout the entire presidency. But Roosevelt's own mix of political skill, courage, willingness to experiment, wisdom, and charisma—that was the ultimate source of his extraordinary successes.

We lived for years in what came to be called FDR's Alphabet Soup—his National Recovery Act, his WPA, CCC, PWA, TVA, AAA, REA, many others I've forgotten, the Social Security Act, and the Workmen's Compensation Act. Rebuilding a badly broken America. Dams, highways, electricity to rural areas, affordable housing, hospitals, schools, theaters. National Parks, National Forests, recreation facilities—in the mid-thirties we skied on trails cut by the Civilian Conservation Corps in New Hampshire's White Mountains. Plays, novels, poetry, paintings, sculptures, music, ballet were subsidized. And FDR's New Deal built the backbone of America's social security net. The remarkable beginnings of democratic socialism, though eighty years later we still lack the universal single-payer health care that Roosevelt—and most subsequent presidents—fought for unsuccessfully. And as of this writing, with Trump, it is but pie in the sky.

America spent its way out of the Depression—a lesson we, and much of the world, have largely ignored as capitalism falters in the twenty-first century.

The New Deal was everywhere around us, and it gave hope to the country and the world, however much some economists may argue that it was really the enormous government spending as we engaged in World War II that pulled us out of the Depression.

~ 5 ~

Why Us, Why Anyone, Mother Dear?

THERE I was, a comfortable, protected life, even in the worst of the Depression. And Puritanism, a work-ethic, frugality, conspicuously inconspicuous consumption were either in our genes or drilled into us. Noblesse oblige was important, but without guilt or apologies on my father's side. It was left to Mother, in her querulous, timid voice, to ask, in effect, whether human dignity should not trump privilege.

After Harvard, my grandfather had trained in engineering in Zurich, the best in its day. As reported in a biography of him, *Only to God*, German became his secret language for his erotic fantasies, recorded, oddly, in letters to his wife, though it seems they were largely unintelligible to her. He became a successful entrepreneur, developing and piping natural gas for consumers in West Virginia and Pennsylvania, and his minor carbon black business was growing. But he insisted that my father walk to school carrying his shoes in order not to needlessly wear them out. Yes, he was an interesting mix, even by the standards of his day.

From my father came a rigorous and narrow definition of, and insistence on, success and earned privilege—productive work, particularly manufacturing, adds to man's well-being. He had a clear view of who qualified. Very Important People, as he defined them, were to be assiduously cultivated. Unimportant People, well, they just were not important, some meriting sympathy and support, some to be tolerated, many to be written off or derided.

Mother, in her wistful way—ineffectual in diverting him—she was quite different, being uneasy and deferential toward his VIPs, but comfortable with those—the overwhelming majority—who did not meet his standards. Individual qualities and equalities were her measures. Merited or hierarchical inequalities were his.

So that conflict was a part of my heritage, too, and it is a conflict still with me. Whether it was or is an influential pattern for the privileged kids I grew up with, even my own siblings, I do not know.

⤔

So who was this kid, this me?

In primary school—just a ten minute walk from home along a brook in the woods—he had been the brightest in his class. The hero of his last year—captain and quarterback of the football team—cheers from the sidelines as his pass connects with Peggy for the undefeated final touchdown. Love notes in third grade exchanged with Diddy—and Buddy, she of the golden hair, just in case. Showing the others how to do stem Christies on the little ski hill behind the football field. Robin Hood for the school play in his last year—though there was that beet-red embarrassment when the target-tender off-stage cried, "Bulls-eye!"—the arrow having stuck in the grass at the archer's feet. He was Humpty Dumpty the year before, just had to sit on a cardboard wall. And the archery disaster is well compensated by the clapping as he goes up to Miss Gibbs for his Excellence Prize, a shiny Webster.

From school hero to his two days of trying out for the

prep school junior football team. Brutal, bruising, crushed under tons of tackling bodies, elbows driven over and over into his ribs. "Here, a hand up. But that's enough, son, maybe next year, and put on some weight. Get over to the track, check with the coach, minimum a mile a day required."

Jogging around the wooden track fifteen times—boring, boring. Well, there was the spring—crew season, when he makes it for coxswain of one of the four-oared wherries for beginner crews. Two years later and he's coxing the first crew, winning their four races in four-oared shells, and then their first and second crews combine into an eight-oared shell for the final race of the season against the Groton snobs. He—well, his crew and he—beat them too, on the Charles River for all of Boston and Cambridge to see. Undefeated, and the next year too—his last before heading West. After every race won they'd swing him, arms and legs, heave him into the lake or the river. The losers would give their school blazers to the winners, coxes too—stacks of them stored in his attic. So, a bit of glory there, and being puny had done it for him.

But the rest, so dreary. And the hazing in the dormitory—he'd board there each spring because of the late afternoon rowing hours. The masturbatory attacks and experiments on us younger boys, the fisticuff pommelings—he didn't have a chance, gasping, holding back the tears. The chapel readings, grace at the evening meal, the headmaster droning on—excruciating. Even science, which he did like, let him down. He was mid-class in most subjects, top-of-class in science. But his masterpiece treatise on the dissected innards of a sea cucumber got only one of several honorable mentions.

And there was the time when Mister Edwards was

teaching about surface tension. Our hero pops up with, "I can float a needle on a glass of water, sir."

"Impossible, show us tomorrow, a prize if you make it."

And float it did, with delicate care, the class giggled, and Sir wouldn't speak to him for months. Only at the end of the year, after incessant reminding, was the prize handed to him—a bottle of warm orange pop.

A college entrance factory, successful too, with a big assist from the legacy factor—almost all the boys had an Ivy League father. That dreary school finally was to be left forever. The drudging through the Latin, the diagramming of English grammar, ass-backward German syntax with the dozens of rules and the hundreds of exceptions, old College Board exams as tests even with college still five years away.

A shy, conflicted teenager boarding a Pullman car, lugging a heavy suitcase in his left hand, a yard of train tickets and Pullman Company reservations and Parmalee Chicago transfers held in his teeth to free his right hand for a peremptory handshake from his father. "Goodbye, my boy." Then, tickets back in hand, a warm kiss and hug from his mother. "Goodbye, dear Robby." Uneasy at the feel of her breasts through his tweed jacket. Overnight to Chicago where he will take the Parmalee van across the city, catch the overnight Zephyr streamliner for Denver, connect there to Colorado Springs. To catch the school's bus, south, then east on their washboard dirt road, out into the sage brush, dodging tumbleweed, past the water tanks, the horse stables, the football field, the tennis courts, the adobe-like Hacienda under its enormous cottonwood, the Dining Hall, Headmaster Froehlicher's private study for German 2 and Philosophy, First House for the younger boys, the Infirmary, the seven weeping willows, to the upperclassmen's dorm.

That's where those tickets will take him, handed back to him by the Pullman porter. Our fifteen-year-old slouches by the window, solitary in the face-to-face plush seats, green and scratchy through his new gray flannels. Relieved to be finally alone, free of the demands, the stiff smiles that make his mouth ache, free of Mother's "Why are you so sad, Robby dear?" And free of the suppressed answer, The burden of privilege, Mother dear.

Free to be alone.

The backyards passing by, the commuters' stations come-and-gone, then slowing, lurching through a switch to another track. Nashes and Studebakers, maybe, Pierce-Arrows, Model-A Fords waiting at a crossing. In the pale reflection he blinks at his near-sighted, spectacled blue eyes, his slicked-back field-mousey hair, his conventional good looks. His meager lips murmur, At last. He shakes his head, his body tenses, shoulders drawn up. He shudders twice, then slumps. Relief—a dog shaking off the rain. Behind his dim reflection, he sees a dark form. He turns, startled, a man is sitting just across from him now, their knees almost touching. Embarrassed, he sits up from his slouch, pulls away from those somehow threatening black pants. A glance at the clerical garb, the parted lips, and he turns quickly to the window. To dead corn stalks, a row of birds on the telephone wire, a water tower on a rise above a stand of autumn oaks—all to be carefully studied, of course. But the priest's reflection still lurks there, his head turned to the boy's image, his hand raising to get the boy's attention. "It seems we will be sharing these seats. I will have the lower berth, you must be assigned the upper. Have you traveled Pullman before? The porter will be here to make up the berths while we're in the dining car."

The boy nods, is silent.

"You were talking to yourself. No, please, I didn't want to embarrass you, young man. I see many young men, of course, and I understand what it means when one talks to oneself. But no, I shan't go into that now. Maybe later, all right?"

He reaches to touch the boy on the thigh, the friendly, reassuring gesture. The boy flinches, turns away, anywhere. Away, away from the mellifluous voice, the parted lips, the touch. He is silent.

Dinner's announced—a large maître d', starch-white uniform, napkin over his arm, coming down the corridor, tinkling a bell. The priest invites the boy to join him. Silence—a star, no, a planet low in the deep blue, still a touch of green at the horizon, must study it, identify it. Silence. He waits a few minutes, then goes to the dining car. Pretending he doesn't see the priest, his friendly gestures, he slips into a single corner table.

Almost two days from the Atlantic to the Rockies, this was his second year, his fifth trip—back for Christmas too, and again this senior year. The dining car experience was for him as exciting as ever. From the rattling clanks of the couplings and the moving metal plates where cars join, a little scary with the jostling, from the stink of soot and urine, on to the kitchen end of the dining car. Steamy smells of cooking, a nod from the chef through the serving window as he shifts pots on the stove. Past the maître d's desk, on into the quite elegant dining room. Wood paneling, discrete lighting, curtains tied neatly back, blinds down on most of the windows. "Those lights, young sir, that's the Hudson River bridge." Murmurs of the diners, clinking glasses. White tablecloths, a black waiter with smiling eyes to greet him, to help him to his chair. The crinkly napkin unfolded halfway for him by the waiter, spread on his lap. The candle in its little chimney, the carnations in their cut-glass vase, the cruets and salt and pepper in their silver rack, the carefully lined-up array of silver-plated Pullman Company knives and forks and spoons, three gleaming glasses the waiter will turn upright as needed. The wine bottles lined up waiting to be chosen—once a waiter, with an exaggerated wink, had actually served him a glass from the leftovers of another table's bottle. Steaming tureens, dish after dish arriving under silver domes, served one-handed, the fork and spoon like chopsticks. The elaborate desserts. Floating islands in custard, chocolate mousse with mint leaves in the whipped cream, cheeses to be cut for you in big wedges and served with a special knife and fork, the enormous bowl of fruit. The demitasse of coffee poured in a long swaying stream, spilling not a drop. The tray loaded with bottles of aperitifs, a tiny glass set before you, but, "Oh, I'm so sorry, sir, I'm not allowed."

As diners depart, trays of dirty dishes are loaded, carried casually over a shoulder as the train lurches through a switch. The bill is worked out with a pencil stub, presented with a flourish on a silver tray. The tip, still a bit awkward for him—his Grandpa didn't believe in tipping, never would—but worked out to be generous, he thought. "Thank you, sir, thank you so much, kind of you, sir." America in the Great Depression.

Back to his Pullman car, he's in the Men's Lounge, toothbrush in hand. Thick with smoke, bright brass spittoons, black leather benches. Two men sitting side by side, they're studying racing forms, talking ponies. Jackets on the coat rack, ties loosened, collars unbuttoned, soggy cigar stubs in their teeth. One spits a bit of tobacco leaf toward a spittoon, misses. Stacks of starched white towels in a rack, the everywhere Pullman Company on a blue stripe down the middle. Passengers Will Please Refrain from Flushing Toilets While the Train is Standing in the Station, he hums the tune that goes with this cast-brass gentile request, the ditty that ends with I Love You.

Past the Ladies, down the corridor, the seats now transformed into two long lines of heavy green curtains floor to ceiling, lights turned down. He finds his berth, a porter holds a two-step booster, he climbs up. There's a crack of light from the lower, a stirring. "Your shoes, sir, shine them up? Just hand them down, there, I'll bring them to you morning time. I'll have a coffee for you. You sleep good now."

Pull the curtains to, button them all. Pajamas, clothes on the big brown hooks, the coat hanger on the curtain rail, the shelf. Reading light out quickly, and soon a snore or two to ward off any priestly gestures. He knows what they mean. A little scared.

⌖

This change of schools became a key step in what seemed to him, even at the time, his escape, his rebellion. Yes, objectively it might appear to be simply a move from one cloistered environment to another, but his inner self was released from the rigors of paternal standards, the putdowns, the constant competitions, the judgments in his inbred home territory. Small for his age, behind in sexual development, though good looking enough, in a WASP-ish way. Introverted, most comfortable when solitary, he was friendly, but not at ease in himself. The tight lips, the stumbled and often unexpectedly malapropos words, the lowered self-esteem—it was not until late middle age that they pretty much disappeared.

Much of the Puritanism of New England was forever left behind—no, he was never to live at his parent's home again, only brief visits, interludes. But the work ethic stayed with him, and he was equipped with a small, a quite small, portion of his father's brain. It was enough, in his new school, now that he was free of the stifling home milieu, to share scholastic honors with his closest friend, Henry.

A brilliant full-scholarship kid, Henry, from the slums of Chicago. He had lost one arm playing in the train yards when he slipped under a rolling freight car. He had, though, created endless better explanations—bank robbing, a lion escaping from the city zoo, gang warfare, the Mafia, or just over-doing his fingernail biting.

Our escapee from the East Coast—he was getting glimpses of other realities, a geographic diversity, a we're-on-our-own-now sense of community, a release from the Ivy League compulsion—Harvard or you are a failure. This new cloister had its doors unbarred for him.

For two years he walked free. With the tutelage and inspiration of an extraordinary faculty, he came to enjoy every school subject and in the end got honors on three of his four college entrance exams. Harvard was the still-inevitable reward.

The final summer before college, he and his oldest brother lived together in an otherwise empty house, Louis to continue engineering studies at Harvard, Robby to learn machine tool skills at MIT and then work in a machine shop in industrial East Cambridge. Bench lathes, turret lathes, drill presses, routers—he worked hard, eager to prove his independent merit. He would drive up in an old heap of a car, work overtime, take on the toughest of jobs, eat from the snacks truck with the guys, make his name into Bob. He was good, very good, but the men seemed to know, the silver spoon was somehow still there.

On an ancient and erratic turret lathe, its iron frame cast in Vermont in 1897, he would tease out stainless-steel valve housings, complicated castings to be turned and threaded—or botched, re-welded, and re-done, damn it! They were destined, he liked to think, for the destroyers that Roosevelt was leasing to the British in his determination to support their war effort in spite of strong American neutralist tendencies—Lindbergh and his America First makes Trump a plagiarizer.

The reality of world-wide war was beginning to penetrate the stubborn resistance of the American zeitgeist.

∼6∼

Heil Hitler

Roosevelt's New Deal—his alphabet soup and huge government spending—was only just beginning to lift the country out of the Depression by the late 'thirties. Though privileged and protected, we kids were vaguely aware of the changes in the world around us. The suicides reported in the papers were far fewer, the soul-destroying grim lines of men and women waiting for hours for the dole, the soup kitchens, the rare day-job—those lines were shorter. There was even a World's Fair on Long Island at the end of the decade, its signature Trylon and Perisphere supposed to represent the World of the Future—a failed attempt to offset its more popular phallic interpretation. It was attended by tens of millions and represented every major country of the world except Germany. We went as a family in 1939, and I went again alone—to my delight—in 1940 as a detour on my way to Colorado for my last year of school.

We were aware, of course, that much of the world was at war again. The relentless progression of events was there for us to see, but they seemed so unlikely and incomprehensible, so foreign and far away across our isolating oceans that they had no personal meaning. They were invisible, just radio news items, black and white photos in Life magazine, journalists' reports in *Time* magazine, the March of Time

newsreels with the cartoons before our Friday-night dou-
ble-feature movies.

⊷

Italian fascism, originating in the 'twenties, was expanding into Albania, North Africa, and Ethiopia over the ineffectual resistance of the League of Nations. The League, re-
sulting from the advocacy of President Wilson during WWI
for a worldwide treaty to achieve lasting peace, was formed
in 1920. It was never joined by the United States due to
partisan political infighting between Democrat Wilson and
Republican Senator Henry Cabot Lodge—a distant relative.

This is the same Lodge who, as a most influential senator, was an essential element in Teddy Roosevelt's empire
building—arch conservative, bigoted, elitist. His grandson
was Henry Cabot Lodge, Jr—also a Republican senator,
though more moderate. An ambassador to Vietnam during
our disastrous war there.

The League of Nations lasted until it was replaced by the
United Nations, achieving several relatively minor peaceful
accomplishments, but never with the strength, particularly
without the United States, to stop the imperial designs of
Italy, Germany, Japan, and Russia.

Mussolini was intent on empire building throughout
his twenty years as Il Duce. Japan's Rising Sun was expanding into the Asian continent. In the early 'thirties, Hitler
commandeered a Germany devastated by defeat and depression, became Der Führer, and quickly built a huge war
machine, annexing Austria in 1938, pushing into Czecho-
slovakia in 1939 while appeased by a Britain more fearful
of a burgeoning Soviet Union than a neighboring state so
recently subjugated, and supposedly on its knees. In Spain's
bloody civil war, Franco's Falangists, aided by Hitler's and

Mussolini's devastating air forces, destroyed the Spanish Republicans' fledgling democracy.

In 1939, Hitler rolled over Poland—World War II had begun—and soon turned on the Soviet Union. By the summer of 1940, in alliance with Italy, the Axis had taken over most of North Africa and all of continental Europe but for two or three harmless, and in fact usefully neutral states.

Even as kids, doing the Cabotian European Grand Tour in 1936, if we had looked we could have seen a Germany readying for war, but the general mood in the United States was for isolation from the messy world and for acquiescence in appeasement. The deep scars of the First World War, which had ended relatively few years before, and the enormous toll of the Depression drew us into an isolationist and protectionist mode and a search for alternatives to failed political and economic policies. Socialism was a popular idea in the U.S. and in England. Under its banner, touted as National Socialism, the Nazi experiment seemed to be effective, as did the socialism, a.k.a. communism, of the emerging Soviet Union. And so too Mussolini's brand under the ancient Roman fasces. Franco's Spain didn't quite fit the pattern, maybe because he had defeated our little private army, and the cynicism of his brand was too obvious to ignore—but never mind.

Many intellectuals such as Hiss, Chambers, England's Cambridge Five, heroes such as Charles Lindbergh, labor leaders, politicians, and some among the remnants of royalty in the Western world turned to socialism and its malign counterfeits, the fascists and communists.

There were many voices trumpeting the truth, exposing the fraud, many calls to arms against the clear danger. The voice that was heeded, though, was Roosevelt's.

~ 7 ~

The Lust for Empire
Forever Drowned in Blood?

In the summer of of 1941 I cranked out hundreds of those valve housings for the war effort in Europe. In the fall I became a seventeen-year-old college freshman. Struggling with calculus, scientific German—another contribution to the war effort—chemistry, history, while excused from English courses because of my stellar performance on the college entrance exams—a much regretted reward, for I never took a literature course at Harvard or Yale. And I never uncovered for myself any academic inspiration at either institution, though it was certainly there if I had looked.

December 7, 1941. Back to the parental home of stone for a Sunday lunch—parents, a sister just moving into her teens, maybe a brother or two. Demitasses in the living room, chocolates from the silver box I have now as a memento of that ritual and of Mother's sweet tooth—and mine. Mother's favorite Mahler on a stack of seventy-eights that slide through automatically with a frightening clatter? No, it's the Sunday afternoon opera on the radio, though not likely The Old Man would have tolerated it for long if it weren't Wagner.

"We interrupt this program to bring you a special news

bulletin. The Japanese have attacked Pearl Harbor, Hawaii, by air."

Silence. Mother is looking at me, there are tears in her eyes, on her powdered cheeks.

Our world is transformed.

⌖

"A date that will live in infamy!" The Churchillian oratorical flourish of our Roosevelt, calling the next day for a declaration of war. Walking back to my room that evening, down the dimly-lit paths of the Harvard Yard, past Widener Library, to the array of freshman dormitories. Book bag slung over a shoulder, my stride determined, my back straight, my head held high. It was the feeling I would sometimes have leaving a Friday night boarding-school movie, alone and in the dark, somehow inspired—perhaps by Victor McLaglen's heroics in *Gunga Din*. Yes, there was a bit of the teenager in me, however much I, in these my last years, enjoy saying that I was never a teenager.

In less than two months I would be eighteen, the minimum age to enlist in the army—though parental consent was required until you were twenty-one, the draft age. There was certainly an element of mindless patriotism in my plan. I effortlessly shed my indoctrination in the horrors of the Great War, the useless slaughter of millions, the war-to-end-war slogans, shed it all without a thought. Yet I was to enlist in a world-wide conflagration that would cause the deaths of eighty million people, destroy many of the great cities of the world, and this time with no promise of ending anything. Almost overnight, Japanese and Germans became universally evil—Japs, Slant-Eyes, Nips. Krauts, Huns, Jerry. Italians were hopelessly inferior, feckless—Dagos, Wops, the Bicycle Boys.

But there was also an element in my newfound buoyant

step of moving into a new dimension—a life of my own, leaving behind the stifling demands of a dominating father, of an anal milieu, enlisting as a private in a vast army, beyond the reach of parental strictures, string-pulling manipulations, privilege. And I would avoid the usual gentleman's route to officer's rank in the navy, the route most of my classmates, my brothers too, were to choose. They would get free rides through college, off to officer training, and then—you're a Ninety-Day Wonder, an ensign, and your kid brother private would have to salute you.

Coming down to earth in a day or two, I decided that though I would be eighteen in a couple of months, it would be prudent to finish my freshman year. I switched my college courses around, taking a double course in physics, the idea being that this would somehow be an appropriate preparation for my upcoming military service. Little did I know of the Byzantine ways of the U.S. Army. I was good in that course, pulling an A on both the exams and the extensive lab work, but came to realize that higher math was probably not within my easy reach and that physics, therefore, could not be my life's work...when I had finished winning the war. In May of 1942, I was among the first in my class to enlist in active military service.

❧

Roosevelt's voice had been muted before Pearl Harbor. His rapid buildup of America's armed forces was called a defense plan. The draft, limited to one year's service until Pearl Harbor. The flow of armaments to England and the Soviet Union was coerced from a reluctant America under the guise of "lend-lease." The enormous needs of our frighteningly hard-pressed allies. But still, it was someone else's war.

With Pearl Harbor, Roosevelt's voice is heard and

heeded. War production and mobilization burgeoned—it is hard to believe the numbers. Within a year or so, America's shipyards were launching five ships a day, rolling off the production lines were upwards of two hundred tanks and two hundred aircraft rolling daily. The military, men and women in uniform, grew from a peacetime volunteer force of a few hundred thousand to a largely conscripted force of sixteen million.

By the end of the war, more than 400,000 of them would be dead. I was not gregarious, I had only a modest number of friends, but from among the few dozen school- and college-mates and neighborhood kids I knew well, I could easily count a dozen killed in action. Imagine, then, what the score would be for a surviving Soviet soldier. The Soviet military lost ten and a half million soldiers and perhaps twelve million civilians, and those millions from a total population not much greater than ours. Worldwide there were twenty million military dead and sixty million civilian dead.

Had the lust for empire been forever drowned in blood?

Freshman exams over, I pull down the blind of my dormitory window, stay in bed for two days, my roommate bringing me snacks. I was hoping that my nearsighted eyes would improve enough to pass the army's requirements.

"Undershorts, socks, everything off, men." A finger jams up my ass. "Good enough, okay." A finger pokes behind my balls. "Cough, cough again. No, no hernia there. Short-arm inspection now, my boy, strip it and squeeze it like a toothpaste tube. Good, not venerealed, not yet. Read this. Good, they'll issue you regulation glasses. You're in. Glad to have you on board, son. Report to the sergeant."

They'd discovered that I had studied and done lab work

on the workings of radios at college, so they kept me out of uniform for a couple of months to take a course in radio repair. "Portable field radios, up on the front lines, dangerous work, essential." So, my higher education appeared to be paying off, and in fact, I ended up for a few weeks being the assistant teacher of the course. Theory—electrons backing up, vacuum tubes, condensers, coils—and soldering and testing and tracing wires. We used a classroom at the Boston Latin High School. I found a dingy walk-up room in a nearby rooming house, rent and per diem courtesy of Uncle Sam.

I had moved to a different world.

↬

Fort Devon, the fall of 1942. Medical probings, lectures, armloads of uniforms and gear, conflicting orders, foul food slopped on mess kits, barracks, never-ending rows of basins and toilets cheek-by-cheek.

Thousands of us, milling about here in what was an old dirigible hangar, hundreds of desks, each manned by a junior officer. They have our records and fat catalogs to match up supply and demand. "German and college math, I see. You're reclassified, soldier, field intelligence work. Dismissed. And smarten up that salute." Sounds important, what now?

They've put me on guard duty. Halt! Who goes there? Yell it three times, if there's no answer, shoot. Two in the morning, two hours to go, thirty degrees below zero. I'm relieving a soldier, they told me, whose eyeballs had frozen stiff. They gave me a World War I Enfield rifle and ammo, how to shoot it I hadn't a clue. And this fort, Fort Devon, Massachusetts—a railhead where they dump us, then just miles of barracks and Quonsets, warehouses, that sort of thing. No crenels and merlons, not even a spiked wooden

Spring, 1943, home on a three-day pass prior to being sent
to the European theater.

stockade. No defenses, just me—and the place no doubt swarming with Huns and Japs. Nothing, just me. The best way, the only way I can figure, is to keep my eyes tight shut. I'll surely hear the officer on duty when he comes out checking on me, and one *Halt!* should do it, I reckon, with a *Who goes there?* for good measure. No dereliction of duty, no court-martial, no lockup for the duration, no waiting for some future amnesty to give me back my civil rights.

Days later, still not quite frozen stiff, they march us—we straggle—through snowdrifts, duffel bags piled in a truck, to the railhead, to the train waiting for us, waiting impatiently, fuming and hissing, MPs strutting about, a first looie, hung over, it's still only oh-five-fifteen, blackout, lights at the dimmest. A first sergeant, old-time cadre, a vet of World War I, doing all the work. Lists and orders, barking out last names and we reply with first names and middle initial.

"Robert M, Sir."

"Sir is for the brass, soldier, not me."

A forlorn looking fellow next to me calls out, "William, but I don't have a middle initial."

"Then you're William NMI, soldier, remember that. Smartly, men, duffel from the alphabetical pile."

Five days we've been on this fucking train. No idea, no one warned us. Our five-day tomb. They told us nothing, where, when, how, or why, nothing. Sealed in, no outside connections, no talking with civilians, the enemy's everywhere, listening, in case you didn't know. A turn-of-the-century coach, recalled from railway heaven to torment us. Five days in a row it serves us—in a manner of speaking. Seats filthy plush worn down to the springs, home for untold generations of fleas, bedbugs, lice. Benches come in sections, face-to-face, four assigned to each seat meant for three. So one of us is usually standing or has managed to climb onto the narrow metal grill of a handbag rack overhead. The cast-iron supports and fittings, their elaborate floral designs, are sticky and mostly black with the grime of uncountable hardworking hands. The one toilet is soon plugged, over-flowing, the trap that should open to drop shit on the tracks just doesn't work. The solutions are varied. The window for a piss, the gap between cars for a shit, frigid sooty air up your ass, or a snowdrift on the frequent watering stops—our engine suffers from hardening bladder, prostatitis, both—and the occasional U.S. Army latrine. Meal stops at army field kitchens, usually in bleak stretches of uninhab-ited landscape in the wee hours, where they slop goo in your mess kit. Except for the infrequent turn on the rack, sleep-ing is just sitting up. Chin propped on your fist, elbow on knee, until the ache in your teeth wakes you, probably thirty minutes at best. No other solutions are tolerated—head on a shoulder, feet on the opposite bench? No way.

Five days, washing just once—at an army field setup in the middle of nowhere. Geography pretty much escapes us. They manage to avoid the big cities, even Chicago, intermi-nably shuttling us round. Shunting yards and empty spaces become our natural habitat.

⮂

Camp Crowder, Neosho, Missouri, center of gravity of the U.S. of A. for a month of basic training.

"Prone position, men. Heels down. Remember, squeeze it off. Ready on the left, ready on the right, ready on the fir-ing line, commence fire!"

Fucking M1, busts my shoulder.

"Rifles on crooked arms, men. Push with your toes. Elbows and toes, men. Get them asses down! That's real barbed wire and real ordnance. Love that mud, soldier. You hoping for an extra hole in your ass?"

Parading in the pouring rain, presenting the colors. What the fuck! Nice umbrella, General, where's mine...Sir?

Better the forced marches, heavy packs, at least we get to see the scenery—if we don't die. And here's me, climbed into this huge pot, scraping at the burned-on goo, and my twenty hours nonstop have just begun. Scrub the ceiling next, no doubt. And when do they tell us how to use a condom? How to kiss ass? Or make a bed?

"Sergeant, that bunk there, check it."

He'll drop a coin on the blanket. Shit, it doesn't bounce.

"Mummy didn't teach you how to make a bed, soldier? Put him on cleanup detail, sergeant."

Cigarette-butt searching in the dead grass, beady-eyed corporal, "Asses and elbows, that's all I want to see. Any goldbricking goof-offs get KP from midnight on."

Field intelligence work? Must be.

It's mostly just a blur.

Another train ride, three days of frigid hell. To pine woods, meadows, snow, red mud, Vint Hill Farms Station in the heart of Virginia. Some serious study—Morse code, Japanese, radio language and traffic analysis, ciphers and codes, radio direction finding triangulation. We are good, mostly old fogies, thirties or more. PhDs, all of them draftees—and a chickenshit, ass-licking, college-kid volunteer me.

And still the useless marching, the close-order drill, more asses and elbows, more polishing, pressing, dusting, tight-tucking, KP duty in turn, extra for your goldbricking GI sins. It's getting to me. There's a sign-up list for those who want to apply for Officers Candidate School. I disdain it still, as a matter of principle. Those who do sign up slave for weeks to prepare for the screening interview. But when the schedule for the interviews is posted, my name is there, and much to the displeasure of the others, I go, am selected, and tentative travel orders are announced. My principles seem to have stepped aside for the moment.

The next day new travel orders are there. My name is in the list for overseas assignment to the European theater, and it takes precedence over the OCS list. My principles are hypocritically reclaimed.

Here, on board HMS Queen Elizabeth, not to the Pacific, that wouldn't do for the inscrutable army that had us learning Japanese, no, to Europe somewhere. Eight, ten thousand of us—we sleep in three shifts, three to a pipe berth, tiered four high, six hours sleep, twelve hours on deck or wedged in some sheltered and blacked-out space—creeping in convoy at the speed of the slowest, U.S. Navy circling on the horizon, flashes, blasts now and then, rumors of U-boats and sinkings. Empty lifeboats drifted by yesterday. Big turnout for chapel on deck this morning.

We survived the Birmingham Replacement Depot, the U.S. Army's repple-depple storehouse of live bodies to replace the dead. Now London. The Luftwaffe is blitzing the city again, well, little-blitzing. It's exciting. They've cranked up the ack-ack battery in Portland Square next door to our requisitioned quarters. We rushed out to Hyde Park to see the show, ducked under Marble Arch for protection. Two of their Heinkels or Junkers made it into London—searchlights and gunfire. They got one, circling down in flames.

Reveille call, oh-five-hundred, me the acting first sergeant. I cajole a few bodies to climb out of their sacks, straggle out to the street, sort of line up. Pitch dark. I snap out, "AttenSHUN!"

An officer's voice from the gloom, "Morning report, Sergeant."

"All present and accounted for, Sir." I salute to the night. And most are sleeping on till the last minute.

We slouch our way from our bombed-out row-house quarters to Baker Street, British Y-Service officer teaching us what could be learned about radio eavesdropping on Jerry.

It's tea break, elevenses, and I'm planning my evening, my dive into the Underground—crowded stations, squalor, every platform jammed with pipe berths layered up to the ceiling—to a play, a concert, vaudeville at the Windmill.

"Your seat number, Sir? Tea and biscuits at the intermission? I'll bring it to your seat. Thank you, Sir, thank you." Solemnly standing for "God Save the King." The audience is jittery—when Air Raid Alert lights up on the proscenium, many will walk quietly out, down into the bomb shelters of the Underground.

Bitter cold, these blackouts in the fog, a few taxis—no private cars—headlights masked down to slits. We grope our way, hoping the few street signs we can see have not been switched around to confuse any invaders.

Sunday, wandering. Just back of Saint Paul's, it's cratered down to Mithraic origins. The pubs, their by-appointment-of, King-certified ales, their bitters and bangers and pickled eggs, rationed. The fish-'n-chips barrows, greasy newsprint cones. "Yes, vinegar, please. Why sure, ma'am, we're glad to be here, glad to help out."

And, most unlikely, sad-sack corporal me lunching at Claridge's with Air Marshal Bomber Command himself—

a most tenuous tie through a U.S. Air Attaché relative of my college roommate. A gesture to the Yankee ranks? His wartime regalia, the kowtowing service, the sherry, whale steaks, cabbage, tapioca goo. Nothing whatsoever to talk about. Is he as uncomfortable as I?

That was Bomber Harris, I'd remember that. The only top British brass denied the Victoria Cross. At the end of the war, the Labour press attacked him. Wanton useless saturation bombing, Dresden worse than Nagasaki, and it just stiffened up Jerry's resolve.

⌀

And now where?

We'd sailed from Liverpool, a P&O steamer, British privates, Aussie privates, and us. We're still corporals, but privileged, put in real cabins and on the traditionally preferred port side—posh, acronym for Port Out Starboard Home, so we're told, the north side, the shady side for the upper-crust colonials on the England-Orient-England passage. Plausible? Apocryphal.

We're assigned to man the fifty-caliber machine guns on the wings of the bridge—all of us noncoms, so they assumed we must be well trained. Nothing like PhDs for protection. Swinging around on the seats, kind of fun, cranking the barrels, sighting on clouds. And yesterday at a Junkers, Jerry's weather plane—at Baker Street we'd worked on intercepts of their daily radioed reports. We actually let loose, tracers, the clatter, though they were way way out of range and the bridge officer suggested we quit.

Yes, sir, just swinging around, checking out the ammo. Experts.

Landfall. Tangier off our starboard quarter, Trafalgar to the north. Hercules straddles the Straits, Gibraltar to Hacho.

The Iberian hills catch the sun, blues to greens. Fields, forests, groves of olives, vineyards, beaches, I reach out, held by the ship's rail, longing. To lie in the sun, a goatskin of wine, bread, manchego, a fig, a friend. Peace even there in blood-drenched Spain.

The P&O, the bitter war, we sail inexorably on.

The Axis, they're beaten, they've lost, for God's sake, it's time to give up. The Battle of Britain, Doolittle's raid on Tokyo, Midway, El Alamein, Morocco, Oran, Algiers, Stalingrad, Attu, Guadalcanal, and the U-boats mostly sunk, I'd guess. Strengst durch Freude, Lebensraum, Drang nach Osten, and the Ever Rising Sun. Lost, what the fuck, can't they see? Hegemonical? Maniacal!

Sailing inexorably on.

⮡

Algiers, a golden city. Teeming with troops, tanks, trucks, the harbor jammed with warships, transports, supply ships, landing craft—hospitals overflowing, they say. Brits, Americans, Aussies, Canucks, they've taken over this Frenchified Arab town.

Allied HQ. Eisenhower, Montgomery, Alexander, are you up there scheming? Did you learn some lessons at Kasserine Pass, old Ike? They really did beat up on you. But Monty, his Desert Rats and a thousand tanks, they'd crushed Rommel at El Alamein a few days before. By now they'd just about pushed Rommel's Afrika Korps into the sea. Scheming, up there at HQ, getting ready for something. Churchill had already told the world in his stirring, though pompous, prose. "We shall strike at the soft underbelly of the Axis before the leaves of autumn fall."

They put us in trucks as soon as we land, no Aussies, no Brits, no other GIs, just our group of PhDs and me. Two hours deep into the Atlas Mountains, a run-down colonial spa, Hammam Melouan—hot springs, baths, filthy cubicles. They put us quickly to work shoveling gravel, day after day.

Weeks of that and I'm looking for reassignment.

A one-day pass—trucked down through the mountains, through Casa Blanca, on to Algiers. I head for Allied HQ. Ike's up there near the top, his palace wrapped in barbed wire. Half way up, I enter a nondescript block of flats, the guards check my dog tags, take me to an office. A captain, the parachute patch on his shoulder, a sloppy peremptory salute returning my GI one.

"So you want to sign up for the paratroops? That's great, my boy, uh, Corporal, we need men like you, men with pluck. You'll hear from us soon and good luck."

He's a friendly sort for one of the brass. Why? Is there something I just don't get?

Back to the gravel—my skills are in great demand. Then at morning's formation, still in the dark, I'm ordered to fall out, report on the double, the CO himself, Major Doney no less, brass of the brass, close to God. What could I have done? The Kasbah, outstayed my pass?

"Corporal, you're way out of line. No paratroops for you. Your transfer's rescinded, I had to cable Washington. We've spent thousands to train you, not to hang you from a piece of silk for their target practice. KP, three days. Dismissed."

⌘

Louis, Murray, Bill, me—we're on a three-day pass together. The four of us, two hours by truck to Algiers from our billet in the mountains. Then two hours west—a rickety bus, Arabs and the four of us—to a village on the coast, Tipaza, Phoenician they say. An empty church, Roman ruins, four thermal baths on the cliff's edge. It was once a rest-and-recreation camp for Roman legions back from the outposts of empire. Like us.

We have a French *pension* to ourselves, a lone inn on a bluff above the sea. Our elderly hosts are effusive, so grateful to be freed at last from Pétain and the Boche. For breakfast, they bring us chicory café au lait—their own cow's milk—croissants, their butter still milky from the churn, maquis honey. Real china, silverware, curtains, sheets on our beds with cats to keep our feet warm. We roam the beaches and cliffs, the ruins. Sherds, a Roman coin in a ploughed-up field, an amphitheater, we quote Shakespeare from the stage to each other, lunch on wine, cheese, black bread we bought in the village. We dash naked into the waves, toss stranded starfish back to the sea. We play Bach on the church's pump organ, see a jittery movie at the village cinema with Garbo in scratchy French.

Bused back to Algiers, we sneak into the Kasbah, OFF LIMITS. I buy a battered gasoline burner for six cigarettes, have a mattress cover stuffed with grass, quilted.

Zeega-zaaga, meesta, fuhga my seesta?

Back to KP and more gravel. While Sicily—Winnie's underbelly—is freed. They manage a very bloody landing at Salerno, roll on to Naples and the slaughter at Monte Cassino.

~ 8 ~

Lily Marlene…über Alles…
Festung Europa…Kaputt

O UR ORDERS finally come—this morning, they called us out, ten of us enlisted men and four officers—ship out tomorrow. We pile our gear on the makeshift parade ground, my mattress, my cook stove—Sure, corporal, no problem—and a scattering of similar loot. We board a small troop carrier for Bastia, Corsica.

Close friends, colleagues—a team of cypher breakers, traffic analysts, order-of-battle recorders—we join a veteran radio intercept company of the U.S. Army Signal Corps, the 117th Signal Radio Intelligence Company. We are the company's Intelligence Platoon. Beginning back where we started our training in Virginia, by the end of the war we will have been thrown together for three years. On leaving Algiers, six of us would be sleeping in the same pyramidal tent or requisitioned quarters for the next two and a half years. We enlisted men are all promoted to tech sergeant. Our war has begun.

The 117th SRI had bivouacked where a German SS Panzer Division had been only three days before. We learn from our radio intercepts, from breaking their ciphers, from tracking their radio signals that they'd crossed over to Italy to help battle the Allied landing at Anzio, near Rome. They had mined their camp as they left. One of our radio operators loses a leg when his truck is blown to bits.

A few days later we climb into our company trucks, jeeps, vans. We are self-mobile, self-sufficient, a traveling circus—dogs and cats, a cage for three songbirds that dangles from a truck stanchion, mattresses, footlockers, stoves, and on and on—convoying over a mountain pass and down to L'Île Rousse on the northwest shoulder of Corsica. Preparing for an invasion of France? They claim—a cover story?—that we'll get better reception there of the radio communications between the German artillery units surrounding our Anzio beachhead. We keep the beachhead HQ informed on where Jerry will move his guns each night.

L'Île Rousse. A tidy little town with its bars, its deserted deluxe hotel, its harbor for the fishing boats, and its gorgeous coral beaches—we have them to ourselves. We've settled in an olive grove five minutes up from the sea, a village of tents and trucks and vans. No more of that wash-shave-bathe in our helmets, hot water scooped from the chow-line mess-kit-washing vats, helmets propped in the dirt by our cots. They have finally gotten around to setting up showers yesterday in the field near the latrine—a deluxe twelve-holer over a trench, the shit burned daily with high-test aviation gasoline. It makes an amazing stench.

Our antenna towers are up, our hilly-billy radio operators tune in round the clock to the Germany military frequencies, scribble reams of ciphered messages over to us enlisted men in our converted moving van. The Intelligence Platoon, cipher breakers in the front, two of us traffic analysts in the middle, two order-of-battle men in the rear sticking pins in their maps. Our officers—three lieutenants and a captain—put together our findings and radio them to Fifth Army HQ on the Anzio beachhead near Rome, radioing on our super-secret Sigaba enciphering machine. Sigaba—we enlisted men could only touch it if there were immediate danger that Jerry would capture it. We were ready to pull the timer lever that would explode the dynamite on which Lady Sigaba sat.

Swimming, wandering the maquis, bar-hopping in the town, forays into the mountains in a borrowed jeep—Little Schmuck painted on her side—to trade cigarettes for fresh bread, wine, laundry, a French lesson. An evening climb to the stone village on the hillside above our olive grove for black bread and cheese and bitter new wine with the family of the girl I'd found to do my laundry—my adolescent lust as usual repressed. A meager dinner in the empty dining room of the Hôtel Napoléon Bonaparte, a brocaded bedroom, a hot bath. I lie in my canopied bed. I weigh my good fortune, I wonder where friends may be. I dream.

Oh-two-hundred, black cold, we jeep up into the mountain barrens of Cap Corse. A boar hunt arranged by a tent mate. He'd befriended a wild Corsican mountain man, a man who only a few years ago had guided a boar-hunting party off a Rockefeller yacht. We hike for hours. By dawn, we crowd into a goatherd's cave, hot bread, goat milk and cheese, eau-de-vie-de-vin. Berets, GI wool caps, assorted firearms—an Italian Beretta pistol, German Lugers, a black-market Garand, Lee-Enfields of the Boer War, our carbines, a World War One BAR, even a bazooka. For hours, we stumble through the maquis in a ragged line, dogs racing about. Shouts, a rush in the bracken, shots, volleys—a feral pig ducks between the goatherd's legs, disappears. We straggle back to our jeep.

A few weeks later, three looies and me as their intrepid, acrophobic guide, we manage an ascent, Monte Padre. Fog and ice and fear and my unerring luck—we make it. And slide down a tongue of snow, down into flowering maquis, then scrub oak, pine, vineyards, figs and olives, the sparkle of distant streams, the call of a goat's bell.

My spring and summer idyll, war gods close at hand. A faintest thrumming, a swelling, a throbbing, filling the air, inescapable, drumming deep to your core. Each day now, in the early morning. Over the mountains to the southeast they come, specks catching the sun, wave after wave, seven hundred, a thousand, our B-17s, our friends, cousins, brothers, the Flying Fortresses, Italy based, Foggia. Thousands of tons of death. How many will be missing on their return?

Last week, those bodies on the beach. A crippled bomber came roaring toward us, faltered, too low, bounced on a rocky reef, twisting, skipping the wave tops, skidding almost to the beach. A parachute pack stenciled U.S. Army Air Force washed up on the sand. Plexiglas turret, its gun bent in a U, water rising in it, blood-red water, white face, eyes staring out, pleading, dead. Another, washed up, his head gently rolling in the wavelets dying on the beach. His last denial, his incredulous No.

A lovely spring afternoon, off duty, three of us are sitting on the grass in the local schoolyard. Our Mademoiselle French teacher—young, most desirable, most unavailable— with her blackboard nailed to a tree, we with a bottle of bitter wormwood absinthe to loosen our tongues, she in exasperation mixing Corsú curses with her French. A rumble of trucks, a small U.S. Army convoy goes by. Till now we'd been the only soldiers around. They stop in a field near the base of the harbor mole, we can see them begin to unload and set up. We go over, watch them, try to figure it out—they weren't talking. Electronic equipment, antennae, some sort of radar is our best guess. And an hour or two later another convoy pulls up, a squad of Rangers, armed but horsing about. They join us for drinks, smokes, and news. Italian-Americans, they'd been parachuted in behind the German lines north of Rome to make contact with partisan groups—sent here for a rest and as guards for this new installation, whatever it was.

Working the night shift a week later, we hear popping down in the town, fireworks maybe, a marriage celebration, no big deal. A banging on our door of our van. It's the officer of the guard.

"They're all dead, every last one. A German torpedo boat had landed, slit the throats of the two men standing guard, shot the rest in their sleep, taken the electronic stuff with them. Keep your carbines with you, ammo clips, always. Captain's orders."

Most nights, when we're not on shift, we doze off in our tent to "Lili Marlene," then "Sing, Nachtigal, Sing." "Ici Radio Monte Carlo" signs off. Mother had sent me the Sears-'n-Roebuck radio I'd had by my bed in a shoebox. We can get the BBC, often drowning out the German radio with the Morse code V, the dit–dit–dit-dah of Beethoven's Fifth, Winnie's V for Victory. BBC news if Jerry hasn't managed to jam them out. And often those opening notes of "The Bells of Saint Clemens"—oranges and lemons—some sort of code message, we figure, maybe aimed at the French resistance, the Maquis. Tonight, we get Lord Haw-Haw, Jerry's pet turncoat, in his Oxford English telling us we are losing the war. They interrupt with the air raid report. "Achtung! Achtung!

Die Luftlagemeldung. Über dem ganzen deutschen Reichs-gebiet gibt es kein feindliches Flugzeug." No enemy aircraft over Germany? That would be most unusual, the RAF by night, the USAAF by day, they're bombing the shit out of them, nonstop, that's what it looks like from here.

⌥

A three-day pass.

"Corporal, show me your orders."

"Yes, Sir, here you are, Sir. Three days, Bastia."

"Carry on, enjoy yourself, observe the off limits. Pick up same place, same time, three days."

I have a school friend, a grease monkey at the Mitchell B-25 bomber base south of town. I find him, and the next morning I'm in the belly of their DC-3 on the first leg of their daily fresh-vegetable-and-ice-cream run—Bastia, Na-ples, Algiers, Bastia. They'd freeze the squadron's ice cream in the cargo bay on the flight back.

I get off at Naples, hitch on another DC-3 to Rome's air-field on the via Salaria. Rome had been liberated a few days before. I join a jeep load to town. Watch out for the MPs, stay clear of the hotels requisitioned for the GIs. In a bar on the via Sistina in my few words of French, I get invited to stay with a family in their cold-water walkup flat.

Rome. It's my first visit, we had not gotten south of the Italian Alps in our 1936 family tour. Delirious, joyful Rome. The fasces and swastikas and blackshirts we had seen in the newsreels—gone. Glowing, beautiful Rome. A city that was to become my home for many years. Gelati, those deli-cious gelati, from a barrow by the Spanish Steps. The piazza Venezia, a herd of sheep under the balcony where Benito once held forth. The Villa Borghese, a band tuning up, a street artist is cartooning the GIs. Me? Sure, why not?

Another hitched ride, back to Corsica, a Mitchell B-25 this time, crouched in the empty bomb bay. Frigid air blasts through the cracks, thin air, they'd warned me, breathless, heart working double time. They let me peer out now and then—Giglio, Montecristo, Elba, Corsica's snowy peaks. I make it to Bastia in time for our company truck. No one the wiser.

Normandy, June 6, 1944, Brits, Canucks, GIs, bloody beachheads secured. We pick up the news on our radios and teletypes. We have orders to follow it closely on our big order-of-battle maps. Rommel is there again, and the colored pinheads on our maps are stuck there week after week. For us, nothing changes. Maybe we're helping, some possibly useful news about German plans—who, where, where to, when—in Italy and France and the Fatherland. The Eastern Front is out of the range of our radios.

Our orders come. Strike tents, fill in the latrines, bring in the radio direction finders from their hilltops, antennae down, mess closed. C-rations now, horrid stuff, dog-biscuit rusks, cans of so-called scrambled eggs, Spam, the sandy no-melt chocolate bar, cigarettes. Pile our traveling-circus gear in the vans.

"Stow it out of sight, men, best not to have it advertised, not just now, chickenshit brass to deal with where we're going."

Our company CO, he's been with this crowd of hillbilly Tennessee National Guardsmen from the beginning—moonshiners, country-store clerks, mechanics, truck drivers, high-school kids made into jittery radio operators, communicating among themselves by tapping Morse code on each other's arms. Morocco, the Kasserine Pass debacle, Sicily, now here. Our CO has learned the ropes, nonchalant by nature, though we noncoms of the Intelligence Platoon see little of him, are always treated a bit apart, newcomers, intellectual types. He's learned not to take orders too literally, it seems.

He leads our convoy to Ajaccio, the embarkation port, by the longer scenic route, up over the top of the island. Our colorful convoy, twenty, thirty vehicles. We stop at cheering villages. We learn of the liberation of Paris. More wine and kisses, tossing cigarettes and chocolate. Then winding our way on, the alpine route, it is spectacular.

But we've missed the boat, we've missed invasion day, August fifteen.

But in a matter of hours they get us on a spare LST— spare, how can that be? We leave in the night, to Saint-Tropez, landing August sixteen, D-day plus one. The big bay is jammed with the invasion fleet. We hit the beach in late afternoon, drop the bow ramp on the shingle, drive ourselves off. No Jerry.

"No time or place or safety to set up shop, men. Stay packed up, close by, we'll move out in the morning."

Some of us stray into a nearby vineyard, gorge on half-ripe grapes. We watch in the twilight, out over Saint-Tropez Bay, dozens, hundreds of ships anchored or moving about, five battleships we can see, dozens of cruisers, destroyers, transports, LSTs, LCTs, LCIs, supply ships, hospital ships, many with barrage balloons on long steel-cable tethers to discourage dive-bombing Stukas. One hits a cable, explodes, setting a hydrogen balloon on fire. A spectacular show. Later a summer storm hits us, lightning strikes several balloons, enormous flares light up the bay. And we shelter in a stone tool shed, spend the rest of the night under its leaky tin roof, stomachs writhing with grapes.

Flowers, wine, eggs, extravagant kisses, whatever they had. We hang out over the slatted sides of our four-by-four trucks, toss cigarettes and candy bars. A touch, a kiss, a cheek moist with tears. Our joyous advance, racing up the valley of the Rhône, the Route Napoléon, the infantry and armored divisions just up ahead trying to catch Jerry in his high-speed orderly retreat. Every town, every village, country roadsides—cheering, welcoming crowds, women, children, the elderly, the few men spared.

Lons le Saunier, Bésançon, Vesoul, each is a stop for a day or two to set up our antennae and listen in on the German retreat, learn what we can of Jerry's plans and problems. A pause while the American Seventh Army and the French First slow their advance to clear out stubborn pockets, to allow rear echelons, supplies, reserves to catch up. And now Épinal, Alsace-Lorraine on the edge of the Vosges Mountains, Jerry digging in, winter closing in.

We've set up in a beech forest. The booming of our artillery is not far off, with occasional much louder return fire from Jerry's eighty-eights. It took a day or so to sort things out, intercept what we can, figure out where their SS Panzer and Waffen Divisionen are, their plans, casualties, strengths. And we're back to our six-on-twelve-off routine.

Free time, time to wander in the autumn, kick up the beech leaves. "Watch it! Willy, the mechanic, he stepped on a mine yesterday, half dead, they say." We find a path through the woods up to a hilltop, to a lone brick structure, maybe a factory once. Over the door is painted:

STALAG

Cautiously we explore the cells—Russian, English, French, German, American, a defiant Star of David, sad scribblings on the walls, pages from diaries, scraps of clothing here and there, prisoners shipped off to the factories of war, of death.

⤚

Here, me, lying in a ward for the wounded, earache driving a spike into my brain. And trench foot, Great War vintage. The mud of autumn, the cold, the soggy boots. They never got around to issuing us winter boots and the wool tuques. I was done in by the freezing wind driving around in topless Little Schmuck. We scrounged chunks of coal in the villages for the stove in our tent—cigarettes and my horded chocolate bars in trade.

Groans—some are mine. Screams, death. An infantry sergeant from the 45th Division on the cot next to mine, half mad from the pain of his wound, reliving two years of his hell. The U.S. 45th had already had two years of combat—the Kasserine Pass, the Sicily invasion, Salerno, bloody Cassino, the Gothic Line, the Rhône, now here. This sergeant was the only survivor of his company's original complement. Half delirious, he's in the foxholes, M1 burning his hands, helmet machine-gun-smashed twice, deaf from the eighty-eights' blasts. Keep going, squad, keep down! Belly crawls toward longed-for death.

The chaplain—a captain—and his sidekick sergeant. What are they here for, another death? Not this time—a box full of medals, Purple Hearts all around. Making their way down the line, like handing out candy, not quite the cure these poor bastards need.

"Name, rank, serial number, soldier."

Me! Fuck that. This fucking war, just fuck off, give me my aspirins… Sir… please.

My neighbor turns toward me, thumbs up, grins, shakes his head—and groans.

❧

There's a break in the weather, our twelve hours are here, the artillery thunder has stopped. We borrowed Little Schmuck from our friendly lieutenant, headed off for a jaunt, and maybe to trade cigarettes for some coal. East and south into Alsace, more German than French, it had switched many times through the centuries. The ghosts of a thousand warriors, they say, still wander here in the Vosges—shields, spears, helmets of leather.

High into the hills, still green through the snow, pine woods, meadows, steepled villages, smoke from stone farmhouses inviting us in for a bowl of warm milk or their eau-de-vie-de-poire, their schnapps. This is the French First Army's sector—random tanks scattered about, washing draped on the turrets, a hammock slung between gun barrels, black African soldiers with their laughing girls dancing to a mandolin's tune. They ply us with eau-de-vie and dried figs.

God! Here it comes again, the GI radio network plays it once an hour, this "Great Speckled Bird." Roy Acuff. He wiped out Sinatra in the army vote. Our old friend "Lili Marlene" is dead. My trusty radio—I smuggled a wire, buried in the muck, two hundred yards from our generators. Here, four of us squeezed in an attic, warmed by the family and cows below us and the mound of steaming, composting manure piled against the front wall—we could step out our window onto it.

Cigarettes still are the best currency—with one carton a week, you can't afford to smoke. Wine, coal, the fresh-baked bread, sometimes an egg or two, a haircut, maybe even a hot-water shave on a trip to the nearest town. And I'm told it takes only six fags to buy sex from the girls.

On to Sarrebourg in the heavy snow. Jerry has just moved out. This house, six of us, it's still warm from the coal-burning furnace, half-eaten breakfast on the table, German magazines lying about. I'll stash away some of these swastika armbands, medals, photos, mail them home when I can.

Bastogne, deep in snow, zero weather, Jerry almost made it, almost got to Allied Rear HQ. The Battle of the Bulge. We had sent back an urgent report warning of a massing of German armies, seemed headed for the Ardennes. Ignored, didn't get to the right command, who knows?

But Jerry's regrouping, we picked it up, reported in this morning. They're headed south—toward us. Did HQ hear us this time? Perhaps—a U.S. infantry division moves forward past us.

Jesus, that's rifle fire! Coming closer. Outflanked, broke through? Jerry's headed at us. Midnight, and they're closing in. Pack, pull out! Retreat into a subzero blizzarding night. To a windowless stone schoolhouse, to sleep on the cold floor, one blanket apiece.

⊸

On the move again. In early March, the U.S. First Army had grabbed a bridge over the Rhine at Remagen, upstream from Bonn. Hadn't the Germans got it mined in time? Or was it, as some were saying, that the German field commanders wanted to let the Western Allies through to occupy as much of Germany as possible before the Soviets got over the Oder?

A PFC from the radio intercept van banged on our door this morning, waving his pad of message forms. He'd copied down a message, in plaintext, German—he couldn't read it.

The battle will be conducted without consideration for our own population, all industrial plants, all main electric-

ity works, waterworks, gas works…all food and clothing…
destroyed…create a desert in the Allies' path. Your Führer,
A. Hitler

Not a comforting message even for a battle-hardened
Prussian.

The breakthroughs have begun, the Rhine is crossed in
several more places, bridges repaired, gaps Bailey-bridged
where the engineers could. We've moved up fast. Into Germany proper, through the Saar, factories smoldering, to
Worms. The worst of horrors—not a building left standing,
bulldozers clearing tracks through the rubble, uncovering
countless corpses, the stench sticks to us for days. Disgusting banter from one of us about a Diet of Worms. This gorgeous city I'd visited ten years before, city of Martin Luther,
of Liebfraumilch wine, the Niebelungenlied, flattened yet
again—the Huns, the Thirty Years War, the French, and now
the American and British bombs.

A woman carrying a child in a bundle on her back is
searching the ruins as we roll by. She stares at us, venomous,
moves on. The shame of victory, I can't sort it out.

Two of our men were stabbed yesterday, left for dead in
a ditch near where we'd camped overnight. One managed
to tell us that they'd been invited to bed by village women.

NO FRATERNIZING

It was posted everywhere. We've heard others have died
when given buzz-bomb juice, the fuel for Jerry's V-1 robot
bombs, disguised as schnapps in ersatz orange juice. De-
monize each other, appropriate a god, drive us to kill and be
killed, this is what you get—in victory or defeat.

Augsburg, we've set up in the outskirts, listen in on the
Germans' last hope. Festung Europa they call it, their final

fortress, rumored to be in the mountains by Berchtesgaden, where Hitler had gobbled up Austria, gave Chamberlain umbrella status, built himself a mountaintop retreat. We comb the likely radio frequencies—nothing, nothing to it. In fact, the messages we do pick up now are in plaintext, even English at times. Generals lining up to surrender, hoping, I suppose, for special conditions. May seventh, the Germans surrender at Rheims. May eighth, again in Berlin.

⟜⟞

Paris on a three-day pass, trucked there, a bunch of us, twelve hours on miserable war-beaten roads. A hotel on Place de la République. A dutiful sightseeing tour, the feelthy peectures at every stop. A four-star restaurant—was it Chez Lapin?—but only passable food, and then the Folies Bergére. Streetwalkers are everywhere, dirt cheap. Twice they almost had me, but...

Back to the Rhine, to Karlsruhe, to the waiting, endless waiting to go home. The Armed Forces Network announces, "Hiroshima ... atomic bomb ... historic breakthrough ... atomic fission ... one element made into another ... major step for humanity." The alchemist's dream, lead into gold, the Midas touch? That's what the announcer seems to be saying.

Humanity? How many killed? Victory, shame?

⟜⟞

Ravaged Germany to bounteous Switzerland. Compassionate leave, they called it, a week's leave for those men who have blood relatives in Switzerland. That's me, yessir. Poor auntie, she'd no doubt need compassion.

The classy train runs smoothly, bridges, tracks intact. The cities in France ruined, stinking of death. We sail on through, Strasbourg, Colmar, Mühlhausen, and the border crossing.

Greenish uniform, cocky cap. "Just your army pass, Sir, that will do."

Sir! I like that. And then the wonder of a normal, undisturbed civilian world, a thriving picture-postcard-chocolate-and-cuckoo-clock-and-watches-and-cheese country. Fat, clean, complacent, they're intensely curious, in their stolid way, at maybe their first sight of a combatant—so-called, I quickly add. They'd issued us Eisenhower jackets, caps with the orange and white Signal Corps piping—our helmets, were they turned in for good, or would they pack us off for the Pacific?—some colorful ribbons, hashmarks, medals, the unit citation patch we'd been awarded, my combat boots would have to do. Do I look enough the part? In Basel, I take a train to Ascona, Lago Maggiore, the south, to the address The Old Man had sent me. No Aunt Katy, but a delightful sunny day with a swim in the lake and a feast of fish and rosé wine. I finally find someone who knows her and gives me her Bern address. I phone, I find her, I zip there in another of their marvelous electric trains. Hugs and kisses and she takes me to the Hotel Royal Palace, puts me in the royal suite—I mean it, me a still somewhat-muddy sergeant—that looks out spectacularly over the gorge of the Aare.

Wined, dined, pampered outrageously, a special banquet put on by the American minister, Leland Harrison, just for me—the OSS chief, Allen Dulles, with his cast of spies, a couple of military attachés, U.S. generals who'd passed a lovely war, and best of all the American minister's gorgeous daughter who accedes to a date for the next day. Toasts, welcomed ego-building questions, my stories taking on some extra height, demitasses, cigars, cognacs, the works.

My date starts with the obligatory sightseeing. The pathetic bears in their pit, the Zeitglockenturm with its mechanical puppets doing their number before every hour, the arcades, the fountains. We go back to her elegant house for dinner en famille. Except it isn't. Our worthy minister is summoned to the phone, comes back to tell us surrender messages from Tokyo are coming in, relayed through neutral Switzerland to Washington. Much excitement, staff coming and going, my date perforce most decorous. Ah well, and if it had come to a pinch? Our sad-sack hero would no doubt not have carried the day.

Aunt Katy puts on a cocktail party to honor her warrior hero. But this time it seems I am not the center of attention, for across the room is a cluster around a white-haired man, introduced by Aunt Katy as the renowned Carl Gustav Jung. Now, who the hell is he?

⤳

A United Fruit Company passenger-and-cargo steamer made over for troops, reasonably comfortable for once. Marseille, the Balearics, out past my blue hills of Spain, Gibraltar, under Hercules' crotch, westward, Europe left far behind. Two days later I'm perched on the prow, my favorite spot, whatever the boat that I'm on. The early sun is warm on my back, a herd of dolphins leads the way. I doze for a moment, wake with a start, the sun is full on my face. Off the port side, I see our wake has become a U, we've certainly turned back. What the fuck are they doing? The skipper forgot his wife in Gib, or the war's started up again, or a U-boat's still out here on the loose, or they've gone back to pick up that chickenshit major, the one we dumped off the stern?

"All hands! We have turned back to Gibraltar. A propeller shaft bearing is overheating."

An hour of seething disbelief, then the sun's on my back

again, All hands! We've found a spare bearing. Repairs are under way. We trust there's been no inconvenience.

No no, most certainly not.

⌁

Land ho! It's Staten Island, not Manhattan, but what the hell. We pull up dockside, decidedly listing to starboard with a thousand men crowding the rails. A band blares music-hall ditties and patriotic stuff, majorettes wave American flags, a few civilians, a lone man in a fedora, and a hot-dog wagon or two. The gangplanks reach up, hands to secure them. The good old US of A.

"Sergeant Cabot, Robert M, report to the bridge, on the double."

Shit, now what have I done? The crew shows me the way, a saloon astern of the wheelhouse. He's there, the fedora, it's… oh fuck! It's The Old Man to greet me, in the flesh. I get it, he's a director of the company that owns this fucking boat.

The demobbing in an army camp somewhere in New Jersey took a week. The heavy pressure to get us to join the National Guard. The paperwork, the lectures about the dangers of reentry into civilian life. A uniform—waist-length Eisenhower jacket, shined up combat boots, cap with the Signal Corps orange and white piping—a duffle bag of this and that, a train ticket from wherever I was in New Jersey to New York, and Harry Truman's signature on my Honorable Discharge.

New York was jammed, not a hotel room to be had. I spent the night in the workout gym of the Pennsylvania Station Hotel, even getting a massage, a bit of the war kneaded out of me. The next morning, in Times Square, I bought the various decorations my service record said I had earned—

six or eight bits of fruit salad on my left breast, various insignia for where and when and how my time had been served, a rifle pin with a dangling bit saying what an expert I had been on the firing range. That sort of thing. Then a DC3 flight into Boston and a doting family reception committee.

⌖

Memories, stories to tell.

Troop transports, four-by-four trucks, jeeps, requisitioned sheds, hospitals, mud, bitter winters, strafing by Messerschmidt jets, dive bombings, limbs blown off. Bodies—American, French, German soldiers, civilians, bloated horses, cattle, smoldering tanks and trucks—scattered on the frozen fields of Alsace. In the last months of the war, we began to hear of the concentration camps. And there were tales of the furloughs, the three-day passes, free time in the euphoria and beauty of deeply wounded, liberated, glorious Europe and her many ruined empires.

Memories of my teammates Louis, Murray, Bill, Emile, Werner, The Hat, Arnold, and many names that have faded away—close friends, colleagues, tent mates. We were a team through it all, depending on each other's wits to divine German intentions, and with some success. Contacts with many of them, by chance and by design, continued for a few years. A platoon mate was my French teacher for a term when I returned to Harvard. One of our lieutenants became a history lecturer at Harvard. Another I chatted with for a time on a Vermont ski hill, though some of the ingrained caution and reticence of the officer/enlisted man barrier was still there. I heard from Louis's sister that he died shortly after returning, an illness contracted in the last months of the war. She wrote, "And all he ever got was a carefully folded American flag." Murray became CEO of a small steel fabricating company in Pittsburg, which had had some dealings with a division of Cabot, Inc. He came to Seattle a few years ago, we dined together—poignant, slipping into dementia. Bill, a stockbroker before the war, retired to Florida. We exchanged notes for a time, then his wife wrote me that he had died of cirrhosis of the liver.

Fall, 1945, demobilized. Greeted home by brothers Tommy and Louis, sister Linda, with brother Ned in crib.

～9～

Starry-eyed America

FROM FIFTEEN years of economic depression, isolation, and then war, America emerged with optimism and vigor, with a far more socially conscious body politic, and with a sense of democratic destiny. Many idealistic goals appeared to be achievable. To redirect our enormously enhanced productive capacity to peaceful ends. To build the infrastructure of institutions—schools, hospitals, libraries, civic facilities—the highways, dams, port facilities, railroads, power stations, power lines, pipe lines. To help rebuild Europe and much of Asia. To construct a world order that could truly control controversy and guarantee peace. To see that the enormous economic bounty and the ideals of a magnanimous America infuse the world. To confront our own shameful racisms, discriminations, inequalities, corruptions.

American politics seemed reinvigorated, bipartisan where it really mattered, and extraordinarily visionary. Even in 1940, the businessman Republican opposing FDR in the presidential election, Wendell Willkie, embraced the unlikely goal of world government. Democrats such as Roosevelt, Truman, Marshall, Acheson. Republicans such as Vandenberg, Taft, Eisenhower, Stassen. They found much common ground. Within weeks after the war had ended, we had hosted and been a prime mover in the creation of the United Nations, the International Monetary Fund, the World Bank. The GI Bill was passed giving free education to veterans.

There were, however, dark clouds about, even in those hopeful years. A feeling of guilt began to emerge at having annihilated two Japanese cities, killing hundreds of thousands of civilians with atomic bombs. Early on, it was apparent that the Allies' saturation bombing of much of Germany into rubble with an enormous cost of human life had little if any effect on the outcome of the war. The realization of the full horror of the Holocaust and the accumulating evidence that the Allies and the Vatican had failed to take possible ameliorating steps was a source of shame and anguish. Our expression of guilt over the internment of Japanese-Americans on the West Coast was increasing. Racism, bigotry, intolerance in America were all too evident. Lynchings, largely of blacks, had taken many thousands of lives and, though lessening, still were happening after the war. Anti-Semitism was rampant. That America's most famous journalist, Walter Lippmann, could be refused entry at a New York hotel made a particularly deep impression on me.

Communism was emerging as a perceived threat. The Allies had made major geopolitical concessions to Stalin, defining vastly expanded Soviet spheres of influence both to the east and the west. This was widely seen as an unnecessary sell-out. The Iron Curtain was rapidly drawn by an aggressive Soviet Union. And soon we were at war again, Korea.

The energy of accomplishment, beginning in Roosevelt's New Deal, gaining power in the war years, and achieving considerable fulfillment in the early post-war years, began to fade as the madness of the nuclear arms race with the Soviet Union became obvious, and as the paranoia of Mc-Carthyism gained strength. A decade later The Bay of Pigs fiasco, the horrors and defeat of the Vietnam War, assassinations—the Kennedy brothers, Martin Luther King, Malcolm X—the widespread riots of the late 'sixties. By the last quarter of the century, our hopes were seriously dimmed.

‡

In the summer of 1947, before heading to law school, I found myself with Stringfellow Barr, Cord Meyer, and many other starry-eyeds at a convention in Luxembourg of the World Movement for World Federal Government. It was an already sadly moribund undertaking. And the clash of ideologies and greed minimized the effectiveness of the new United Nations as the Cold War heated up.

An aside. Cord Meyer, a seriously wounded war hero, a founder of the World Federalism movement, and a famous young aide to the American delegation at the San Francisco founding of the United Nations, later became a dirty-tricks CIA bigwig. He was even accused by Howard Hunt, a White House "plumber" in the Watergate affair, of orchestrating the assassination of JFK. Meyer's former wife, Mary Pinchot, was a mistress of JFK. She was later mysteriously murdered. On his deathbed, Meyer said she was murdered by JFK's assassins. CIA's notorious dirty-tricks chief, James Angleton, was caught apparently trying to burgle her home for her diaries. And another scenario was making the rounds—that Meyer had been part of an JFK assassination team masterminded by Lyndon Johnson!

Titillating, these conspiracy theories, though one seems to preclude the other, and they are way beyond improbable, given the continued silence of the large network of conspirators that would have been necessary to these theories.

⊸

Nevertheless, for America's youth, particularly us veterans, those were the brightest of years. We were offered extraordinary opportunities, and we either seized them immediately or relied on them to be there for us when we were ready. I was, it is true, starry-eyed, but it took some time for my stars to settle into place. Studies, geopolitics, societal values, fun, friends, careers.

And women—for some time they were, for me, dazzling galaxies.

∾ 10 ∾

Birds and Bees

THE IMMEDIATE world I entered in 1924 was, at least on the surface, almost entirely male dominated. I believe my mother sincerely considered herself to be of an inferior sex—less intelligent and knowledgeable, inept at fixing things, at numbers, at joining male conversation. She was a loving mother. She ran her household well. She was good and tireless at reading aloud. She ordered food every morning by phone to be delivered by the local mom-and-pop grocers. She was good at mountain hikes, good with horses and dogs—no cats—and with family members from her line. But when she was thrown in with the Cabot line, she considered herself hopeless. And her husband agreed with her and often as good as told her so—however lovingly. Yet even in him, there was an element of bafflement, of awe—yes, in some ways he did hold her in awe. And there was enduring love between them.

My sister Linda suffered acutely from Mother's lack of self-esteem, considering her to be nestled in downy isolation, unable to endow her daughter with even basic household practicalities. Linda once told me that the only practical thing she learned from her was how to fold and hang bathroom towels properly.

Mother was, however, clearly better at horsemanship

than her husband—and she knew it. She was an avid rider—trail riding, drag-hunting, point-to-points, pack trips. There is speculation that she deliberately acquired difficult, even dangerous horses for herself to outdo her husband. She went through several racetrack mares who knew nothing but the track and the jockey, who shied violently and regularly at the unknowns of the bridle trail—headstrong, bucking, throwing her, on occasion, as well as several others in the family. Well beyond her husband's patience and capacities.

Of course, her low self-esteem was by no means warranted. It was imposed on her by the accident of the familial, cultural, and historical world that she found herself in. Few women within my early horizons broke out of that world, a world that fortunately came under increasingly successful attack as my century progressed.

In the Weimar Republic emerging from a Germany defeated in World War I, women got the vote in 1919. The rise of the Nazi party was largely through democratic processes, but the women's vote for the Nazis was considerably less than the men's. In 1920, four years before I was born, women got the vote in America, the result of decades of heroic work. In the United Kingdom, though single women thirty and over got the vote in 1918, universal suffrage did not come until 1928. In France, it was 1944. In Switzerland, 1971. And still, in much of the world, even if there is an election it is usually rigged, meaningless, and largely women-less.

The bit of the world that received me in 1924 was dominated by the Cabot line. A characteristic of that line then was repression—emotions, dreams, mystery, art, sex, joy, spontaneity. Happiness was a goal but defined strictly as an uplifting and intellectualized event. Natural beauty was noted and announced as such, to be appreciated as an intellectual given.

Anal prudes, that Cabot line, at least what I knew of it. As a child, maybe seven, I wandered into my parents' dressing room, my father standing naked in front of me. I was reprimanded for asking, What's that thing? I was led to believe that I'd said something naughty, dirty. Later, when we brothers were required to swim naked with naked him, I was permanently embarrassed—I still find men's locker-room scenes gross. I don't remember ever seeing my mother naked—even breast-feeding was out.

In childhood and even up to my leap into the war, certain words, mostly four letters, were never pronounced, never written, entering my consciousness only with a considerable degree of guilt. In cases where communication required some reference to otherwise prohibited subjects, we used indirect words or gestures. For us, "shit" became "moody"—derived from bowel "movement". Among us boys, sexual intercourse seemed to have no word at all, just a finger of one hand plunged into the other fist.

We got the birds-and-bees sex education from our father, done with mystery and finality. Later, as we headed into puberty, he would tell us of the evil involved in premarital sex. "Think of your mother and her disappointment if you were ever tempted." And the delights of masturbation clearly should be, but weren't, firmly suppressed. In that first half of the century, there was still the word out there that the onanist risked insanity.

And yet on my mother's side, the Wellington line, I still hear stories of families that seem to have lived a home life uninhibitedly. Often entirely naked, male and female inter-mingled even in the most—private?—bodily functions. I hear of cousins in pre-pubescent all-out sexual experimen-tation, becoming ever more fun in puberty—so they told me. I, to my great regret later, heeded the paternal admoni-tion, remaining, though just barely, virginal until my first wedding night. That seems almost unbelievable in the world I live in today. By now, there is almost a sense of shame in such a confession. I don't know the statistics on this, or if there are any, but I would guess that this was rather com-mon in the 1930's societal niche in which I then lived and that transgressors in that niche experienced at least a modi-cum of guilt.

⊕

But hindsight sees a far different world. There were six-teen million in the U.S. military in World War II, almost all men, and they were given fifty million free condoms each month. Eighty percent of the U.S. military who had been away from home for two or more years—in that war there was no home-and-back rotation—admitted to frequent sex-ual intercourse, and one third of them were married. And of course, it went right to the top. General Eisenhower's driver in England, Kay Summersby, became his mistress. Roosevelt had his private secretary, Lucy Rutherford—he even called her to his deathbed rather than Eleanor.

More than a hundred GIs were executed by the U.S. military command for rape and murder. As hundreds of thousands of GIs flooded in to occupy Japan, they descend-ed in droves on the Japanese "comfort stations." These had been a regular feature of the Japanese military. There were thousands of them, peopled still with tens of thousands of enslaved "comfort women" drawn from throughout the

Japanese empire. And the dreadful stories of the women and their horrors are still coming out.

✧

In 1900, one in five adult American women worked outside the home. They were mostly unmarried and were running against the mainstream belief that women should stay at home, supported financially by their husbands. In World War II, fifty percent of adult women, and this time most of them married, joined the work force, which included many imported workers, largely from Mexico. An old codger with a tiny gift shop behind the taco stands on the Alameda of the Mexican town where I wrote some of this memoir, likes to talk, codger-to-codger, of the years he spent in Detroit on the Sherman tank production line.

Millions of women learned that they were as good as or better than men at their jobs. They built aircraft, they flew them to the combat zones. And though they might be riveters, wear a welder's mask, or run a company, they were still attractive to the men they met on the job.

The war brought about major changes in the role of government. The enormous costs were borne by heavy taxes— by 1945 the top marginal income tax rate was 94%—and by unprecedented deficit financing. The withholding tax on wages and the income tax gave the government ready access to everyone's earnings and income. Deficits exceeded the entire gross domestic product. Yet at the end of the war, the country, far from being depleted, was the economic powerhouse of the world. The role of government in the social welfare of its citizens had been revolutionized by the depression of the 'thirties. By the end of the war, the role of the U.S. government in the world economy and hence in the geopolitics of the world was dominant.

By extension, the American woman was gaining new power. The attack on gender discrimination, the revolution of women's rights was underway, though it still has a long road ahead.

↭

This was the world that millions of us young American males returned to, back from years of war. For some it was years of repressed urges, for most, it was years of one-night stands, wherever they could be found. For all, they were years of absence from the normal, whatever that might have been. We expected that normal to be there for us on our return. Many of us clung to that, at least for a time, not ready to accept the irreversible changes that the war had brought about.

My romantic notions about girls, women, their place in the world , were, of course, far from any reality even before the war. To cling to those notions on my return perhaps shows the strength of the societal and familial imprint that I bore—or just another character aberration?

↭

There were three girls on my sixth-grade football team. Peggy and Betty were guards, Buddy was a tackle. Padded pants, shoulder guards, floppy leather helmets—bruising, tough, determined. The ends, the backfield, the light-footed ones were puny boys—Sandy, me, I've forgotten the other names. Yet in class, when the teacher wasn't looking, I slipped folded bits of paper with crayoned hearts and flowers, an I-Love-You to nearby girls. Though girls could act like boys, their world was a mystery.

Girls, women. The warm embrace, breast to yearning heart. The laughing eye, the perfumed-dancing-swirling-away—away, beyond the touch of a timid hand. The colors, the shadows, the loss, the passing, the tears, the farewell. And, maybe, the call, the far-off ghost of a reply. The forgiveness, the return. The question, the promise.

↤

I returned from four years of war, uniformed, polished combat boots, sporting my ribbons, my modest decorations and achievements, with the ruptured-duck patch of an honorable discharge newly sewn on my Eisenhower jacket sleeve. Shown off by my parents and my U.S. Navy desk-officer brothers as the battle-hardened Intelligence Platoon sergeant, I traveled across the country with my father by train—modestly fêted, speeches, a curiosity in the civilian and desk-officer world. On to my oldest brother's lavish U.S. Navy marriage.

I was quite willingly on display for a short time, then was swallowed up in the hordes of far more meritorious veterans. Back to college, charged with ambition to make up for lost time—girls, fun, studies, career—but vacillating on how, when, and where to proceed.

Girls were everywhere, yet I was awkward and timid. A few tepid dates, one or two heating up only to be quickly resisted…by me. Deb parties with me the self-made wallflower. But then an ardent two-year friendship with a remarkable girl, Ann Resor. Flaming red hair, bookish but fun, popular, offering close friendship but never more, despite my fumbling proposals of marriage. Studying together, skiing weekends from the college cabin below Mount Washington, a summer visit to her family's lavish Wyoming ranch. A cruise on my family's forty-eight-foot yawl skippered by old seadog me, sailing from the Chesapeake to Maine. Ann, four or five college mates, theoretically chaperoned by a just-married college mate and wife. Kevin Andrews, his bag-piping from

Lounging with Ann Resor in Jackson Hole, Wyoming, 1947.

the bow echoing off Manhattan's skyscrapers as we sailed up the East River—dear Kevin who became a strong influence in my life until his enigmatic death, drowned swimming at dusk out into a Mediterranean storm. I shall refer to him again.

Ann, two good years of friendship, coming to a tearful end. A last glimpse as her New York apartment door closes me out. Some years later she was to marry Jay Laughlin— friend of Ezra Pound, founding publisher of New Directions. Sadly, she was to die of bone cancer much too young.

Returning from a summer in Europe on a converted troop transport, I met Charlotte Fitzpatrick, she of the black hair, the Irish eyes. More skiing, more weekends down to Manhattan from Yale Law School, and my marriage proposal accepted.

✣

But first, back to my remaining college days. What am I here for, what are we back in college for? To catch up, make up for lost time, get on with—what? Four years of war, from eighteen to almost twenty-two, four years of longing to return to a familiar world, but years that had shaped us and the world profoundly and in unexpected ways.

Like many privileged school kids, I'd not had a plan for my life. I was uneasy with my privilege but unfocussed on what to do with it. I had done a lot of reading, had written some interesting short stories in school, and was uncomfortable with my societal niche. Still, to prepare for some sort of job in business seemed the path of least resistance, and while overseas I even half-heartedly signed up for a correspondence course in economics. The nurture pull was strong. But by the end of those four war years, I was readying for something else.

First, I would finish Harvard, and in a hurry—two years with summer school, a mishmash of courses, none in the least inspiring or memorable. It was not a grind, though—B to B+ grades. And with a modest amount of fun. Skiing, beer parties with 10th Mountain Division veterans, collecting jazz records. The weekly tea party—black tea spiked with rum, cakes and cookies from the Window Shoppe, early jazz from my small horde of 78s—our tea party in our dormitory living room was the focus of my friendships. Ann, Helenty Estin who'd escaped from Eastern Europe with her family and a sizeable chunk of treasure as the Germans arrived, Twit, and three or four other Radcliffe College girls. Kevin of the kilts and bagpipes and classy British stammer, dorm neighbors, a variety of college mates, and roommates Art and Larry.

With roommate Larry Lunt at Harvard College, 1946.

Art Eldridge, a neighbor and schoolmate in primary school, in World War II had served in the Tenth Mountain Division. Some of his brutal experiences in both the Aleutian expedition and the Apennines are retold fictitiously in my novel *The Isle of Khería*. He died, still a young man, sitting peacefully in his favorite easy chair, pipe in hand. I'd known Larry Lunt since we were toddlers. He enlisted in the U.S. Air Force, served as navigator on a Black Widow propeller-driven night fighter. His unit was based on one end of Iwo Jima while at the other end of the island many thousands of U.S. Marines and Japanese were dying in that famous battle. I speak of Larry's death later in this memoir.

I usually managed to tolerate the tyranny of The Old

Man on occasional sails on his yawl between terms at college. Before a summer term at Harvard, I took a few days off to join him and Mother to explore a ranch that his company rented for employees' and clients' R & R in Colorado's Sangre de Cristo mountains, climbing the fourteen thousand foot Culebra in spite of my suppressed acrophobia.

Many of us were drawn to the idealistic energies of the times—toward moving the world under a rule of law rather than of raw competing power—Willkie's "One World", World Government, the United Nations seemed a promising beginning. I resolved to go on to law school, international law, to eventually apply to the UN's Office of the Legal Adviser. Education, for us veterans, was free, thanks to the G.I. Bill—and that enormous boost was a key in propelling the U.S. into decades of growth, prosperity, and ever greater world hegemony. And propelling me—though I could have afforded it—into Yale Law School.

Graduation from college was a small moment for me, but that Harvard Commencement of 1947 was a major moment on a historic scale. Sitting in a sea of graduating gowns in the stifling humidity of a New England June, in the ritual drone of self-important Harvard. First, T. S. Eliot was honored and spoke eloquently. Then, General George Marshall, the leader of the American military victory in World War II and by then the Secretary of State, announced the intention of the Truman administration to undertake a massive plan of aid to help reconstruct much of the world so devastated by war—the Marshall Plan, as it came to be called.

~11~

Best of the Best

TRUMAN, the folksy haberdasher, a nonentity from Independence, Missouri, Roosevelt's last vice president, had been catapulted into the White House upon Roosevelt's death. It had been his decision—he of "The Buck Stops Here" Oval Room desktop reminder—his decision alone, to introduce the peoples of the world to the potential of total self-annihilation, to make the choice to drop the atom bombs on Hiroshima and Nagasaki. This was a decision made in the first few weeks of his tumultuous and ill-prepared presidency. As VP, he evidently had not been aware of the existence of the atomic bombs. It is said that Roosevelt disliked him and kept him out of the White House decision-making process. President Truman was briefed on the bomb by Jimmy Byrnes who had been a close adviser to Roosevelt. But Byrnes had expected to be Roosevelt's VP, was resentful of Truman, and was a strong advocate for the immediate use of the bomb on Japan, as was the War Department. A vast majority of the scientists who were in any way associated with the development of the bomb were opposed to any use of it beyond a relatively harmless demonstration to the Japanese of its destructiveness. Szilard, Einstein, Oppenheimer—sixty of these men signed a letter to this effect, but it very likely never got to the president. Truman was ill-informed. Even then, though, his decision to use the bomb on Japan was to be restricted to its use on a military target, and his radio announcement of the bombing called Hiroshima a military target. Both Hiroshima and Nagasaki were overwhelmingly civilian targets.

Truman announced in early 1947 his determination to take a hard stand against Soviet ambitions of world communist hegemony—the Truman Doctrine—and thereupon put it to work in supporting the Greek royalists in a bitter civil war against a Soviet-supported fiercely anti-fascist movement. This Truman Doctrine was a key early step in shaping the Cold War, though its application in Greece proved highly divisive and misdirected. I was later to hear much about American follies there from Kevin Andrews, who went straight from that Harvard Commencement to spend the rest of his life in Greece, identifying deeply with her agonies.

It was this humble, seemingly small-bore Truman who later threw a reinvigorated American military might into the rescue of at least the southern half of the Korean peninsula from a communist invasion that had very nearly succeeded. He courageously fired the enormously popular World War II leader of the Allied victory in the Pacific, General Douglas MacArthur, who had led the American expeditionary force that had helped drive the communist armies out of South Korea. MacArthur had gone on to occupy most of North Korea only to be driven back to South Korea by an enormous Chinese army. He leaked his plan, against Truman's orders, to bomb bases within China. Truman flew to Guam to confront and remove him from command. Firing him for his reckless insubordination was perhaps the most politically unpopular decision in presidential history.

In putting his essential weight behind the politically risky and historically unusual Marshall Plan, a plan to pour enormous resources into the reconstruction of former enemies as well as allies, Truman again acted with extraordinary political courage. Though the Soviet drive toward world hegemony was already evident and its "containment" had already been announced in the Truman Doctrine, Marshall Plan aid was nevertheless offered to the Soviets. They rejected it.

Both Roosevelt and Truman were generally ready to listen to and act on the advice of extraordinary cadres of wise men both in and out of government, men such as Dean Acheson. Acheson, in official and unofficial capacities, was instrumental in the shaping and implementation of American domestic and foreign policies from the early years of the New Deal through the Nixon administration, forty years of extraordinarily effective public service. There were many like him, and the presidents they served, both Democrats and Republicans, were wise enough to seek and give weight to their often uncomfortable and contrary advice. This was notably not the case with presidents George W. Bush and Donald Trump.

∽12∽

My Cheapo Tickets

MY PLAN had evolved. Early aspirations toward becoming a writer faded away when the world went to war. The war-effort-inspired idea of becoming a scientist I had aborted when I realized my dislike of and inability with advanced math. A desultory dabbling in economics at Harvard, with a view to mindlessly following the paternal path into business, died a quick death. No, I would go on with free education, get myself another free degree, and use it to launch myself into this heady activity of reshaping the world. A law degree seemed to be the best choice as an entry ticket.

That I could realistically and seriously contemplate, and later pursue, so many and so relatively exclusive paths speak, of course, for the enormous advantages that I was born into. Looking back, I am content to recall that I was always acutely aware of my abundant and usually unearned privileges, though in those early years I was not much of an activist in bringing about change in my country, in helping to level the playing fields.

My father, though he espoused and acted on his principles of noblesse oblige, gave the sense that his privileges came to him not by luck but rather by work. His philanthropic efforts were significant, both as giver and as highly successful fundraiser for the educational and scientific projects meaningful in his world. His giving of time and money were intellectually focused and bore elements of self-aggrandizement, a need to be given credit. His name is on buildings at Harvard, on professorships, on various plaques in public places around Boston. In that world, yes, he was effective. His leveraged giving was astute. For example, believing that the human population explosion was the direst threat of all to the world, he often would say that of all his extensive and impressive charitable giving, he was proudest of his relatively small gift to help enable the writing of the legal brief that gave legality to abortion in Roe v. Wade. And he was glad when his five offspring nevertheless produced hordes of descendants, all destined to be privileged and therefore, he believed, effective levers for good in the world.

⤸

In those years, my grasp of national and local politics was slight. With the exception of the men with whom I served for my four war years, the adults around me had been, I believe, almost exclusively Republicans. I soon began to form my own preferences, my rebellious inclinations nudging me. Those preferences were, and have been ever since, almost always Democratic. I believe there are still some die-hard Republicans in my extended family, supporters of Bush II and McCain/Palin, Romney/Ryan, but many had already opposed the Republican extremism of Goldwater, Reagan, and Bush II if not Bush I, and most swung to Obama. I would be surprised if any one of my siblings and their families supported Trump.

Yale Law School, small and liberal, for me it would also serve as a rebellious mini-step away from more conventional Harvard or Columbia, to which I had also been accepted.

I don't recall any parental comment about my decision, but it was against the advice of my grandfather.

Boston's Beacon Street, a street of traditional power and old wealth running up to the golden-domed State Capitol. Godfrey Lowell Cabot, an imposing name, an imposing town house. Elevator, chinoiserie from a trip-round-the-world year, lush but subdued, gloomy, gloved servants. He sits stiffly, watery eyes, bald, white moustache, impeccably suited. My teetotaler, Puritanical, unknowable, and most awesome Grandpa. "A dubious choice, law, my boy. You will be dealing with the quarrelsome, wasteful side of life."

Good advice, I'd say, but I really had no intention of becoming a lawyer. So off I go to New Haven in my shiny Studebaker coupe, bought two years before with my mustering-out pay and my silver spoon.

Three years in New Haven, singularly uneventful, getting by with as few hard law courses as possible. Writing papers wherever permitted instead of enduring the Socratic method and the massive exams. Philosophy, land-use, fact-finding, papers published in other law reviews on exchange control and international legislation.

There were, however, adventurous interludes for me during summer breaks—it being peacetime, the law school did not offer a summer term. I already mentioned my role in the doomed World Government Convention in Luxembourg. We were totally out-matched by sovereignty. It seems a dubious idea that mankind will improve its innate behavior, its penchant for violence, that there can be life without bloodshed, without greed. But efforts to control, to police our urges after two devastating World Wars in quick succession seemed worth trying.

That summer I went on to the Swiss Alps for a day or two of glacier skiing at Jungfraujoch, easily leaving Weltschmerz behind. Then a visit with Aunt Katy in Lausanne, she of Jung's bevy of patients-cum-mistresses. In that visit, I learned a lesson in how to gracefully reject seduction.

My one foray into employment in the corporate world was a job my father offered me to collect a wartime debt owed his company by his agent in Copenhagen and to then work under the tutelage of his vice president to do some snooping around England preparatory to opening a carbon black factory there.

The debt collection got no farther than a mammoth meal in the Tivoli Gardens and several time-bomb shots of ice-cold Genever gin. The snooping was more productive. It included climbing onto the vice president's shoulders, holding a camera over my head to blindly photograph a competitor's Cardiff factory hiding behind a broken-glass-topped brick wall. And a memorable overnight sleeper train trip to Edinburgh to see what creosote could be bought as a raw material for soot-making. Tablemates in the dining car were the Reverend Reginald Churchill and wife, he the chaplain to the king. That, in turn, led to tea at their house in the park behind Windsor Castle.

Then am I in London's high society. Through connections made before college—a cousin of a sister of a classmate was Sharman Douglas, daughter of the U.S. ambassador—I joined several beer parties at the ambassadorial residence, which in those days looked over Hyde Park. One evening, Foreign Secretary Bevin dropped in and joined us for a bit. A few days later, six or so of us, men and women, bicycled in the Cotswolds, going from inn to inn.

Another college classmate had talked his way into the

royal family with his soft southern accent. He invited me to join a small dinner party in a posh Mayfair restaurant with Princess Margaret. She was close to blotto. Later it was rumored that she had a two-year intimate relationship with Sharman Douglas. This classmate connected me to Emily Grigsby, once a gorgeous redhead southern belle with intimate connections to three generations of the royals. Invalid and ancient, she still loved to reminisce and gossip. She insisted that Prince Philip was gay.

Lots of contacts, but much to the distress of my father I already displayed propensities to deliberately leave potentially useful connections with the rich and powerful quite unexploited.

My outspoken support of Zionism and the creation of the state of Israel particularly distressed my father. On one of my summer adventures, I found myself on a plane sitting next to a South African man in his thirties who was on his way to Jerusalem and planning to move his family there to join in the War of Independence. I recently came across a copy of a letter I wrote to him speaking of my enthusiasm for the cause, and I found letters to various newspapers stating that I intended to join the cause and offering to freelance stories to them. I don't know whether my father ever realized how close I had come then to walking my talk.

Another set of summer adventures seemed to have involved primarily girls. Ann, Rosselle, Sissel, Charlotte, Sally. That first summer Ann and I still saw a lot of each other, though her firm No showed no signs of weakening. By coincidence, we were both in London. I had rented a cheap nondescript apartment off Baker Street. She was living in the Ritz Hotel with her mother. The modestly inconspicuous Boston wealth versus the extravagant New Yorker. In those early postwar years, the Ritz was an island of opulence in deeply wounded, heavily rationed London. Under the guidance of Ann's father's business acumen and her mother's extraordinary ad-art creativity, J Walter Thompson had become the largest ad agency ever. Their wealth was certainly conspicuous—an enormous posh ranch in Jackson Hole, Wyoming, a lavish home in Greenwich, Connecticut, valuable art acquisitions for New York's Museum of Modern Art, and themselves. Ann asked me to join her for a weekend at the Cambridgeshire home of Augustus John, Britain's foremost—and very expensive—portraitist.

On the River Cam, 1948, Cambridge, England.

She would sit for her portrait. He was a shaggy, dominant presence in a chaotic, multi-family country home. He tossed off a red-chalk-on-paper sketch, as I recall, rather like what you might get from a street-fair artist. They did say he was past his post-impressionism and portraitist-of-the-famous prime. So be it, and it would appear that at least a bit of the Bostonian judgmental abstemiousness persists in me.

By the next summer, I had been decisively told that my presence was intolerably clinging. Her door had closed to me. I signed up for a *cours de vacance* put on by the University of Bordeaux in Pau on the edge of the Pyrenees.

Pau, high above its river gorge, its handsome boulevard framing the distant Pyrénées, its castle to Henri Quatre. Peaceful, almost apathetic, still tainted by its recent Vichy-Nazi past under Pétain.

A summer course for foreigners—language, literature, history, the works. Dreary lectures I really couldn't comprehend, didn't want to. But the weekends were delightful—piling in a bus, wine and songs, Pyrénéan hikes to glaciered cirques and mountaintops. Boots, wool trousers, beret for our professor, patent leather high heels for a gorgeous señorita—she managed with them even on the rocky mountain trails. Not another American, just me. And the swimming, tennis, dancing, a try or two at the casino. School-kitchen meals—omelets, greens, sausage, warm baguettes, cheeses, the solid goat-milk yogurt in a tinfoil tube to dip in sugar, the never-ending wine. And my sweet Norwegian Sissel, my friend right from the start.

∻

During my law school years, my weekends were regularly in New York. At first, I was still clinging to Ann. When I was definitively rejected, I turned for a time to the friendship

An outing in the Pyrennes with Sissel Jensen and fellow Pau University *cours de vacance* students.

of her roommate Twit. And finally, on a student ship converted from a Kaiser-built mass produced troop transport returning a crowd of us still starry-eyed from one of those summers in Europe—seventy-five dollars round trip—I met Charlotte. Game, kind, and truly good, academically inclined, employed then at New York's Museum of Natural History. Our December wedding at her home in Saint Paul was conventionally lavish, bridesmaids and groomsmen of our sisters, brothers, friends. I had moved from a dormitory to a garage apartment of an uninhabited country estate outside New Haven where we settled in for my last term. For token rent, we were to keep an eye on the place.

With my LLB in hand, I struggled with the DC bar exam. I had learned very little law and had to endure an acutely depressing cram course and take the exam twice. That summer, we went to The Hague where I sat through a boring course at the Academy of International Law at the Peace Palace, now seat of the UN's new World Court. Given that the course was in French too, I again learned virtually nothing but sallied forth with yet another piece of paper.

College, law school, for me there was not much difference between them. After the triumph of my last years at school, I had settled into a B-to-B-plus norm and was to be never again academically inspired. Perhaps I learned something about the value of the generalist as well as the specialist, learned something about the processing of information. But I retained very little of the information itself. I would have made a mediocre physicist or economist or businessman or lawyer. The degrees, though, and from prestigious institutions, they served me well as admission tickets to my several varied generalist jobs as a government servant over the next ten years.

Even at the time, I had realized that I was on the fringes of hypocrisy. Still today, I seem often to be taken as knowing more than I actually do, and I am afraid I still do on occasion feed into this perception—and sometimes, to my chagrin, catch myself or am caught at it. For many years, I felt that forces quite foreign to the real me, particularly my father, were pulling the puppet strings of my life. My rebellions were to some extent driven by my need to escape these strings—name, father, accent, and degrees too. Yes, it was not long after I had coasted through to win those degrees that I began to move away from them. A message on a birthday card to me from my dearest Penny, my wife for the past forty years, is a quote from William Blake.

No bird soars too high, if he soars with his own wings.

∼ 13 ∼

From His Everlovin' Boss

T HE UNITED NATIONS, created in 1945 in San Francisco, held its early meetings in London. Not until 1951 did it move into its new Manhattan headquarters building, designed by a team of renowned architects including LeCorbusier and Niemeyer, on a site bought from John D. Rockefeller. When I went for an interview in 1950, it had moved from London and was temporarily housed in the massive, now dormant, plant of the Sperry Corporation—munitions manufacturers—at Lake Success, Long Island, not far from the site of the 1939-1940 World's Fair that I had enjoyed.

The UN Office of Legal Affairs was glad to accept my application and was optimistic of approval. However, there were hints of warnings. The member-nation staffing quotas were rigorous, seniority could not be jumped, and much of the job looked to be extremely dull. In short, a secure route to ineffective obscurity, disappearing forever into first a bomb-sight factory and then a glassy palace on the East River, there to watch a ghostly yawl sail by, bag-piped to the Cock 'o the North.

Look elsewhere. On to Washington, to the jovial advice of Tommy the Cork. Tommy Corcoran, once one of FDR's Happy Hotdogs, now a major presence behind the scenes, one of the many senior counselors to whatever administration held the power. My father arranged the meeting, having known Corcoran through, I believe, their mutual connections to the United Fruit Company. United Fruit was a notorious influence in Central America and on U.S. foreign policy there. Another wing of the American empire. Fruitful territory for sage advice—lobbying, it would be called today.

Will it be Irish or Scotch? Rocks? Now, listen to ol' Tommy & Son. Materials, raw materials, son, that's what ultimately drives the world. Start, though, with their extraction and their flow into our war production, our gearing up to win this war in Korea. See Stu Symington, senator, retired, you know, he's Truman's man to make arms production happen for this new war. I'll call the senator. And keep an eye on your dad, he's likely to run into rough stuff in the fruit company's dealings.

I'd meet him once again when I was about to take on an assignment with the U.S. economic aid program in Thailand. He gave me the name of a young friend whom he said he'd arranged to have sent to Bangkok. A job in export-import, he said. When I got there and looked this person up, it was obvious he was an undercover CIA type.

⊶

Washington, 1950. An eleven-foot-wide row house in Georgetown next door to a barely surviving black mom-and-pop corner grocery store. A daughter Kathleen just born. A short streetcar ride down Pennsylvania Avenue to my job in the Executive Office Building on White House grounds.

A famous building, built just after the Civil War, a flamboyant aberration in the midst of the Greek Revival architecture of most of governmental Washington. For Harry Truman, the EOB was "the greatest monstrosity in America" but was worth saving from the many attempts to tear it down. An enormous granite and cast iron and slate French Second-Empire intrusion. A parody of a huge French faux-château.

In its early years, it housed the Departments of State, Army, and Navy together. By the end of World War II, it housed the White House Offices, the Office of the Vice President, the National Security Council, the Budget Bureau, Presidential Commissions, the National Economic Council, and many other activities close to the White House. Several presidents have had hide-away offices there. And me.

The main tool Symington's office used in reviving America's huge military industrial output potential, which had rapidly turned to peacetime production after World War II, was a rather arcane but effective tax incentive—the granting of accelerated depreciation tax allowances to defense industries.

Symington had a lush upper-floor office in the EOB. I only saw it once. But in the bowels of that monstrous building in a small, dark room, sitting behind battered desks, was the guy in charge of the day-to-day operations and his assistant, me. So far as I recall, there were no other staff. We were responsible for dealing with the avalanche of phone calls from top management of American industry, for getting the recommendations from the relevant government departments, evaluating them, and passing our conclusions on to Treasury over Symington's signature. But there I was, this kid just out of an undistinguished three years of law school, me and my tolerant and brilliant boss-colleague, at the controls of the U.S. war effort—it seemed. Yet at the time, I thought nothing of it. In fact, it was soon quite boring.

Most of the avalanche of work had been dealt with in

a few months. Lunching in the Executive Office Building cafeteria with a friend, a lawyer with the Budget Bureau, I was told of a new project getting underway in the EOB, the staffing of a presidential commission Truman had arranged, the President's Materials Policy Commission, made up of big-name businessmen, an editor of *Fortune* magazine, and chaired by William Paley of Columbia Broadcasting System. There was a major concern that the country was running out of raw materials to feed its enormous maw. Let's find out the facts, do our best to project where we'll be twenty-five years from now. Under the direction of a young economist and two young lawyers—in later life they would become a college president, a State Department Legal Adviser, a Harvard law professor—a staff was assembled. Materials experts—petroleum, steel, copper, etc.—economists, population projectors. And a handful of generalists like me to pull things together. The bulk of the report would focus on estimating the materials reserves, the costs of extraction and refining, and projecting demand. But the Commission decided that one chapter of their report should take a critical look into the maw itself. Can anything be done to take some of the edge off our appetites? And they chose the construction industry as an example of where new technology, more sensible building codes, and other policy changes might make significant differences. That was my charge, me and an assistant, an old codger who had been in the lumber industry for decades and who had an extraordinary intuitive sense for the job we were given. That I had been chosen for this job, a callow fellow with no expertise whatsoever, is a reflection of those heady years when innovation was okay, and the need for generalists was well recognized.

We did a good job, my colleague and I. We farmed out

some of the work to think tanks, technology wonks, building-code experts. There was much writing and phoning to ferret out information about a hugely complex industry—often corrupt, clearly wasteful, hamstrung by outdated, confusing, and often scandalously skewed regulations. We put it all together in a few months, came up with a list of policy changes that governments might consider, and it became a chapter in the bulky report that eventually emerged from the Commission. The several volumes of the report were published months later—and largely disappeared into obscurity.

I recently Googled the report and found an index of the archives of the staff's work that still is stashed away somewhere, hundreds of boxes of memos, reports, letters, contracts, records. Buried in one box was my name—in parentheses. When our projected twenty-five years had passed, there were a few casual attempts to evaluate the accuracy of our projections and the efficacy of our recommendations. We were way off. Even our population projection was critically underestimated.

In the year and a half that I was in Washington, I had three very different jobs in the government. Each time I moved into a new job, I moved several steps up the civil service ladder. With my role in the Paley Commission winding down, and again through the cafeteria lunch mechanism, I joined a staff of twenty or so in a new office established by Truman to oversee all American foreign aid. Economic aid—the Marshall Plan and its successors. Military assistance—particularly weapons, as the Cold War heated up. And the secretive monitoring of the severe restrictions America was imposing on trade with the Soviet empire. This staff was headed by Averill Harriman, a man of unique

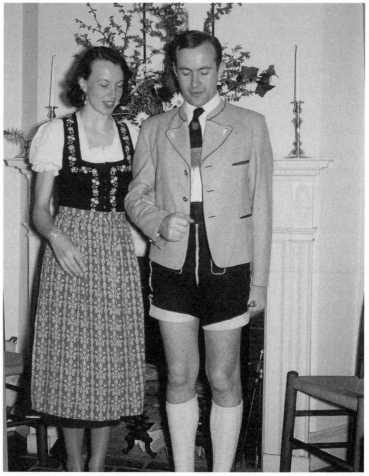

Charlotte and I dressed for a Washington costume party, 1949.

stature in the world of business, finance, diplomacy, and politics—and the founder of the Sun Valley resort where I'd skied on spring break from my Colorado school, and again with Charlotte on our honeymoon.

My role there turned out to be primarily the preparation of the elaborate and voluminous presentation books put on the desks of every member of Congress to back up the Truman administration's requests to Congress for foreign aid funds. I would often go to Harriman's morning staff meetings, sitting at the foot of an enormous conference table, headed in the distant gloom by the icy and largely silent Harriman. I never met the man. I don't recall ever speaking at those meetings. He surely did not know I existed.

Though I had no real need to see the vast flow of classified information dealing with U.S. foreign policy and its execution, much of it poured across my desk. Maybe it was assumed by the bureaucracy that any member of that prestigious staff was entitled to see all but the super classified. In any case, it was fascinating to me. And I would often carry a batch of Top Secret telegrams home on the streetcar to leaf through.

Heady stuff, sitting by the seats of power. But I was never much good at taking advantage of my contacts there. For me, the glamour of my unlikely jobs—and I never fully realized at the time how glamorous they should have seemed—wore off by the time I was well into this third job there in the EOB. I had concluded that the real action, the effective workings of our highfalutin government policies, were out closer to the receiving ends. That took our little family to Italy.

One of the last visitors to that tiny Georgetown house of ours before we packed up and sold it—I'd bought it for $17,000 and sold it a year and a half later for $25,000—was my father. He came for dinner. We served him a special culinary treat, a casserole made of three cans of tuna fish, a can of condensed cream of mushroom soup, and potato chips sprinkled on top. And there was a salad with handmade dressing including a garlic clove dangling on a thread inside the little cruet—the garlic came loose and ended up in my father's teeth.

He had been living in Washington in an apartment near the State Department, occasionally visited by my mother. When he was squeezed out of the presidency of the United Fruit Company—as he would tell it, the company's directors rebelled when he objected to the political skullduggery and bribes, the "gunboat diplomacy," that were a way of life for the company—he was drawn into the Democratic Truman administration in the number three position in the State Department as the Director of the Office of International Security Affairs. That he was chosen partly as a token moderate Republican businessman in an attempt at bipartisanship by a Democratic administration, he would often state himself. However, his extraordinary knowledge, his bear-trap mind, and his clout in the seats of power were of considerable value.

As usual, the Executive Branch of the national government, particularly at the higher levels, included many appointee businessmen. As the CEO of an important burgeoning industry, and with his obvious acumen, he should have been a good pick. His role in government, however, was short-lived, at least in part because Congress and the administration, as they seemed to do every year or so, yet again fiddled with power structures of the various foreign aid bureaucracies and a year or so later abolished his job. Harriman's new position reporting directly to the president took over his role and other responsibilities as well. My father was shunted aside.

He had hoped to get back into a high-level government position. When Kennedy came into office ten years later, he asked me to promote him with my friend and neighbor,

Adam Yarmolinsky, one of the talent scouts, the "king makers" of the new administration. No one was interested.

I believe my father left a mixed record in Washington. Despite his brilliance and clout, his people-skills were uneven. He was judgmental by nature, impatient with consensus making. By coincidence, years later I was assigned by the Agency for International Development to be program officer for the large U.S. economic aid program in Thailand. My boss, the head of the aid mission, Bill Shepard, had been an assistant to my father in the State Department. Bill was an admirer of my father, but it was quite clear that he had these same reservations about him as an administrator.

My father's close associations with many VIPs in and out of government were insufficient to get him back into a Washington position. I had met several of these associates—I hesitate to say "friends," for by the usual meaning of the word I still do not think of any of them as true friends of his, nor do I know of anyone who would qualify as such, at least by the time he had climbed well up the power ladder. During his tenure in the State Department, he would give cocktail parties, inviting Charlotte and me. Supreme Court Justice Frankfurter, Secretary of State Acheson, Senator this-and-that. Much to my father's distress, I took no advantage of these and similar contacts, remaining private, shy, uneasy, and largely silent throughout my fifteen years in government service.

⊷

Trunks, suitcases, Plymouth car are picked up to be shipped to Rome. We get a cabin on the maiden voyage of the S.S. *United States* on the next deck below first class. Light and airy, but small—baby Kathy sleeps in a bureau drawer. Truman's daughter and other VIPs are up there, traveling with the press. Daily newspaper, movies, shuffle board, bouillon brought to our deck chairs in the summer sun. A record three-and-a-half-day crossing to Southampton—much too quick—then on to Le Havre. Train to Paris, plane to Rome, Embassy car to a hotel. Hotel for a month until we find a lovely country cottage off the via Appia Antica—flower gardens, fig trees, a vineyard, soon friends with Italian and Irish families living across a field of artichokes. Four-and-a-half fine years there, joined by baby Sara, and by two rough wonderful country girls who took care of us, our daughters, and our little house.

Defense Program Officer, the job I angled for back in Washington. Three bright, hard working young Italians as my assistants—they became close friends. The job, with the Cold War heating up, was to try to direct our military assistance to Italy into procuring weapons, planes, vehicles made in Italy rather than made in the U.S., thus stimulating local defense production and the economy—two birds, one stone. And, as with much of U.S. economic aid, for every dollar we directed into Italy, the Italian government would appropriate the same amount in lire—the "counterpart funds"—over which the two governments had joint control, and which we helped program into economic reconstruction and development. A third bird, same stone.

There were three U.S. ambassadors in our years there. Ellsworth Bunker, a businessman who moved into diplomacy, becoming perhaps the most experienced and praised diplomat of his time—a gentle man who later, unfortunately, became infamous as the ambassador to Vietnam during the war. Clare Booth Luce, author, journalist, editor, Congresswoman, socialite, Republican wheeler-dealer, wife of *Time* magazine's Henry Luce. And J. D. Zellerbach of the lumber company. There were also three heads of the economic aid mission, and since they held the purse strings, there was considerable question for the Italians as to whether they should go with hand outstretched to the embassy or to the aid mission across the street.

The Marshall Plan actually drew to a close about the same time that I was sent to Italy. Its mission during its active years, 1948 through 1951, is described by its official title, the European Recovery Program. In those three-and-a-half years, Europe's economy far more than regained its prewar level and was well launched into its extraordinary period of growth and prosperity in the 1950s. There is still an active debate among economists and historians as to the role that the ERP played in this remarkable resurgence. There is general agreement, however, that the psychological impact, the sense of support and hope engendered in Europe by the ERP, was crucial.

The mechanism of the ERP was essentially to replace Europe's drastically depleted foreign exchange, its inability to buy raw materials, fuel, food, fertilizer, and machinery, by supplying them from largely U.S. sources, bought with Marshall Plan dollars, and in return requiring the recipient governments to deposit equivalent sums in local currencies to be used for reconstruction. It was, to a large extent, improvised rather than planned from the beginning. European governments and experts had major roles in its development, and of course, in its execution. The program got fully underway in mid-1948. It was staffed by an extraordinary group of men—very few women. They were largely drawn from business and academia. Favoritism and nepotism were almost non-existent. The recruitment process was extraordinarily rapid, a matter of a month or two from the initial contact to employment. It was notably bipartisan—more than that, apolitical. More than half those brought in to run the program were Republican. A member of the ERP mission to Greece, speaking of the enthusiasm of these men and women at the time, said:

> We had a goal; we had fire in our bellies; we worked like hell; we had tough, disciplined thinking, and we could program, strive for, and see results.

Politically, the Marshall Plan was not an easy sell in America. Senator Robert Taft led a conservative and non-interventionist Republican opposition. Taft was a chronic presidential candidate and hoped to follow Democrat Truman into the White House. It is thought that a reluctant Eisenhower, a national hero as leader of the Allied victory in Europe who had turned down a presidential candidacy in 1948, finally agreed to oppose Taft in the Republican primaries and convention for fear that an isolationist Taft presidency would dangerously embolden the Soviet Union. He only barely won in a bitter convention, then beat the Democrats' Adlai Stevenson in a landslide.

By 1951, the euphoria of the first two years of the Marshall Plan began to wear off. Routines were established. Many of the best men returned to their professions. The Soviet threat and the Korean War gradually eroded the non-political character of the European Recovery Plan. The communist threat became ever more urgent. Soviet expansionism seemed dangerously effective, and perhaps a third of the electorates in France, Greece, and Italy was voting communist. Increasingly, the program looked for ways to be used as a lever against communism, and that, to many, seemed to tarnish its image. Congress, too, lost some of its enthusiasm and whittled away at the autonomy of the Economic Cooperation Administration which ran the ERP, creating instead an agency—its name and some of its details changed often thereafter from ECA to MSA to FOA to ICA to AID—which was moved closer to conventional government departments, particularly State. A few years later, the agency administrating U.S. economic aid was fully integrated into State.

We went to Rome in the spring of 1952. Truman was still in the White House. Ellsworth Bunker was the ambassador in Rome, Vince Barnett the head of the ERP. They were both kind, generous men, both entirely accessible even to a newcomer like me. They both still carried the fervor and idealism of the Marshall Plan. I was surrounded by brilliant economists—Barnett, Chenery, Clark, Doggett. They went on to professorships, a university presidency, a number two spot in the World Bank. Ambassador Bunker was a strong advocate of the original intents of the Marshall Plan. Yet my job as the newly minted Defense Program Officer was to head a small piece of the aid mission that had just been set up at Washington's insistence, a job that was a considerable departure from those original intents.

The idealism was slowly draining away. Defense had virtually nothing to do with the earlier goals of the Marshall Plan. But the growing threats of the Cold War and the intractable communism of European electorates shifted the goals. NATO, the North Atlantic Treaty Organization, had been formed in 1949 in response to the early warnings of Soviet aspirations for world hegemony. Its first Secretary General, Lord Ismay, famously stated that the organization's goal was "to keep the Russians out, the Americans in, and the

Germans down." It was at first, largely a political association, but the Korean War and increased Soviet incursions caused it to begin to flesh itself out militarily. It became U.S. policy as much as possible to provide military aid to NATO countries by using dollars to stimulate European weapons industries.

I was dropped into a job that reflected a new dimension for U.S. foreign economic aid. And in hindsight, it seemed antithetical to my nature. Me, already of pacifist inclinations, later to become an angry opponent of the arms race, the bomb shelter mania in the U.S., Kennedy's rattling of his nuclear weapons, the better-dead-than-redders. Me, who as the Vietnam War burgeoned, gave up my government career, moved to Italy to write novels and essays of protest, and at one point was even ready to renounce my U.S. citizenship. Me, whose closest Italian friends later were members of the Communist Party. Yet there I was, 1952, a minor Cold War warrior in Rome, helping to rebuild Italy's military industries and hoping to pull its electorate away from communism. I was never a totally determined ideologue, however, and in those early days of the communist threat, our new policies, NATO's policies, must have seemed incontrovertible even for the likes of me. Yes, a show of determined strength should do the trick.

<e>

Italy in the early 1950s still showed much of the post-liberation euphoria and energy that I had sensed in my brief AWOL visit from Corsica during the war. Though Italian national politics had quickly moved from dictatorship to a labyrinthine democracy smudged by the Mafia, the feeling on the streets, in the villages, was still of joy and novelty and improvisation. The people, the landscape, the economy bloomed. And the traditional country ways were very much there, too. Often we would see flocks of sheep being herded through Piazza Venezia, just under Mussolini's famous balcony where he would soak up the *Duce! Duce! Duce!* of the docile and terrified multitudes. The sheep were on their traditional migration between summer mountains and the winter pasturage of Lazio.

Almost every weekend, and in holiday times, we would drive off in our Plymouth, shipped to us courtesy of Uncle Sam. Mountain towns, coastal villages, archaeological sites—Charlotte was an inveterate lover of the art and artifacts of the past and present. Often as not, our somewhat battered station wagon with its Corps Diplomatique license plates drew crowds. Get away from the cities, and you were in medieval times.

Avowed fascists and Nazi sympathizers had quickly disappeared, either through denial or retaliation. In one town where I later lived, they had strung up their notorious local quisling by the ankles and hung him head-down over the well in the central piazza. There were exceptions, though. When the war ended, the new government ostensibly would expropriate the property and the civil rights of former fascist officials. But if they formally recanted, all was forgiven. My Aunt Katy's second husband, Count Vincenzo "Cencio" Visconti da Prasca, had been a much-decorated colonel in the Italian army, commanding troops in the Balkans. He refused to recant and remained a firm believer in the fascist ideology. He lost all his property and was scraping along by fishing in a one-lunger off the Ligurian coast when he met my aunt. She had inherited a villa in San Remo where she and Cencio would often entertain lavishly.

Cencio came to represent for me one of the dangers of labeling, particularly in the convoluted ambiguities of Italy.

He was a wonderfully ugly man, sweet, generous, thoughtful, funny. His defense of fascism was a wry mixture of descriptions of the failings of Italy's mafiosi attempts at democracy, and, on the other hand, descriptions of a benign autocracy which he readily admitted was unobtainable. He visited us often in Rome, always with little gifts, "sorprese," for our daughters from Zio Cencio. More than once, when given by a waiter a splash of wine to taste, I saw him spit it out onto the floor with a colorful oath—an oath, however, directed not at the waiter but at the vineyard.

Charlotte and I once attended a dinner under the palm trees by Katy's San Remo villa, a banquet to which he had smuggled from France across the border two members of the exiled Italian royalty. At the appropriate moment, he rose to his feet and offered two toasts, gesturing to us all to rise. Winking at me, a member of the American diplomatic corps, he cried, *Viva il Re!* We all raised our glasses and solemnly repeated the treasonable invocation. Then he looked up into the palm tree hanging just over the banquet table and toasted the "palm-rats-at-play"—these were the only words in English he claimed he ever mastered—thanking them for their unusually restrained behavior this evening.

I would commute to work in a tiny two-cylinder Fiat Topolino, down the Appia Antica lined with statues of Roman heroes, past the catacombs, through San Sebastiano gates of the Roman wall, past the Forum, around the Colosseum, up via dei Serpenti, up via Veneto, to park behind our offices. I would usually lunch in a small restaurant nearby— the extended Roman siesta lunch—with one or two of the Italians who worked in my little section.

Corrado was a street kid from Naples who had learned English running errands for American soldiers during the war. He was a socialist unionist, shrewd, knowledgeable. He had developed good connections in Italian defense agencies. He later became a key leader in UIL, the left-leaning labor union.

Giancarlo was a graduate of the elite naval academy in Livorno. He was later to go to Harvard Business School, work for a time for the Italian branch of my father's carbon black empire, and teach at a business school in Milan.

Luigi also was a naval academy graduate. He later married an American who'd worked at the U.S. Embassy and retired to his family's holdings in Sardinia. We later learned that he was a count in the old and now outlawed aristocracy. All three of these men were socialists and most likely voted for the communist party. That was the ideological leaning of most of my Italian friends then as well as later.

⊷

At an amusement park with Aunt Katy, Zio Cencio, Charlotte, early 1960s.

With the 1952 presidential elections, a major change in the American political scene occurred—the 22nd Amendment to the U.S. Constitution, ratified in 1951 in response to widespread unease with the experience of FDR's election to four terms. "No person shall be elected to the office of the President more than twice, and no person who has held the office of President, or acted as President, for more than two years of a term to which some other person was elected President shall be elected to the office of the President more than once." Truman had already served more than three years of FDR's fourth term and was reelected in 1948, but he was specifically exempted by the amendment from the two-term limit. He began to campaign for a third term but withdrew after a poor showing in the New Hampshire primary. In 1953, Eisenhower became president. A Republican was in the White House for the first time in twenty years.

The arms race was already under way. We were headed into an era of Mutual Assured Destruction. Soon after the end of World War II, euphoria and hope were tarnished by fear. Faced with the threat of total annihilation, paranoia crept around the globe. At home, we were deeply into a Red Scare reminiscent of the fears arising from the Russian revolution at the end of World War I. The populist and socialist ideals that recur often in American history had reappeared significantly during the Depression. Many intellectuals were drawn to communist ideals. My father's father, a staunch Republican conservative, publicly opined that Christ and the Pilgrims were communists—a remark that caused my father to lose his security clearance until James Killian, the president of MIT, interceded with Eisenhower.

For years, America was absorbed in the drama of the trial of Alger Hiss, a senior member of the State Department. He was accused by Whitaker Chambers, editor of Time magazine, of revealing classified information to the Soviets. Lots of surprises came up during the trial that kept us riveted—a pumpkin-patch drop-off point for microfilm, a typewriter's peculiarities. Hiss landed in prison in 1950 for four years.

An excess of national paranoia caused enormous damage. The harsh tactics of the House Un-American Activities Committee and its junior Congressman, Richard Nixon. The vicious grandstanding and groundless accusations of Senator McCarthy. The blacklisting of hundreds of prominent Americans. The dismissal of many loyal government servants. The trial and executions of the Rosenbergs, found guilty of passing nuclear weapon secrets to the Soviets.

McCarthyism was in full swing, and Eisenhower turned a timid and blind eye to it. In the spring of 1953, nine months after my arrival in Rome and with a new ambassador in place, Clare Booth Luce, the U.S. Information Service library—it was on the ground floor of our offices—was visited by two of McCarthy's assistants, Roy Cohn and G. David Schine. They were on a tour of USIS libraries in Europe. They reported that over 30,000 books in those libraries were by "pro-communist" writers and demanded their removal. Dashiell Hammett, DuBois, Melville, Steinbeck, Thoreau—thousands of books were immediately removed. With the advent of the Red Scare, *Moby Dick* had to go. Though there were many comparisons made with the Nazi book-burnings, fear of McCarthy's ruthless tactics muted what should have been an outcry.

An aside: Roy Cohn, with a reputation as a ruthless lawyer, represented Donald Trump in Trump's early business career.

Another front in the evolving Cold War was the struggle for the Third World. By 1950, most of the colonial empires around the globe were weakening, some had collapsed. Japanese, Dutch, French, British, German, Italian, Spanish, Portuguese—gone or greatly diminished. The American Empire relinquished the Philippines in 1946, the Panama Canal in 1977, but it would bring into statehood two of its territories, Hawaii and Alaska. Its economic, military, and cultural grip reached around much of the globe, ever stronger.

The Soviet Union likewise had vastly strengthened its huge empire. The largely less-developed countries of the world were becoming ideological battlegrounds in the Cold War contest, each of these two massive empires vying for influence and control. Each was pouring huge amounts of energy, money, arms, propaganda, and advisers into Africa, South and Southeast Asia, Latin America, and the Middle East. It was a struggle for influence, alliances, markets, ideologies. The European Recovery Program and the reconstruction of devastated Japan had been largely accomplished by 1953 and were replaced by a much more cynical, brutal, and at the same time subtle conflict, a contest for hearts and minds around the globe. And it was overshadowed by the nuclear arms race, a race running wildly out of control. In a very few years, the hope and euphoria of the World War II victories had turned into desperation and fear—and in the West, into consumerist profligacy as well.

During the formation and execution of the Marshall Plan, many Europeans had opposed it on the grounds that it was essentially America asserting its values on a Europe that was widely disdainful of America. The American planners and administrators were aware of this attitude and went out of their way to avoid any element of truth in it. But widespread Yankee-Go-Home graffiti came much later, and for valid reasons. The tag end of the Marshall Plan and the quite rapid shift to a Cold War economic-military aid program around the globe brought in a more crass ideology—and thousands of less excellent, less dedicated men and women who were often insensitive to local feelings and circumstances. Let's-remake-the-world-in-our-American-image became prevalent. At every level, the men and women we sent overseas were increasingly mediocre.

In Rome, the attitudinal change was dramatic. Ambassador Luce was well to the right of center politically, subtly ruthless, and with a one-minded anti-communist bent. The contrast with Ambassador Bunker was pronounced. The position of head of the economic aid mission had been moved from a place of independence and virtual equality with the ambassador to the position Minister for Economic Affairs in the Embassy itself. Henry Tasca became my boss. He was a hard-nosed, scheming, egocentric man. He was later made ambassador to Greece and gave every appearance of being a perpetrator and supporter of the vicious Junta dictatorship.

For a time, most of the rest of us on the economic aid staff remained as holdovers from Marshall Plan days. A few had been victims of McCarthyism—Stassenated, we called it, Harold Stassen being now Eisenhower's director of what had just become the Foreign Operations Administration.

I continued for a time in the role of looking for ways to stimulate Italian defense industries with U.S. aid dollars. Visits to ammunitions factories, an aircraft factory that was ready to duplicate U.S. jet fighters, guns, and so forth. I made many overnight train trips to headquarters in Paris to compare notes with colleagues from other capitals. I was sent to Washington for a month to help in formulating the administration's request to Congress for aid authorizations and appropriations. While there, I spent some time at the Pentagon because of the military aid component of my job. I got to know Jeeb Halaby there, a former colleague of my brother Louis's when they were both working on naval aircraft design during the war. Jeeb became the CEO of Pan American Airways, his daughter became the queen of Jordan.

Where you lunched in the Pentagon depended on your rank—measured by your diplomatic or civil service level. I ate in the generals' mess hall—me, a twenty-nine-year-old kid who'd boot-strapped his way up through four government jobs in two years to a temporary high rank. Weird, as I saw it even then. I don't think it went to my head, partly, perhaps, because I still sometimes saw myself at the reluctant end of puppet strings held in puppet-master Dad's manipulating hands.

Ambassador Luce took a shine to me, or more likely saw me as an ally who might help her understand and deal with Tasca's ambitions on the one hand, and with the more liberal mind-sets of the Marshall Plan staffers on the other hand. My age, my name, Harvard and Yale—a likely ally, she must have thought. She was shrewd and drew attention to herself in flamboyant ways. She had me come to her morning staff meetings, often the only representative from across the street, though I was considerably junior to several of the economic aid staff. She would always arrive a minute or two after the rest of us were seated. She would wear a fresh flower in a test-tube pinned to her jacket, and once or twice, with much gesturing and cooing, would direct her next-in-command to please fill it with water.

I broke my leg skiing one winter at Monte Terminillo. Invited to her birthday party by her deputy, I arrived on crutches and was led to a chair, a cushioned footstool slid under my cast. Up swoops my ambassador, demands a pen, and proceeds to write on my cast, "To poor dear Bob, from his everlovin' boss, Clare Booth Luce." I had let no one call me Bob, and let no one write on my cast. Lesser lights rushed to sign up too, but no, I would keep that bit of historic memorabilia exclusive, however craven that is. And it was snipped out carefully, enshrined in foil, and must now be stored in a box in some attic somewhere.

The ambassador's official residence was the Villa Taverna on six acres of parkland—gorgeous gardens, catacombs beneath them—at the north end of the Villa Borghese, Rome's enormous central park. Parties there—we went a couple of times—were lavish. I once wandered around a bit beyond the range of the party crowd—antiques, a banquet table set with place plates with the gold seal of the United States, Republican party memorabilia, Ike's signed photos with Clare and Henry Luce, the works. I figured there must be a storeroom someplace where the Democrats' stuff is stashed away till the next switch. I didn't get a chance to search for it—a polite Marine guard in a splendid uniform led me back to the party.

～ 14 ～

"Having Been Cremated, I..."

IN THE early 1950s, in what was once, I believe, a gloomy mausoleum on the eastern edge of the Villa Borghese, lived the painter Manlio Guberti with his companion, Anna Khiel, a Swiss journalist. The ancient stone structure had been converted into a tiny living space and a barely adequate studio. The whole thing was no bigger than a railway boxcar. It had been made available from year to year by the City of Rome to promising artists. Manlio became among my closest and dearest friends for the rest of his life. He was there for me in several of the crises that life brings. I was fortunate to be at his bedside on one of his last days.

Manlio was a Renaissance man. His university degrees were in philosophy and mathematics. He was, for a short time, a concert pianist. He had been forced into the Italian army as a lieutenant, but when the Badoglio government surrendered to the Allies, he managed to escape the Nazis who took over what was left of Italy, deserting into the mountains as the Allies advanced up the peninsula.

He designed and built innovative sail boats and wrote a definitive book on seamanship and sail, *La Vela*. He published several volumes of beautiful poetry—one he touchingly dedicated to me. He and Anna were accomplished gardeners.

Manlio's paintings and drawings are in many private collections and museums. There is a museum in Russia largely dedicated to his art, and his son is promoting a similar museum in Italy. His style developed from a reduced realism of landscapes and people into a form of cubism tending toward the abstract. He spent a year in Arizona on a Fulbright grant, painting the desert with a mystical passion. He became known there as the "singer of the desert"—and was made Honorary Mayor of Tombstone. His pacifism, his gentle nature—in a bear-like body—his ability to listen, to see, to express, were extraordinary. He was a deeply thoughtful man with a passion for clarity and truth.

Over the years, we saw much of each other. He and Anna soon moved into the Lazio countryside, first an old farmhouse, then further out into the sheep-grazing lands—narrow valley bottoms, brooks, grasses, cane, between scrubland ridges of tufa from the Bracciano volcano. There, in the dry overgrazed maquis, they built a home of tufa blocks, a studio, a well, a garden, a vineyard. They planted around them a small forest of pines and eucalyptus. An oasis of peace away from the turbulence of Rome. In later years, when I returned to Italy, I would often join them there. Weekends of long walks, quiet meals together—their own vegetables and fruit, their home-baked bread, their own dark red wine. Long afternoons, Anna perhaps writing an essay for a Swiss journal, Manlio at his easel or at the piano with his sublime Chopin.

Sailing together, crewing for a friend who had entered his sloop in the classic Giraglia ocean race—San Remo, around Giraglia Island off the tip of Corsica, to Toulon. Sailing in Manlio's flat-bottomed fifteen-footer, pulling her up on Adriatic beaches for a swim, a bottle of wine, cheese

Manilo Guberti and Anna Khiel, 2002, Castelnuova di Porto, Italy.

and black bread, a siesta. In the early years, we spent lovely days together when he was living and painting in a Spanish watchtower on a cliff above the sea. That tower became a souvenir shop for the tourist plague. He and I made several tries, hiking the rocky coasts of Gargano and the island of Giglio, hoping to acquire a bit of land over the sea, to find a spot to build a hut for deeper retreat. But the developers always beat us to it.

Manlio was profoundly troubled by the degradation of the planet and the greed of mankind. Anna, I too, would try to lead him away from what at times became obsessive. His poetry increasingly mirrored his despair. He had lived for the clarity and truth of the Mediterranean sun, the desert sun. Now "…anche l'ombra mi ha lasciato," even the shade has abandoned me.

Christmas time 2003, I received a card from Italy. It read "A cremazione avvenuta, vi comunico di essere morto il 12.XII.2003—ore 17.30 c. Manlio." His elegant Italian loosely translated might be, "Having been cremated, I communicate to you that I died 12/12/2003 at about 5:30 p.m., Manlio." It was signed in his handwriting, unmistakably his, though a bit shaky. The date was filled in in another hand. Manlio was not a believer in an afterlife, but Manlio's story is the basis for the third novella, "Touch of Dust," in my novella collection, *That Sweetest Wine*.

After a year or so in my defense production role, U.S. dollars had put some vigor into the Italian arms industry. Tasca asked me to take on a new job. I was to work for and soon replace the mission's Productivity Division chief, a man who had to be squeezed out for incompetence. Here I was again being put into a job I knew nothing about, my only qualifications being lack thereof—being a generalist.

It did seem a good idea to try to increase the productivity of Italian industry. It had become clear that the best tool we had to this end was to send key Italians—midlevel managers, union bosses, small businessmen, a few well-placed politicians—to the States for a few weeks or months of exposure to American industry. This was a job in my Productivity Division, handled by one low-level individual who'd been doing it for years effectively, easily, without fanfare.

Our other activity was to bring so-called experts from the States to somehow demonstrate how to increase productivity in their field. The only success that I remember was in contracting with an American university to establish a business school in Italy. Otherwise, the caliber of the men brought over was usually pathetic. To his credit, Tasca saw this and tacitly put me in the job of sending them home as painlessly as possible. By the time I left Italy three years later, this had largely been done.

∼ 15 ∼

Mixed Messages

IT WAS NOT easy to leave Italy. It had been a good life—close friends, interesting jobs, a lovely country home, a most beautiful city and country, many trips, generous home-leaves back to the States—our little girls learned English staying for two weeks with grandparents. Interestingly, though I was in close and friendly relations with many American colleagues in the Aid Mission and the Embassy, my closest and lasting friends from those years were Italians—artists, journalists, and Giancarlo and Corrado, my office colleagues—and two American sculptors and their families living permanently in Rome.

But if I were to continue a career of government service, it was time to move on. Except for tag ends of counterpart funds, the use of which needed to be worked out, the Marshall Plan had effectively ended. U.S. economic aid and military assistance, which had been at least loosely connected for a time, went their separate ways. And economic aid, under the rubric Point Four, expanded to underdeveloped countries around the world.

The fourth point in Truman's 1949 inaugural address, a year after the Marshall Plan idea had been launched, announced a new policy—provide technical assistance and economic help to underdeveloped countries. It soon became a central part of the foreign aid program. Thailand is where they sent me in 1956 as Program Officer—later I became Acting Deputy Director.

The emphasis in U.S. foreign economic aid became to help the development of poorer countries that were at least potentially oriented toward the West, hoping it would thus strengthen the resistance to the spreading Soviet communist dominance. There was, of course, a humanitarian aspect to this aid, but its main reason was to further our Cold War aims and our economic hegemony. The prevailing theory was that a relatively small infusion of technical advice and training, carefully targeted, could guide underdeveloped countries to a "take-off point" after which their development would continue self-sustained. It was argued that prosperity, if not gratitude, would keep them in—or entice them into—the Western bloc.

Until the collapse of the Soviet empire, this ideological conflict was perhaps a standoff. Spheres of influence between the West and the Soviet Union kept shifting. During the Eisenhower administration, the Korean War was finally brought to a standstill, Eisenhower refusing to throw in the vast reinforcements necessary to drive out the Chinese or to use nuclear weapons. He was not willing to risk a likely Soviet military response and a world war.

Eisenhower had to confront other situations, which to some advisers seemed to require military intervention, but to his credit, he chose caution and negotiation each time. When the French were backed into a hopeless situation in Dien Ben Phu in northern Vietnam, the U.S. was urged to jump into the war. Eisenhower said no, it would be a hopeless blood bath, though he realized that this meant the end of French Colonial Indochina. He helped to bring the two sides to the negotiating table. Vietnam was divided up into two countries at the 17th parallel, with North Vietnam in communist hands and South Vietnam clearly a new American responsibility.

In 1956, Israel attacked Egypt in the Sinai and France and England invaded Egypt to take over the Suez Canal. The Soviets asked the U.S. to join them in taking up arms against these three American allies. Eisenhower refused, of course, but he called Eden, Britain's prime minister, and gave him such a tongue lashing that Eden broke down in tears—and the takeover was called off.

The two small islands of Quemoy and Matsu were controlled by the Nationalists under Chiang Kai-shek who had holed up on the island of Formosa (Taiwan), driven off the Chinese mainland by the communists. These islands were close to the mainland coast. Mao began to shell them, testing the sole possible protector of Chiang, Eisenhower. Ike's response was to play a poker hand of guarded threats and nuanced patience. The shelling stopped.

At about the time of the Suez crisis, the anti-Soviet tension in Soviet-occupied Hungary became a rebellion. Hungarian quislings were being executed. The Red Army moved in and brutally crushed the uprising. Eisenhower's response was deliberately mild. He was far readier to humiliate his allies, Britain and France, and effectively write them off as world powers, than risk World War III.

At the time, I was not a great admirer of Eisenhower. He was not even good material for hero-worship. He was no Patton or Montgomery or Rommel, no Marshall, no FDR, no Churchill. As a president, he seemed gutless against McCarthyism. But he did clearly have a deep fear of military adventurism, particularly in the new age of nuclear weaponry, and his skills in avoiding military confrontations, now that I look back on the period, were superb. His final words before turning the presidency over to Kennedy in 1961, words of caution, have been too often ignored by his successors.

> In the councils of government, we must guard against the acquisition of unwarranted influence, whether sought or unsought, by the military-industrial complex. The potential for the disastrous rise of misplaced power exists and will persist.

In that same speech—equally visionary and urgent, though rarely quoted, he also said:

> We...must avoid the impulse to live only for today, plundering for our own ease and convenience the precious resources of tomorrow. We cannot mortgage the material assets of our grandchildren without risking the loss also of their political and spiritual heritage. We want democracy to survive for all generations to come, not to become the insolvent phantom of tomorrow.

⊷

Thailand, next door to France's Indochina empire, had never been ruled by a European power, though it had been occupied by and then allied with Japan during World War II. It did have a history of close commercial ties with Europe, being a major source of teak wood, tin, and other minerals. During the war, it had been ruled by a military dictator, Phibun, who was forced out for a time but was back in power when my family and I were there. In fact, his residence was just across the quiet side street where we lived for two years—putting us in the bullseye for a coup, I suppose.

Our house was built around 1900 by a Danish import-export manager. It was a lovely rambling home—screened porches, louvered partitions, a separate building for the cookhouse and servants' quarters, a large yard with flowering vines, a mango tree, a special little spirit-house shrine. There was an enormous terracotta pot buried in the lawn, which was intended as an air-raid shelter in the war, big enough for an entire family to squeeze in. Daughter Sara, thinking to try it out, lifted its cover and discovered that it was the home of a family of cobras.

We had two kittens, Siamese, of course, Nit and Noy, which I think meant Little and Bit. Kathy still has a rather attractive little scar near her eye when Nit punished her for trying to drag her out from her hideaway under the bed.

Our compound backed onto a khlong, a local canal that fed into the large network of canals and the Chao Phraya River. In those days, Bangkok had only just begun to evolve into the megacity of today. The khlongs, most of which were later to be filled in to become city streets, were the lifeblood of the city. In true faux-colonial style, we would sit on a back porch sipping gin-and-lime gimlets brought to us by Asai, one of several servants that came with the house when the U.S. Aid Mission rented it for us, and we would watch the life on our khlong. It was a narrow, filthy, stinking sewer—yet the heart of a teeming, colorful, rich culture. We could watch the daily lives of our many neighbors in their little wooden homes. Their ablutions in the khlong, washing behind a brightly printed sheet or towel, ladling water for teeth brushing or for pouring over themselves to cool off. Life on their khlong-side rickety platforms—cooking on charcoal braziers, dining, cool open-air sleeping on their rush mats. Long flat-bottomed boats, poled or paddled, hawking vegetables, rice, charcoal, candles, Coca-Cola. Taxi boats, bus boats, tiny canoe-like boats paddled by monks in their saffron robes, their begging bowls held out. Scratchy radio music, laughing children, screeching parrots. I would often take a khlong bus or hail a khlong taxi canoe to the warehouse-like building the aid mission had rented and converted into our offices.

In those years, U.S. aid to Thailand was primarily technical assistance. It was one of the larger of the post-Marshall Plan economic aid Point Four programs. There were several hundred American technicians we had hired—working in our offices, in various Thai ministries, in schools, in the fields and rivers and roads of the country. As was my experience in Italy with our productivity program there, the most effective of these projects were those conducted by American educational institutions—universities, medical schools, teacher colleges, engineering schools, public health faculties, even a police academy, though more on that one later. There were many good men and women, a few freeloaders. Perhaps to accept assignment to unfamiliar steamy Thailand took more dedication than did the dolce vita of Italy.

Our job in the Program Office, a staff of several economists and secretaries and me, was to serve as the planners, the screeners of ideas, the monitors of ongoing projects, and the principle day-to-day contact with our counterparts in Washington. In turn, we were the working staff for the chief of our mission. It was natural for his deputy to take his place when he, the Bill Shepard I have referred to before, suffered a stroke, and for the Program Officer, me, to become the acting deputy chief.

One of the principle criteria we looked at in attempting to plan ahead and to evaluate proposed technical assistance

With colleagues inspecting the North East Highway Project,
Thailand, 1956.

projects was the "multiplier effect" measure, the ability of a
proposal to trigger a widespread multiplication of its particular innovation. As an example, public health technicians
had discovered that one of the main sources of disease in
rural areas was from the widespread custom of uncovered
village latrines, simple pits usually. They designed and built a
solution, a concrete slab of a size to fit over the pit, two holes
in it with hinged covers. It worked exceedingly well, but the
trick was how to get this idea, and the forms and concrete
and hinges, out to the tens of thousands of villages across
Thailand. It was calculated that a couple of public health
people with one or two Thais going from village to village
would take some hundreds of years to cover the country.
The idea needed to be standardized, replicable, advertised,
and pushed out through a network, governmental and non-
governmental, that would predictably and quickly multiply.

The opposite approach we called the "missionary effect". Religious missions, the theory was, worked in one very restricted place, perhaps showing the way to make significant improvements in the lives of the local people, but without much of a plan to multiply those improvements. We tended to ridicule the missionary approach. But before long, some of us began to question this. Though we might decry the spiritual conversion that was a goal of most religious missions— the arrogant imposition of an entirely foreign religion on an already deeply spiritual people—we wondered if there might not be advantages to bypassing cumbersome and usually corrupt networks and instead looking for organic, unstructured processes for the multiplying of good ideas. The drop of oil on a surface of water, the admittedly discredited but appealing "hundredth monkey effect." And the genuinely humanitarian aspects of the missionary approach in comparison to the often politically motivated, self-serving, and corrupt government-level approach, were appealing.

I was told once that in some "underdeveloped" country an American agricultural adviser noticed that the farmers all used short-handled hoes to tend their crops, with the resultant almost universal crippling of farmers' backs at a young age. He put a long handle on one of their hoes, went out to the fields and worked with them for a few days, getting far more hoeing done with far less effort than the farmers working beside him. He soon returned to the U.S. Within a year or two, every farmer in the country was using a long-handled hoe. Unbelievably, in California it took farm-labor organizer Cesar Chavez until 1975 to finally get el cortito, the short-handled hoe, outlawed. Agribusiness had resisted this, claiming that crops would be damaged by stand-up hoeing.

It turned out that I became the person in the aid mission in closest friendly contact with second level officers at the U.S. embassy. We worked together informally on a frequent basis, one reason being that at that level we had jointly concluded that the aid program was bloated, way overblown, its anti-communist rationale coming from our new ambassador, Max Bishop, largely groundless. Its real purpose was simply to advance Bishop's climb up the Foreign Service ladder. The number three man at the embassy and I had become friendly with the *Time* magazine correspondent for that part of the world. He heard us out often, and in July 1956, *Time* issued an unprecedented full-page indictment of our ambassador. Bishop was soon out of there. He was, for a time, State Department adviser to the Naval War College, but he had no further foreign assignments and soon withdrew from the Foreign Service.

The most expensive U.S. aid program to Thailand in those years was the building of the Friendship Highway from Bangkok out past the airport and on north, eventually all the way to the Laos border, 380 miles. Max Bishop was a heavy-handed promoter of the project. We had brought in American engineers, then a major U.S. construction company—Halliburton-esque—with its shiploads of equipment and materials. A major, wide-shouldered, heavy-duty highway was in progress during my tenure there. Why so far above local standards and needs? There was a certain low-profile military staff that was attached to the Americans building this highway, giving some hint that its purpose was related to the increasing turmoil in neighboring divided Vietnam. To mix a military component to the supposedly altruistic economic aid program was anathema to many of us.

Another project proposed by Washington that came

across my desk was to bring police academy personnel to Thailand to train traffic cops. Several of us mildly objected, not having heard any request for such from the Thais, and not having observed any particular need. At this point, a young man I knew in Bangkok, the one whom Tommy the Cork told me to look up, came to my office and expressed his enthusiasm for the traffic cop project. With our objections overruled, the so-called police trainers came. Before long, I copped on to the truth—it was a cover for anti-communist espionage training.

That was a major element in my decision a few years later to resign from government service.

‹❧›

Again, though, they were good years, those two in Thailand. The challenges of the job could often be met with success. The exposure to a different culture and environment was rewarding. The Thai people were delightful, with exquisite grace and beauty. Bangkok was only just beginning to be plagued by its famous traffic jams. Its temples and palaces were fairylands for our daughters.

We were often invited by members of the aristocracy to join them. Parties. Waterskiing on the filthy Chao Phraya. To a country home on a jungle river, swimming there as an elephant approaches, splashing down the middle of the river carrying an enormous teak log in her trunk. To their racetrack and country club, where we were allowed to join them in their swimming pool despite our "…rather repulsive pink flesh." We managed a trip into Cambodia, wandering among the jungle temples of Angkor Wat in a rickshaw.

The aid program helped set up a medical school in Chiang Mai in northern Thailand, contracting with the University of Illinois. We were invited by the Thai government to visit. Charlotte and I took a day off to hike far up into the mountains to the northwest of Chiang Mai, up toward the Burmese border. Through jungles, into drier high valleys, one of which was brilliant for many acres with poppies for the opium trade. In the center was a Hmong village of huts.

We then were invited to join a Thai government expedition to float down the Mae Nam Ping, a major source of Bangkok's Chao Phraya River, for a week. The traditional way to get massive construction bamboo down to Bangkok was by convoys of rafts. Our convoy was to be one of the last before a large dam would stop that commerce. A government ministry had commandeered eight or ten rafts. On each raft, there were huts of woven bamboo with palm-leaf roofs. There was one big kitchen raft. The smaller rafts, each with a bamboo and reed hut and a man to pole or paddle, were the sleeping quarters for several government officials, for three or four of us from the aid mission, and for the government scientists who were ostensibly testing the water quality and the flora and fauna that would be affected by the dam.

It was a remarkable trip. The river of clear, fast-flowing water ran through jungles, agricultural land, deep gorges. Wild country. Elephants spraying river water at each other with their trunks, monkeys screaming on the pink cliffs, hordes of chattering parrots, night-birds shrilling, snakes swimming with us. Lunch while floating down the river was brought by canoes from the cook raft to each smaller raft. At night, we would pull up to a sandbank shore. A bonfire, hot food, singing, some of the raftsmen dancing.

One night they sacrificed a ferocious black pig they'd bought in a village we passed and had kept in a pen on the cook raft's stern deck. Mugs of blood were handed around.

He was turned on a spit over the bonfire, sawed into steaks, ribs, his testicles a special reward to the captain of our flotilla. The hairy black head—tongueless, eyeless, brainless, his penis clenched in his teeth—was left on a pole stuck in the sand to deal with evil spirits.

One or two nights, a couple of men paddled across the river and set fire to the jungle, again to deal with the spirits, and for the fun of it. Passing cultivated fields above the high banks, we floated by enormous wooden water wheels turned by the current, scooping up water, lifting it high into irrigation ditches.

✦

I was sent to Ceylon for a month to join a group of American technicians, economists, and generalists to map out a new economic aid program with the government of Ceylon. The group was headed by Jim Grant. Jim became a good friend. We worked together, we played together. I joined his economic aid programming staff in Washington a couple of years later. Jim was originally a Canadian, born in Beijing, his father being a medical missionary. He lived in China until he was fifteen. He got an economics degree from UC Berkeley, became an American citizen, and after Harvard Law School he went directly into a lifetime devoted to foreign aid, diplomacy and, for fifteen years, Under-Secretary of the United Nations in his role as executive director of UNICEF. He was a warm, loving, dedicated man who, in his fifty years of devotion to the vision of a healed world, to many of us was a great and largely unsung hero. His commitment to the work of UNICEF, hugely expanded through his tenacity and charm dealing with hundreds of the world's leaders, may well have saved the lives of tens of millions of children, children who would have died of disease, poverty, wars, and natural disasters. In his statement following Jim's death, United Nations Secretary-General Boutros Boutros-Ghali said:

> Very few men or women ever have the opportunity to do as much good in the world as James Grant, and very few have ever grasped the opportunity with such complete and dedicated commitment. He will be remembered as a most distinguished servant of the United Nations and as one of the greatest international public servants of his generation.

President Clinton awarded him the Presidential Medal of Freedom saying:

> Throughout his long career, Jim Grant was a visionary leader — one of the most distinguished international public servants of our time.

When I left government service, for many years our paths did not cross. Then...I was flying with my young son Alexis to Florida for his spring break from school. Cramped into economy class, I was walking down the aisle when my name was called out. It was Jim, headed to Haiti, I think it was—a UN Deputy Secretary-General traveling economy class. He said that the members of his staff were of sufficient rank, by government regulations, to travel first class and they usually did. He never had.

My role in the aid mission to Thailand also took me on trips to Taiwan and Laos. And Charlotte and I had two much needed respites from the oppressive climate and the intensity of work and life in Bangkok—one to Hong Kong, and a year later to a highlands retreat in the Philippines.

Yes, they were good years, full, interesting, and exhausting.

Another friend in Bangkok was Jim Thompson. Jim was a left-leaning Princeton graduate socialite, who, to escape his largely Republican family, joined the U.S. Army Air Force and was assigned to the OSS, the predecessor of the CIA. During World War II, due to his fluent French, he was dropped several times into Nazi France to make contact with the French resistance. After the war, he became, for a short time, the head of the OSS office in Bangkok. Although he soon officially abandoned intelligence activities, many suspected he was still an agent under cover. During the Vietnam War, his closest friend was a USAAF general in charge of air operations over Laos and Thailand.

By the time I knew him, he had ostensibly moved into private business, founding the famous Thai Silk industry. His wife had refused to move to Bangkok, and they were divorced. He built an exquisite traditional Siamese teak home where he was living with his Thai boyfriend when we met. Years later, he disappeared while on a walk in the jungle near Kuala Lumpur. A tiger, another secret agent, a new identity? There is still no official explanation for his mysterious disappearance. His Bangkok home has become a museum.

One last Bangkok scene. Only a few days before we were to leave Thailand for an assignment in Washington, Charlotte, the girls, and I had gone to the Olympic-size pool next to the racetrack. I had swum to the far end of the pool. As I climbed out, there was a woman—in her stolid matronly thirties, I'd say, standing a few feet away purposefully looking down on me.

"You do not recognize me. I am Sissel Jensen—the *cour de vacance*, Pau, the Pyrénées? I am married to Norway's Minister to Thailand. I have been here for several years. I knew you were here. My husband and I were actually at the costume ball at the French embassy that you attended. You came as a Mississippi steamboat gambler. I know you are leaving. I wanted to say hello and goodbye, but I didn't want in any way to intrude awkwardly into your family life here."

Many years later, I found her address in Oslo through an inquiry to the Norwegian Foreign Office and sent her a copy of my novel, *That Sweetest Wine*. I gave the page references to the passages that described our time together. And I wrote a few words to her about my feelings at the time I left her, my quite suddenly overwhelming sense that I was not ready for a deeper relationship. It was an apology, yes, and she did reply to it generously, thanking me for finally giving her some sense of what had happened between us.

We had no more conversation there at the poolside. She turned to rejoin her husband. Charlotte graciously accepted my explanation of my disoriented state, my recounting of that strange encounter with a prior life.

~16~

Gloomy Weltanschauung

I RETURNED to a Washington in transition. The roles I was to play there, the forces that I was asked to play with, were soon to lose much of their meaning for me. Looking back now, was my return to that epicenter of the world the moment a seed of decision was planted, the ending of one mode, the beginning of quite another? Was that a pivotal time for the world, for all of us? Or for just me?

Four years as a soldier in the United States, England, Algeria, Italy, France, and Germany—a just war if that is possible, an interlude of study, an exciting year or two next door to the White House, then six years in Europe and Southeast Asia. Those were years when my country was offering an effective hand in saving and reshaping the world, by most standards largely for the better. Those were years of opportunities in which I could gladly participate. And they were years that followed a decade in my childhood of my country's heroic efforts to correct the injustices and despair of the Great Depression.

The Washington I returned to was a place where corrupted power, desperation, and bigotry seemed to have largely replaced the ideals that I had thought were obtainable. Where willing sacrifice for those ideals was replaced by greed and consumerism. Where the voices of my heroes seemed lost in a cynical snarl, by the growing dominance of corporate and military power, by fear.

Oh, there were moments, many moments, when to be there again, back at the proclaimed center of the world, seemed to offer hope and reward. There were good people still, those who resisted the distortions of good intentions into the madness of mutual assured destruction, of ends that sanctioned means, of irreversible waste in the name of urgent necessity or simply thoughtless expediency. Maybe, too, my Weltanschauung was personally jaded by the years. Time to look inward?

⊕

Eisenhower in the White House, it is true, had pursued a restrained public foreign policy. But he was an active promoter of many covert CIA foreign adventures, and most of them were to lead to disaster. The support of Iran's Shah in a coup against the fairly elected Mossadeq. Similarly, in Guatemala, and again in the Republic of Congo. He assumed responsibility for the new South Vietnam as a bastion against the spread of communism. An insurgency was already building up supported from the North by Ho Chi Minh. American military advisers, money, and arms began to flow into Saigon.

He had thrown down the gauntlet of nuclear weapons. The arms race with the Soviets was on, there was no turning back. The world was racing to develop nuclear fusion hydrogen bombs, which could be thousands of times more destructive than the fission bombs dropped on Japan. Stalin died in 1953, but any détente with Khrushchev failed when Ike's U2 spy plane was shot down by the Soviets, and its pilot lived to testify to the world that it was indeed a spy plane.

Ike was a man of good intentions, but he lacked the vision and the intellectual energy to find another path. He was not interested or engaged in domestic affairs, his silence had permitted McCarthyism, and his determined though relatively mild Republican bent was chipping away at the Rooseveltian form of democratic socialism and liberalism that many of us had come to believe in and rely on.

An alternative, a way to perhaps reverse this perceived decline, was beginning to show itself—Kennedy. As a Democratic senator, he had shown his intelligence, his charm, his thoughtfulness. He was gearing up to run for president, and his Republican opponent would be Vice President Nixon, who had often shown his hardline conservatism and ruthless cynicism.

In 1959, I arranged to meet with Kennedy. He asked me to see him in the library room of his Harvard Fox Club, the Harvard equivalent of a fraternity. I presented myself as wishing to join his presidential campaign, perhaps my very Republican family name being of particular interest to him. He was receptive, but he asked me to wait some months until he was closer to throwing his hat in the ring officially—but not to wait too long or it would seem like simply an opportunistic attempt of a presumably Republican turncoat to jump onto his bandwagon. I later saw him casually once or twice at Washington's Metropolitan Club. But that Fox Club feeler, though I continued for a time to be tempted by the offer, proved to be the last move I contemplated of staying in government service.

I had a kaleidoscope of jobs in Washington during those last two or so years. On Jim Grant's policy planning staff for a stint. Writing speeches for Ike's economic aid chief. Meetings with congressmen in their offices seeking this or that legislation.

My last job in the U.S. government was as Assistant to the Director of a newly formed Development Loan Fund. As a representative of the DLF, I would find myself sitting in on State Department policy planning meetings, contacting various departments of government regarding project proposals coming our way, watching the unfolding on a coded teleprinter of status-of-forces agreements with NATO countries gearing up for the Cold War. Hanging out in the Senate gallery to see and phone back to my boss the latest about on-going relevant debates—Senator Lyndon Johnson back-slapping, gesturing across the aisle, orchestrating, conducting the Senate. It may sound glamorous, but I contributed very little. I was a well-paid, unnecessary observer. In fact, useless.

I continued to climb up the temporary civil service ladder, often associating with VIPs, a visit once to the White House with my boss to meet with one of the staff. My friends and associates seemed to regard me as somewhat of a key player. In reality, I felt I'd become a mediocre bureaucrat hiding behind a weird mask that I had never intended nor wanted to wear. In truth, I was an ever-smaller frog in an ever-bigger pond, bored, disgruntled, uneasy with what was happening to the image and the actions of the U.S. at home and overseas. Uneasy at what was happening to me. This was in contrast to my earlier years in public service. In the army, in the Executive Office of the President, in my work in the foreign aid program overseas, I felt I was doing good work. Now, back in a new Washington, this was no longer the case.

As I withdrew my energies from government service, I turned more to family life. We rented a house on the outside edge of suburbia. Our daughters walked to school—across

a field, past a small pond where we often skated. I took as
much time off as I could get away with. Rapid-water canoeing, camping with the girls, a vacation in Denmark and
Greece, skiing—once in Canada's Laurentian Mountains
with fellow hotel guests Bobby Kennedy and a couple of his
sisters, one of whom I had dated years before.

I was good friends with several men and their families,
men in key government jobs, in law firms. Roger Fisher, who
went on to become a Harvard law professor. Tony Lewis,
New York Times reporter covering the Supreme Court, later
a columnist. Adam Yarmolinsky, headhunter for Kennedy,
who became Provost of the University of Maryland. Our
families have remained close friends, friendships unaffected
by several divorces—including my own.

We joined several families in buying a spectacular property over the Potomac River. We built our houses, a community tennis court, and swimming pool. I bought a tiny island
in the river, ferried two goats to it in a canoe, and watched
them raise a family—and walk away in a drought—an island I eventually gave to my daughters.

Private lives, good lives—but I could no longer continue in jobs that seemed increasingly meaningless within
an atmosphere that had become intolerable. I took a leave
of absence, audited a course in philosophy for a time at
Georgetown University until I found it impossible to follow,
studied the *Divine Comedy* with a Dante scholar for a couple
of months at American University, and soon resigned from
government service for good.

I had dropped Kennedy's invitation to join his campaign staff. To have possibly ended up on his White House
staff would have turned out to have been particularly painful and hypocritical, for I became increasingly vocal in op-

position to Kennedy's saber-rattling. His campaign scare tactics about a mythical "missile gap" in our arms race. His heavy-handed build-up to the Vietnam war. The Bay of Pigs fiasco. The encouragement for the building of private bomb shelters—"...provocative and inviting the killing of shelter-less neighbors," I would say and write.

The military buildup in South Vietnam in response to threats from the North. The confrontation with Khrushchev—the nuclear missiles the Soviets were installing in Cuba, the game of who blinks first. I would have had to resign soon from that White House—if they hadn't fired me first.

My resignation became my response to that Washington, to that new world, a response that many friends, family, and colleagues considered perverse and disloyal.

∼ 17 ∼

Est, Est, Est!

WE SOLD our house, sold our car, packed up, sailed to Italy, and made our way to Tuscany. Not something a career civil servant would normally undertake. I had saved most of my salary over the years, we had lived relatively frugally, and largely at government expense. But a co-enabler of that move was the portfolio I had inherited from my paternal grandfather. I had used it very little, but its presence, its modest heft, its seeming permanence whatever the vagaries of the economy—it all helped as at least a subconscious underpinning in sending us on our way.

I'd been writing, often voluminously, for most of my life. School, college, I survived law school largely by writing thick papers—stunningly boring to write, excruciating to read. Then government—much of my many changing jobs involved endless reports, letters, analyses, cables, speeches. Thousands of pages I must have written.

I'd had it. But the writing I enjoyed most was the bits of fiction I'd tried my hand at, several items published in school magazines, long, often-fanciful letters home during the war, one of which was published. I wanted to turn now to writing a novel. I had read every novel in reach in my early years, hundreds of them. Now I'd take a turn at writing one—or more.

And we chose Italy because we'd lived there during the Marshall Plan years, loved it, longed to be there again as just private people, in a culture where the driving force seemed to be community, friends, food, fun, love—politics and world affairs kept well in the background. "Expatriates" was an uncomfortable label, but that's what we would become. For Charlotte, it also meant the chance to enter deeply into the history of Italian art, her particular love. For the girls, it meant leaving friends, but they were excited, they remembered Italy—though they'd lost their Italian and would have to learn it this time by brain, not toddler's ear. I had already made an exploratory trip to Italy and had found a school for them in Florence as well as a *pensione* where we could stay until we found a home.

When we arrived in Florence in the spring of 1961 and were settled into our delightful *pensione* with its lush gardens, my job then was to go out and find us a place on the sea for the summer. A home for the winter we'd look for later. For me, the sea meant an island, a rocky hut, not a beach resort. I took ferries to several islands in the Tyrrhenian Sea, hiked over them, got fishermen to putt-putt me around. Each was quite wonderful, each had a problem. One was a penal colony, another had been discovered by the summer tourists, another seemed surrounded by molested signs saying Trespassers Will…and so forth.

Then—Isola del Giglio. I was, it's true, saving for the last what I hoped would be the best. I had been there briefly many years before when we were living in Rome. I went with my mother and young brother, Ned. We stayed in a scruffy *pensione* in the little port. We did not explore the island. Instead, we hired a fisherman to sail us—he was disdainful of his ancient cranky motor—to another island,

Giannutri, a two-hour trip in a good breeze. A tiny island, we walked across it in a few minutes—pines, palms, the resinous maquis—we snorkeled in the clear water of a cove, exploring the submerged Roman ruins and artifacts. One caretaker farmer, that's all, he offered us plates of spaghetti and his own green wine.

But Giglio—not for its *gigli*, its lilies, but for *aegilia*, its goats. An enchanting island. Except for a handful of summer tourists hauled in on the daily ferry—and they kept to the port, its one *pensione*, a restaurant, a small nearby beach, sunbathing on pink granite rocks—it had hardly moved out of the Middle Ages. I got a fisherman, this time he had a reliable motor, to take me slowly around the island, maybe three or four hours.

Round a lighthouse with its keeper's house, down the northwest side, facing Montecristo on the horizon—the island I'd seen from the bomb-bay of a Mitchell B-25 returning from my AWOL adventure seventeen years before. Ahead of us, a curve of white beach, a sickle, its handle a long rocky point on its far side. A few fishermen's huts, boats pulled up, a stone tower defending the islanders from Saracen pirates. Pirates had more than once headed for that beach, up steep hillsides to the south, up to the fortified town, Giglio Castello on the top of Monte Pagano.

Half a mile before that merlined tower, I had asked my boatman to stop the engine. Above us, above a slight dent in the rocky coastline, above terraced plots, some abandoned, some with scraggly grape vines. Fig trees, patches of vegetables, three once-whitewashed stone ovens for drying figs. And higher, beyond a grove of umbrella pines, is a slightly larger shelter hut, whiter, well-tended surroundings, it seemed to be still in use. The boatman told me it belonged to Ede and Giuseppe and that they might, just might, rent it.

Struggling up to Giglio Castello in a rusty blue bus, oodle-oodling at every switchback, I found Ede, warm, immense, and delighted to rent us the hut, and for very little. Giuseppe volunteered to finish the work he'd started on a rudimentary bathroom, using water from a tiny spring behind the house, drop by drop into a tank. He showed me a basin, a shower, a toilet—gray water fed to a barrel, black to another. His vegetable garden cut into the hillside, his grapes, his olives, cherries.

In the year 1111 AD, Henry V of Germany was headed to Rome with his entourage to be crowned Holy Roman Emperor by Pope Pasquale II. An envoy was sent well ahead of the travelers to taste the local wines. If he found a passable one, he would write "Est" conspicuously at the entrance to the town. When the imminent Emperor's entourage arrived at the gates of Montefiascone, there was written "Est! Est!! Est!!!" Today, it's on the wine bottle labels of the region.

I sent a telegram to Florence, "Est! Est!! Est!!!"

We quickly found a place for our winters too, in the hills a few miles to the west of Florence, off the road that winds up to Impruneta. It was on a dirt track down through olive groves. A crumbling-stucco house, Villa Guidarelli, ugly nineteenth century, it totally failed in its owner's attempt to call it a villa. An abandoned chapel to bolster the pretense, a sad palm tree in the unweeded courtyard, virtually unheated, no telephone, unfurnished, no appliances, electric wires tacked to the walls, bare bulbs. But it did have a spectacular view of Florence in the far distance. Beyond farmhouses, hay barns, dovecote towers, a church or two, the requisite cypress-treed cemetery, the loggia of a villa above umbrella-pine branches, and on to that stony city hunkering on the Arno.

Close by our shabby new home lived two families of subsistence farmers. Their ancestors were no doubt tenant farmers for the villa's owners, remnants of feudalism. One family consisted of dour, withdrawn, sullen communists eking out a minimal living on their miserable plot of land. The other family, nostalgic royalists, worked the villa's still quite ample farmland—olive groves, modest vineyards, their white oxen to do the plowing, chickens, pigs, there might have been a milk cow and calves for the milk-fed veal, I don't remember. There were the traditional three generations of that family living together. The grandparents to tend the money, the chickens, the sickling of green grass to feed the cattle. The parents, Dante and Teresa, to do the heavy work of plowing, the firewood, the cooking. The daughter, Fiorella, was drafted into whatever she could be persuaded to take on. And everyone would join, neighbors too, in the fall grape harvest and winemaking, the winter olive harvest and oil pressing, the pruning. And so forth. That family, too, was always there to advise and help us, to be amused by our ignorance. They became good friends, friendships lasting over many years.

And there was Rina and her family of lively communists just down the dirt track in another cluster of two or three farms. She would do a bit of housework for us, but mostly she'd show up for a good chat. We saw a lot of these two families, joining them for family events, for vendemmia feasts. I remember a breakfast at Rina's that consisted of yesterday's leftover spaghetti, fried, and boiled rabbit meat—most of these farm families would raise many fat rabbits for meat, feeding them fresh greens in their cages.

Our landlord's south-facing vineyard bordered a pine grove, dropping down steeply to a brook. In the pines just above the borro, I had built a tiny studio, maybe five by ten feet, with a fireplace and a propane light. Just room for me, a few books, my typewriter, and Laglia, our white sheepdog who would keep me company, lying by the fire on a goat skin or out on the sunny pine needles.

On Giglio, Ede and Guiseppe let me use an abandoned stone shelter as a studio, a ten-minute walk from our little home across terraces, through dense maquis, stands of cane in dry watercourses. A barrel-dome stone roof, a badly weathered door, which still could be locked, a barred window into which my typewriter cover would just fit when I chose to block out the world entirely. A dirt floor, maybe two paces wide, three long. One rickety chair, one small table, alone with the lizards and spiders, the occasional snake. Laglia would stay with the girls.

In those two cell-like studios, year after year, my first novel unfolded. It came to be called *The Cell*.

The dropping of nuclear bombs on Japan had ended World War II, but had launched the Cold War and the ever present terror of massive, even total, annihilation. A dramatic shift for the thought processes, the hopes, the attitudes of mankind. For me, it was the beginning of a search for how we can best deal with the possibility, even probability, of worldwide doom. Ignore it, enjoy it hedonistically, dwell in the past, seek radical new forms of government and social organization, hurry mankind's evolution to artificial intelligence? In my austere cells—barred windows and all—self condemned, as we all are, to *The Cell*, my novelistic response became a description of that cell and escapes from it through anscestral elegiac memories.

The Cell never quite made it to publication, but its two or three rejections went far beyond the courtesy of boiler-plate, giving me essential encouragement. And most of it I adapted as passages and thoughts in later novels and in this memoir.

❧

During those summers on Giglio, Charlotte spent much patient time helping the girls with Italian, with their summer homework, reading aloud to them. She did a great deal of her own reading and studying too. And there was the small vegetable garden to tend. With a half gourd tied

My writing studio, "the cell," Isola del Giglio, Italy, 1961.

to a long cane pole, scooping water from a trough filled by the overflow from our tiny spring, tossing the water over the rows of tomatoes and eggplants and peppers. And the housework—she and I shared the cooking.

The three of them and Laglia would swim for hours every day off the rocks in our cove of pink granite ledges. A twenty-minute walk down through the macchia—rockrose, lentischio, juniper. I would join them for a bit before lunch. Afternoon rests were in hammocks strung up in a nearby small grove of umbrella pines. Sunset time we would climb up behind our wee cabin—Stella Marina—step onto the barrel roof, crawl to the top. A bottle of vermouth, a bottle of water for the girls, crackers, crumbled cheese. And as the sun touches the mountain peak of Montecristo, out would come the harmonica. A distinctly imperfect rendition of "Taps," maybe a try at "Saint Louis Blues." Sleep well, Edmond Dantès, Count of Monte Cristo.

We had bought the smallest, cheapest car that Fiat could make, a miniature station wagon, its two-cylinder engine hidden under the rear floor, maximum speed on the flat maybe fifty miles per hour. The four of us could just squeeze in. It did, though, manage the steep winding Chiantigiana to and from the coast quite gallantly, year after year.

So, all set, ready for a switch from the luxuries of an architecture-prize Potomac-view home on the fringes of a power-center of the world. As dramatic a switch as I could manage without a full-fledged family rebellion. Our expenses were kept modest for several years. And I suppose all that austerity was about what a casual ex-pat friend would expect that a government drop-out type could afford, this rather eccentric fellow of thirty-seven, however brilliant he may have been at skipping from job to job in a few short years, up the ladder of success. And giving up that no doubt glamorous career, much too soon for a fair-sized *pension*, couldn't have saved up much, what will he do for a living?

There were more switches coming, too, as the dimensions unfolded of my extreme reaction to the way the political, economic, and cultural world was heading. And my determination to write.

I had been listed in Who's Who for a couple of years. Why? Job titles, the Cabot name, maybe paternal string-pulling? I wrote the editors, saying that I did not believe I merited the listing even by their standards, that I objected to the whole concept of the important and the unimportant people of the world, that I refused to buy a copy of the latest edition—with me in it. I demanded that I be removed from all future editions. I was. Would I now refuse to be listed by them on the merit of my published works of fiction? I don't know—is hypocrisy an essential part of life?

Then there were the family prohibitions, the in-house austerity. No Beatles—I can't remember my reasoning. And what was Charlotte's opinion? Just the dominant male getting away with nonsense? (Much later, to the relief of my families and friends, I finally learned of the cultural and musical value of the Beatles. Penny and I played them over and over as we sailed the Mediterranean—and Paul Simon, Cat Stevens, Peter Paul & Mary, Moody Blues, many more. Ah well.) No television too, but that was easier, reception would have been minimal, and in those days, there wasn't much to receive in Italy.

The heating of that house was absurd. In a closet at one end of the main hall, there was a wood- or coal-burning forno the size of two shoeboxes, which was supposed to heat air passing up through terracotta pipes maybe the diameter of an overage mortadella sausage. One pipe, strapped high up on the wall, led to the far, very far, other end of the hall and into what we used as a living room. The other pipe went up through the ceiling into the upstairs hall. We'd get this so-called furnace going white-hot, and we'd still feel nothing. Whatever heat we could generate stayed in the closet. We put a little terracotta fireplace in our designated living room, and later a kerosene heater. That was where we largely spent our winters, there and in my cell with its mini fireplace. And a couple of those winters were graced with major blizzards, deep snow, frozen pipes, olive trees exploding if their sap had already started to flow.

Our bedrooms were frigid. We heated our beds with *suore* or *preti*, wooden racks with earthenware pots of embers from our fireplace hanging in them, slid in between the sheets. The *prete* was long and low, a flaccid priest, the *suora's* dome shape was a pregnant nun. The trick was to avoid any ember that might give off a spark. Several of our sheets succumbed.

⌁

Florence in those years, to me it was a strange place. It seemed determinedly isolated from the rest of the world, different from Rome. Its architecture and public statuary were stern, hands-off, remote. The few exceptions—the colorful, delicate Duomo, the Battistero, Giotto's Campanile—were reminders of what could have been, of what most of the rest of exuberant Italy is, despite its history of city-state warfare, its fortifications, its victories and defeats. Florence was largely a city of careful understatement, of a deliberate plainness and intellectuality, its foundations were in commerce, it relied heavily on its past, its Italian was elegant,

With Charlotte and daughters Kathy and Sara in a trattoria
in Florence, 1961.

carefully avoiding the colorful vernacular of rural Tuscany.
It was reminiscent of my birthplace, Boston.

And was not Florence strangely out of place in that glorious Tuscan countryside? How could the warmth and beauty
of its surroundings—the villages, the farms, churches, hills
and mountains, the rivers and brooks, forests, orchards,
vineyards, the country roads, the other Tuscan cities decorated with delicate beauty—Siena, Arezzo, Pisa, Lucca—how
could the generous and welcoming people of Tuscany have
brought about this stony heart? I have no answer, but there
it was, at least in my eyes.

Giglio Castello too. A severely fortified village perched
on a cliff, a cliff still stained with the village's trash and
the morning contents of the village's chamber pots. A
dank, cold village—a few twisting cobbled alleys just wide
enough for a loaded donkey, the sun squeezed out, the
whole wrapped in a formidable wall with one entrance only,
a great medieval double gate. Acrid smells, harsh sounds—

the shrieking donkeys, roosters who knew no dawn, the oodle-oodle-oodle of the rickety bus climbing the switchbacks from Giglio Porto, arriving in the piazza outside the threatening walls, unloading its cargo of shrieking goats.

Outside the walls was a relatively new schoolhouse, one or two homes, including that of Amerigo, Giglio's only teacher who helped our daughters regain some of their Italian. And again, an overwhelmingly glorious countryside—mountainous, only the one treacherous road up from the port, a branch road off to our side of the island. Cliffs, pink rocks rising straight from the sea, terraces of grapes and vegetables and wheat and olive trees—terraces hacked out of the granite hillsides over the millennia. Groves of umbrella pines, clumps of cane in the watercourses, and everywhere the Mediterranean maquis—rockrose, lentischio, rosemary, junipers bent and dwarfed by the winds, aromatic mints, laurels, mastic, myrtles, wild figs, thyme. And the surrounding sea, the dancing sea, stretching out to Tuscan islands—Giannutri, Elba, Pianosa—to the volcanic hills of Lazio and Tuscany, to the snowy alps of Corsica on the horizon, to the sun setting behind the peak of Montecristo.

These were the contrasting settings of our new lives—a village and a city living grimly in austere pasts, countrysides offering exquisite beauty.

⌔

I certainly realized when I withdrew from government service that I was making a major course change, but its consequences were by no means thought out. Looking back on it, I was on a path leading by degrees to atheism, later often revised to agnosticism, atheism requiring a faith in no faith, revised to a determined attempt at literary asceticism, to vegetarianism, socialism, pacifism, even benign anarchism for a time—and there will be other isms to be added and subtracted in later years. The austerity we moved into in Tuscany seems now to have been a natural setting for such a path, and it was no doubt also an attempt to deal with the inequity and injustice of my largely unearned, inherited money. But little of this was due to farsighted planning, let alone omniscience.

⊖

Charlotte's aesthetic bent led her to work in the Harvard art history library of I Tatti in Fiesole on the outskirts of Florence. Willed to Harvard, I Tatti had been the residence of Bernard Berenson—art collector, historian, and art authenticator. Berenson's relationships with women were complicated and extensive. His surviving lover, Nicky Mariano, who had lived with him and his wife in an uneasy à trois, became a friend of Charlotte's. Other contacts developed in Florentine society, particularly for Charlotte—scholars, aristocrats, foreign residents. I tended to stick to my studio.

I did see Manlio frequently. It was during those years that he and I searched on Giglio and the Gargano coast, a bit of land for our own, a stone cabin, a place of unthreatened isolation. In vain.

It was in Florence that my forty-five-year close friendship began with Lubomir "Luba" Radoyce. As a teenager in Belgrade, he'd been a part of the resistance to the Nazi occupation, was imprisoned and tortured. He eventually escaped and joined one of the guerilla groups. After the war, he studied in Heidelberg, Paris, London, Yale, and West Virginia. He acquired an MA but never stuck it out to a Ph.D. He was richly fluent in Serbian, Russian, German, French, Italian, and English. His field was comparative literature with the emphasis on Russian.

Several years before I met him, he had moved to Florence with his second wife, an Italian painter, and their three young children. Within weeks, he had mastered Italian and landed a book contract to translate Tolstoy's essays on art into Italian and to write a long scholarly introduction to the book in Italian. He later became a professor of comparative literature at the University of California, a rare exception to the Ph.D. norm for professorships. He divorced for a second time in the midst of violent quarrels with family, academic colleagues, and UC Riverside. He moved to Paris, taught at the Sorbonne, and was in a short, disastrous marriage with one of his students. He finally returned to Tuscany where he continued with some of his research and writing, but spent his last years, before succumbing to lung cancer, in legal battles with his mentally unstable ex-wives numbers two and three, with his neighbors, and with the University of California.

A discouraging story—he had so much that he never managed to offer to the world. He was stubborn and incorrigibly litigious, both within his family and in the various governmental and university justice systems—he was prone to call them injustice systems. But his warmth, his love of literature, history, and art, his brilliant mind, his touching will-o'-the-wisp search for comfort and joy, his unassuming nature, his old-world charm and gentility drew his many friends to him.

We traveled together, adventured together, worked together, lent each other support often. His response to that first novel of mine, *The Cell*, gave me crucial encouragement. Literature, writing, were common grounds.

~18~

Too Plushy?

THOUGH living quietly in rural Tuscany, I was not out of touch with the world we had left. Radio, newspapers, news magazines, letters from family and friends back in the States. And as usual, the news was mostly bad. The botched Bay of Pigs adventure. The confrontation with Khrushchev off the coast of Cuba. On a gloomy day in November 1963, I was listening to a radio news broadcast when they broke in to announce the assassination of Kennedy.

The proliferation of nuclear weapons—Britain, France, China, Israel, and many more no doubt on their way—doomsday, the annihilation of much or all of life on Earth, was a finger-flick away. A badly worded communiqué, a navigation failure of a bomber or a submarine, anger and hate, despair, or simply one person's petulance in a nation's capital or in a missile silo—the end was close at hand.

There was no avoiding the barrage of doomsday scenarios. Firestorms that would suck the oxygen out of life, nuclear winter that would cover the globe with ice, radiation that would deform and maim and torture and kill, the horror of slow death to any survivor. Or maybe hopes of escaping to a sparsely populated untargeted southern hemisphere would cause desperation and death to millions stampeding south at the last moment from ground-zero northern population centers. School children around the world were drilled to duck under their desks when the sirens and the bells cried out— only much later realizing it would be safer to head for the aisles. Bomb shelters, evacuation routes, feckless plans for the survival of key persons, their genes. The novels, the movies, the television screens in every home and bar, the screaming headlines. Every plane that flew overhead, every siren, every church bell, every massive firecracker or gunshot, every un-claimed piece of baggage. Doom was in every quiet corner of our lives, and of course still is—and more so after 9/11, more so as the tipping points of climate change arrive and as terror-ism spreads around the world. I began to research and plan for a second novel, a post-doomsday story of a few survivors.

Was a cold war perhaps not worth fighting? Must paci-fism mean likely death? Private bomb-shelters, would they not effectively mean the murder of clamoring neighbors outside when there was no longer room for them within? Would not a red world be better than a dead world? These were questions I pondered and answered in a flurry of let-ters and articles. My answer for each was a tormented Yes.

And Vietnam, the war there was building up.

The consequences of America's decision to take over the responsibility for whatever would be left of Indochina from the French after the Dien Bien Phu defeat of the French forces—catastrophic. The missteps were huge. To install a Catholic as dictator in a Buddhist country, to back him up as he proceeded to slaughter Buddhist monks—a weak, ruthless, ineffectual leader. To stage a provocation in the Tonkin Gulf—alleged attacks on American destroyers. President Johnson commented, "For all I know, our Navy was shooting at whales out there."

Why? So that we could start pouring thousands of tons

of bombs on the civilian populations of Vietnam? To falsify reports, to poison millions. To gloat over daily body counts, to cover up horrors like My Lai. To lie to Americans, as did Johnson and Henry Cabot Lodge, McNamara and Bunker, with light-at-the-end-of-the-tunnel victory-in-sight, when we now know that privately they were despairing. To promise quick withdrawal, as did Nixon and Kissinger, only to continue the war for eight more years, with tens of thousands more American soldiers and another million Vietnamese killed. To expand the war secretly into a bombing and invasion of Cambodia and Laos.

My outrage this time joined a swelling chorus.

⌖

Was my response to the violent and devastating chaos of the world a deliberate, meaningful response, something to look back on with pride? Or was it simply a pleasant escape to the essentially pacifist culture of beautiful Tuscany, to a self-indulgent attempt at writing novels, a retreat to a comfortable, simple lifestyle? Would I have been truer to myself and a more effective voice had I been a conscientious objector rather than a volunteer in World War II? To have stayed in government service of some sort, rising as far as my abilities—not the imagined ones, the true ones— would have allowed, raising my voice as much as possible, rather than finding a voice in writing novels and a flurry of largely unheard protests? Would that not have been the best response? Were there middle grounds of validity behind these questions?

⌖

Whatever the answers, those early years in Tuscany were good years. School was giving the girls a decent education. Charlotte continued with her library work, her social contacts growing. And she joined in on many rigorous adventures. I was starting another novel.

We bought a canoe, at least the Italian idea of a canoe. We explored several rivers in Tuscany and Umbria, something in those years rarely, if ever, done. The four of us, the girls sitting amidships on the bags of gear—tents, sleeping bags, food, pots and pans—we made our way for three days down the Ombrone from Buonconvento near Siena to the sea. There were no river maps, lots of unknowns. We had scouted it a bit by car but found we could rarely get near it. Luckily the few rapids were easy, though there were several small dams to portage around. We found lovely isolated spots to set up camp. As I've usually found in canoeing or kayaking or rafting many smaller rivers—Italy, New England, Virginia, West Virginia, Arkansas, Washington, Thailand, Canada, Costa Rica, Britain, France—they provide us with a look back to a time when nature was largely left alone.

The Ombrone. An occasional riverside farm, a lone fisherman, two or three bridges. A ferry angling across, pulled by the current, fixed to a cable by a pulley. A walled town high on a cliff, ignoring the river. The last day of that trip was down into marshlands, sand dunes, the sea, camping there in the dune grass, swimming in the sea.

In those years, we also canoed the Arno in the Mugello Valley and down to Arezzo, a rough and rapid stretch with formidable dams to portage. And the Tiber from the heart of Umbria to Todi—again remarkably isolated except for an industrial zone near Perugia, a lovely countryside, many good spots to camp. Todi, from upstream, carried down with the swift current, is spectacular, standing behind its walls high on a cliff, remote from the river, though a sand bank where we pulled out was a popular swimming beach.

⟜

We did get back to the States—a piece of a summer. Families, friends. We were invited to join in a pack trip in the Canadian Rockies by Rick Bronson, an archeologist friend from Florence. Ten days in those glorious mountains. A guide, pack horses to carry our food and gear, saddle horses who knew how to deal with the mountain trails, the boggy tundra, how to alert us to a slinking mountain lion, a herd of caribou. We climbed once to a snow cornice, looked over the edge at a mountain goat, tossed snowballs his way.

Rick and I canoed for three days down the headwaters of the Athabasca—a small, fast stream there through wilderness. Loons, trout, a wolf, a fox with her cubs, mosquitoes in clouds.

A conversation by our campfire: You know, Rob, if you ever want to spend real time in a wilderness like this, on your own entirely up to your skills and perseverance, like that mountain man we came across the other day, fed up with surveying for railroads, in his shack, his animal skins, alone for years, he'd lost count, now is the time, before one has put on the weights of too many years.

That endless wilderness, that stretch of virgin river, our total dependence on our own resources—those words released in me a pent-up dissatisfaction. Had my response to what we were doing to our world been incomplete? Did privilege still weigh on me, still the puppet master back there somewhere? I would seek further, deeper into wilderness. I would know, I would survive.

I had admired Farley Mowat, his writings of his Canadian wilderness, his search. I knew from his later books that he was retreating now, that his wilderness was no more, destroyed by the never-ending snarl of our NORAD bombers patrolling over the Arctic. But had he looked too far, was there not wilderness still obtainable less grand than the entire sweep of arctic Canada? I would find him, I would ask him, I would begin my search.

Farley was living by then on a tiny island just off Burgeo on the southern coast of Newfoundland. I flew into St. John's, found a rooming house for a few days, settled into the city library and the city archives. Homesteading laws were still on the books, and vast tracts of Newfoundland were available Crown lands. I poured over the maps, settled on Willis Island in Bonavista Bay on the eastern coast—uninhabited, large enough to support game, a couple of small ponds with short brooks emptying into the sea, no harbors or sheltered coves to attract intruders.

I wandered the waterfront, waiting for my ferry to Burgeo—I would go there first. Docked against the pilings of a sagging pier was an ancient Portuguese three-master. She was being provisioned, some of her rigging replaced, readied to head out to the cod-fisheries of the Grand Banks. There were dozens of dories nested together, tied down on her decks, stacks of oars and short masts wrapped with their sails, tubs of hand-lines. A sailor, he'd been scrubbing bait barrels, invited me on board, showed me around. The fo'c'sle was dark, stinking, lined with tiers and tiers of cubbyhole berths. The captain's quarters were not much better. It was the schooner's last trip—the fantasy last voyage for Kipling's *Captains Courageous*, written almost a century before.

The harbor is a large perfectly protected anchorage. Its narrow entrance is between two headlands. I walked out to the stone tower on the northern headland—Cabot Tower, in honor of John Cabot's landing there in 1497. Giovanni Caboto, a seaman from Genoa who found sponsors in England to explore lands to the west, to outdo Columbus by sailing on a shorter northern route where the longitudes are closer together. Caboto sailed the Matthew from Bristol on letters patent from Henry VII. There's a rather ugly stone Cabot Tower on a high point in Bristol built in 1898—a much delayed commemoration. There are members of today's Cabot clan that like to think John Cabot was a forbear. I know of no hard evidence of this.

Prominent in St. John's's—fun, that punctuation—St. John's's government liquor store was Cabot Tower Demerara Rum. Mowat had written of that rum with special fondness. I took him a couple of bottles. He remembered me for that when he agreed to write the forewords for two of my novels.

Our meeting in Burgeo—I stayed with roly-poly, bearded Farley and his wryly indulgent wife for a couple of days—was warm and boisterous. We sailed a bit among the islands in his red catboat that he'd written about. He gave me no advice whatsoever about my homesteading scheme—just a quizzical look. I flew out in a floatplane, hitchhiked to Bonavista Bay.

At Burnside, a settlement of fisher folk, I got a lobsterman to take me out into the bay, pass by Willis Island for a look-see, and to leave me at the next island's still functioning fishing village, Saint Brendan's. He wouldn't stop at Willis Island, making it clear between squirts of chewing tobacco that he had to get back to Burnside before dark and that I must be particularly dimwitted. "You can't get in or outta there from November till April, ice moving, can't walk, can't boat. Sealing we do out further where current's less. Nobody never ever lived on Willis, not even Willis."

It was about then that I realized he was right about my

wits. And I learned nothing by putt-putting along the shore of Willis for a few minutes. Heavily wooded with scraggly white and black spruce, no clearings that I could see, low rise in the center, steep-to rocky coast, no shingle or sand beaches, no decent coves.

I stayed in Saint Brendan's for a couple of days waiting for a ride back to the mainland. The forests of the island succumb to soggy tundra on the northeast, ending in a fair-sized harbor. The town there once had a population of more than a thousand, thriving as base for the cod-fisheries. Each family would build a schooner, a "floater," living aboard much of the year. At one point I was told that as many as thirty floaters would be anchored there. What I saw was no more than a slowly dying village, maybe a few dozen families, a little church, a bit-of-everything shop with the elderly owners living in back. They put me up in a spare room. Being a rare curiosity, I was invited to several homes—a moose-meat stew maybe, or eggs with thick slabs of their own bacon, coffee, canned milk. In the kitchen of every house I visited there were shelves loaded with dozens of sealed jars of moose meat. That was the winter staple, though there was still some salted cod stored away from the heyday of the cod-fisheries.

There were spectacular views from the village out over the near and far islands, the open ocean, but I noticed that whenever a window might look out on that view, it was small and curtained. That's the last thing I wanna see, son, that sea, we hate it. There was a strong similarity among all the folks I saw there, a kind of blank-stare monosyllabic quality. Evidence of the dangers of inbreeding in small, isolated, tribal configurations?

So ended that adventure. How serious was I about it all?

Was I ready to pack up and leave my family for months, a year? Did I really think I could survive alone there, starting with virtually nothing? Or did I just need to run through that look-see, knowing full well the outcome, a kind of reality check? Was it my need to push to its logical conclusion the absurdity of finding a right and a wrong to life's choices?

Well, that was the best I could do with it then, searching my perhaps slightly less-dim wits while traveling back to Tuscany. There were many adventures and misadventures yet to come before I began to see that it is not the choices we make that matter, but rather what we do with those choices.

By now, dozens of kayakers pass by Willis, many in tour-guided flotillas. None seems to be drawn to stop there, though if they had spotted a cleared landing spot, a hut, some sign of something, they no doubt would have invaded. They were all on their way to Flat Islands, one of the well-known historic outports evacuated by the government in 1957 when the cod fisheries collapsed. Those islands are now stripped of all trees. There are, I read, a few squatters' summer cabins, their outhouses overflowing as kayakers sneak in to use them, conscientiously avoiding covering the islands with yet more toilet paper and garbage.

So it goes.

~19~

Trading Treasures

I RETURNED from that Newfie adventure to our tranquil routines, writing, studying, Charlotte's work in I Tatti's library, weekend expeditions, summers on Giglio, our friendship with Ede and Giuseppe ever closer. But my relationship with Charlotte had become somehow rather distant, less of the warmth and enthusiasm that I had known. It was disturbing.

Both of us were becoming exasperated at the needless inconveniences of our pseudo-villa home. Giglio? No problem. But Florence? Brutal winters, constant annoyances. We'd heard that a Swiss acquaintance was giving up on his botched attempt at remodeling a very small abbey on a beautiful subsistence-farm with remarkably preserved Renaissance landscapes that had been decreed as untouchable. We bought it. We engaged an architect friend to suggest a remodeling plan of action. We, far too easily by my taste at least, acceded to his approach. What we got was clearly an expression of his saccharine taste, tainted with his cloying brand of Catholicism.

A stunningly beautiful place, though, comfortable, everything in working order, the farmer's wing of the little abbey still occupied by three generations of the tenant farmers. The twilight of an almost medieval subsistence farm—white oxen for the plowing, a milk cow with calf for his veal, rabbits in their cage, chickens, fan-tail doves, an eternally chained guard dog, a vegetable garden, olives, fruit trees, a vineyard with the vats and barrels and demijohns and fiascos in a dank stone-vaulted cellar, a stand of oak trees with acorns for the wild boar, on the migratory route for songbirds for the hunters to slaughter. I built another studio down in the oaks, similar to my studio just up the way. I rarely got to use it.

My writing had ground to a halt. There was the year or more of distractions with the remodeling, the settling in, with the visitors, the house guests, and the entertaining. Several years living in Florence had made a number of firm friendships and connections, particularly for Charlotte, and now there was the new home with its four bedrooms, dining room, a double living room, a large terrace looking out over that countryside of ancient farms, vineyards, olives, umbrella pines, cypresses, dovecotes, villas, a herd of sheep, oxen plowing. Secluded, near Florence, an ideal place for house guests, for dinners, for cocktail parties. We seemed to have become landed gentry with tenant farmers in our service, however close our friendship with them became. We had entered a firmly classist society.

I found that new life unfolding around me to be increasingly uncomfortable, a betrayal of my rebellions. I had not just let it happen, either, I had played a part in bringing it about. I had helped set in motion a serious deviation from my original choice, my determined response to the world as I saw it, my chosen role as a would-be conscientious objector. And it seemed to be adding to the distance between Charlotte and me.

It was my original choice, my response, largely my ini-

tiative to leave America. And it was my perception that this
new life in our lovely new home was a betrayal. But what
about Charlotte and our daughters? What were their values,
their perceptions, their hopes? I still bear the shame and
the sorrow of not knowing the answers, of not having had
the clarity and the courage to work this all out openly with
them at the time—openly for me, openly for them. Of not
having the foresight to deal with the dangers, forestall them
before they engulfed us in pain and disruption and divorce.

⟿

After several years of summer peace and isolation in
our little stone hut on Giglio, the tourists began to flood in.
Our tiny cove where we would swim every day, diving from
the pink granite ledges with our sweet sheepdog Laglia, had
been discovered. It was often left a disgusting mess. Was this
the end of our summer idylls? Let's try Greece. I found a
young Greek student at the university to teach me a bit of
Greek for a month or two before we went.

Maria. A young woman from a town in rural Greece
desperately trying to get on with her university courses in
architecture but with inadequate preparation. Her father, a
doctor, had found ways to propel her into studies that clearly
did not match her abilities. Soon I was helping her with her
course material, Greek language studies going by the board.
Italian was our mutual language. And soon I was obsessed
by this seemingly warm, needy woman. She was not a great
beauty—light brown hair, blue-green eyes—not at all the
fiery, dark stereotype of a Greek woman, no Irini Pappás.
But she had a way of drawing one in—warm, welcoming,
and vulnerable. She had the ability of intuitively discerning
and then filling whatever gap one appeared to need, of being a mirror to those needs. It was a psyche trap, not a sex

Maria Anagnostopulu, 1968.

trap. This, I believe, was the mechanism and blindness of my obsession.

In our few years together, I would often see this ability of hers work on others, too—on mere acquaintances, on family, even quite dramatically on trained psychotherapists. And I was soon to learn that to be a brilliant mirror meant to cloud over any consistent personality. Much later, tragically later, I was to awake to find I had evidently been living with some mirrored need of mine—pushing the metaphor, with a bit of silvered glass in a plain frame—and had failed to seek and find Maria's true personality.

Soon after meeting her, I was fantasizing withdrawing

from the social scene that was increasingly uncomfortable for me, from the formalities and conventions, from a cooling relationship with Charlotte. Perhaps this Maria could be a companion, to live very modestly in rural southern Italy or Greece, to quietly write, maybe to open an after-school center for needy children—the missionary approach to offering help, an approach that I had once decried. But I should have realized that, given our extreme differences, our hopes were incompatible.

Charlotte recognized my obsession almost before I did. Coming on the heels of my Newfie misadventure, she must have seen me as half-crazed. The result was Charlotte offering me the space of separation to work through my obsession. She would move to the States with Sara to live with my parents for the winter, Kathy being already enrolled in an English boarding school. A sad, cruel ending to a loving family, a chapter of my complicated life that is still excruciating to recall. We all soon realized that it would be a final separation of Charlotte and me.

That was the fall of 1966. Within days of their leaving, one early morning I watched from the top story of an apartment block overlooking the Piazza della Signoria as the Arno flooded through the city. Michelangelo's David stood silent in the alluvione, buses afloat around him, cars tumbling by, one hurled through the storefront window of a bank, the city silenced in the roar. A devastated city—thousands of priceless books, works of art left in the mud, monuments, bridges, treasures everywhere trashed.

My dear friend Luba invited me, with Maria, to join him and his family in Riverside, California, where he had just taken a professorship in comparative literature at the University. At her father's insistence, we had bent the regulations and exaggerated Maria's record to get her admitted to a master's program at Stanford—though she had no university degree and would be starting a month or two late.

My writing was not going well. I let myself be almost constantly distracted. The mounting horrors of the war in Vietnam, the drama of the African-American civil rights movement. The tragedy of Luba's wife going insane almost overnight—spirit writing as the bride of God, messages coming to her from electrical wall-outlets, a chase after her down the streets of Riverside, through a church with a wedding in progress, ending in a psychiatric hospital commitment.

And my difficulties dealing with Maria's unfolding personality. Her flirting with a young Greek student, with Luba —making sure I saw her. Her wide mood swings, her growing jealousies of my past, doing her best to deny or erase it. Ominous beginnings, but not enough to overcome my obsession.

With Maria enrolled at Stanford for her year living in the grad students' dorm, I bought a used Ford and a small trailer, moved to a trailer park in San Jose. That became my base, it was there that I began work on my novel *The Joshua Tree*.

✢

The Southwest had had a particular draw for me ever since my father took brother Louis and me on a pack trip in Arizona's Superstition Mountains when I was maybe twelve. Our father was an expert horseman and guide. Three saddle horses, one packhorse for our food and gear—self-sufficient for ten days. Desert to pine forests in the high country, legends of lost gold miners, Indian encampments.

While with Luba in southern California, I had driven up into what was then the Joshua Tree National Monument, later to become a National Park, and had hung out with old-timer Bill Keys, who'd been allowed by the Park Service to stay on his ranch for life.

I went back there to Bill's homestead, a ramshackle bit of the past, parked my trailer against Park Service rules, well hidden from the rangers behind a red-stone tooth of the earth, and spent weeks with Bill, his memories, his stories, the scattered shards of his life. Bill became Will Spear of *The Joshua Tree*, the principle setting for my novel was his ranch. I backpacked for days, for many miles, up into his world of the red-stone teeth, the willowed washes, the cactus, the cat claws, vultures and eagles and mountain sheep, rattlesnakes, the arms of the trees of Joshua reaching out to the Promised Land. My attraction to the past, to simple living closer to our natural surroundings.

My writing style turned out to be a development from that of the unpublished *The Cell*. I was never schooled in the art of the novel or poetry, but I had read voluminously, particularly novels. I had come to feel that most prose followed too many conventions—syntax, past tenses, abstractions, punctuation, names, explanations, quotations. One of the rewards of much poetry is that conventions are loosened, even to the point where only verse form and rhythm remain. The rhythm of every sentence in my novels has been important to me.

We usually do not think in sentences, names are often replaced with images, feelings are unleashed, time ignored, verbs often left out. Associations carry us into revealing places. Memories are present events. Life lives in the present tense.

And our minds work in many unlikely ways simultaneously.

Most of my fiction is in the present tense, largely in the first person, and in the case of *The Joshua Tree*, I attempted to encourage a reader's associations arising from the written word with bits of marginalia on every page. There is also a consistent rebellious and elegiac theme in my fiction, and a longing for a close sense of belonging to the natural world.

Results—fine reviews, scant revenue.

I continued work on the novel while doing the requisite time in a Reno motel to get that cruel divorce from Charlotte. And when Maria had gone back to Greece, with me to follow when I'd finished the first draft, I moved my trailer to the top of the coastal hills above Palo Alto, above the city smog. I parked it under a twisted, dying apple tree, home of a mother opossum, her brood peeking out of her pouch. I loved that place, I worked well, I finished the manuscript.

And several times a week for a month or two I subjected myself to hours with two Jungian psychiatrists. Lots of dream analysis, trying to understand my need for my rebellion from my father, from my earlier life, from my wife. I got no further than, *It had to be.*

Before a Greek Orthodox wedding in Greece, I had to go through a pro forma ritual of being accepted into the Church. New shirt, white and tie-less. New name, Nikódhemos—the Pharisee who coined "born again."

We rented an apartment in the heart of Rome—cheap, scruffy, top-floor next door to the central synagogue, with spectacular views over the ancient ruins, the Pantheon, St. Peter's Basilica, the roofs, the bell towers, the domes, the pines and palms, the Albani Hills. And soon our son Alexis was born into this Roman life.

I had bought a thirty-two-foot sail boat in England, put her, *Aeoli*, on a flat bed, drove with the Welsh truck driver onto a Channel ferry, through the streets of Paris and Versailles, and on to the launching in Cannes. With Maria and two equally inexperienced friends, sailing to Fiumicino at the mouth of the Tiber, a few days in the apartment, then sailing on to Corfu, Piraeus, and the Aegean. Soon I had

bought a tract of wild land on the far side from the village of the small island of Koufonissos, east of Naxos. We built a house above the coral beaches in 1970 our little family moved there from Rome each summer, mooring *Aeoli* in a nearby cove.

Sailing in the Aegean. Often with friends—Harry a British Grecophile, William an expat architect living in Rome, Paolo and Ulla—Italian communist journalist and German wife, Manlio and Anna from my Marshall Plan days. Cruising from island to island—adventure and beauty. The summer winds from the north, the meltémi, could often blow at gale force for months. Cloudless skies, fierce sun, steep breaking seas, often rail under with only a minimal storm trysail, naked in the salt spray. Swing in behind an island, dead calm, coast into a cove, drop anchor off a wild beach, a swim, cold retsína, a lobster with lemon juice and olive oil. Or maybe lower sails when you've swung into the lee, motor in to a fishing village, drop a stern anchor, nose into the pier, ashore for a beer, bits of grilled octopus, a khoriatikí salad, a grilled barboúni just caught, oúzo, a thimble of coffee thick with sugar, a clarinet slurring the notes of an island love song— finger rolling on a violin string.

⟡

It was during those times that I began to receive reviews of *The Joshua Tree*, which, after several rejections, was published in 1970 by Atheneum. They were many and gratifyingly, effusively positive. Years later, a second edition was sprinkled on the dust jacket with excerpts from these reviews, much to my ego's delight. Bloomsbury (London) did a third publication of *The Joshua Tree* in paperback in 2011, later issuing it as an e-book.

⟡

But there was a growing dark side to my brief years with Maria. The storm of jealousy when Maria sees a postcard I have received from my daughter—she stops breathing, her face blackens, she vomits. The extorted love. The quizzical looks of the islanders when, in her queenly way, charm becomes overt flirting. We wintered in Rome where Alexis was born. Often I would escape Maria's vicious moods, he in a carrier on my back. We would explore the piazzas, the markets, the ice cream bars.

On Koufonissos, he and I would wander the beaches, the limestone cliffs over the whitecap sea, the fields of asphodels and junipers twisted by the meltémi.

My daughters were living in Italy. Kathy in Rome with her future husband, Michael Fitzgerald. He was teaching, but would soon move into a long successful career as a movie producer. Sara in Florence at Italian public schools and then an American school. She soon married Gulrez Arshad. Two weddings, first in Rome with me, then in Florence with her mother.

Maria's bitter jealousy of my past lives concentrated increasingly on my daughters, alternating between displays of hospitality and slammed doors. It was frightening. I tried to get help for her in Rome. Some psychotherapy there, and later in Canada where she went for a month or two to a "growth center." but it was as if it were a contest with the therapists, a contest she seemed to win.

❧

Rome was a good choice for our winters. Maria thrived on the latest fashions, sometimes pulling me into them too. I managed to get another novel written there, *Nima*. It was received enthusiastically by a New York agent, but quickly dropped when it got a couple of rejections. It was story of an epileptic and his dog, set in the American southwest, Italy, and Greece. It remains unpublished. Much of it took place on an island similar to Koufonissos, and I've used some modified passages from it in my novel *The Isle of Kheria*.

It was good to reconnect with old friends—Manlio and Anna, my American sculptor friends, several others. Some were entirely supportive of me whatever the wild swings of my life, others were quizzical though accepting. And I was grateful for several close new friendships—an Irish poet, an Italian painter living downstairs, a journalist for the communist paper *Paese Sera*, a documentary film maker, an architect, Linda and Mike, collectors of antique dolls and typewriters. It was a pleasure to become part of the Roman kaleidoscope. To be greeted at my morning espresso bar as part of the scene, to shop nearby in that most exotic of all open-air markets in those days, Campo dei Fiori. To roam the artisans' alleys, discover hidden restaurants. To hear the cries of the knife-sharpener wheeling his bicycle, the hundred church bells calling, the street minstrels. The swallows skimming rooftops in the dusk, the gipsy children by the Coliseum practicing their pickpocket trade on the tourists. In those days, Rome for me was full of adventure, offsetting the growing agony of my relationship with Maria. And often Alexis was with me exploring that kaleidoscopic world.

I have spent long periods of time living in several countries other than my own. But the usual feelings of being foreign, of being an odd intrusion, and in the last analysis unacceptable, was not so in Rome. A large and cosmopolitan city, millennia of history sweeping through its streets—one became just a part of the mix. Rome was also an interesting place from which to observe world events. Many different points of view were vigorously promoted by local friends, journals, the Italian press. And, as I had begun while living near Florence, I would hear and read much about emerging countercultures, particularly in America—historians arguing, columnists, poets, novelists. A flurry of opinions, passing fads, rebellions—the search for paths to lead out of ourselves and out of a world that had tolerated racism, discriminations and prejudices, genocides, lynchings, consumerism, the brutality of religions, the destruction of the natural world, and always war as a solution.

I loved that Italy, its ability to observe the world without being swept into extremes, to stay true to its own culture. In response to my despair about my culture, the America I thought I knew, I even seriously considered becoming an Italian citizen.

✧

By the time Alexis was three or four, Maria's demands on me had become obsessive. A bigger apartment, a new car, a bigger sailboat—I resisted. Her flirtations became more blatant. There was one feckless and seemingly more or less unwitting fellow she began to concentrate on. I confronted her often about this, but she would not back off. She began to look for another apartment for herself, putting ads in the classifieds. Her tantrums, her histrionics, her mood swings increased. She would tear at me—often in the presence of our toddling son—ripping at my shirts, scratching, screaming, if, for example, I were to make a forbidden phone call to one of my daughters. She seemed to both want me out of her life and to need to be utterly in control of my every hour.

I sought advice—therapists, mutual friends, Maria's sister who also lived in Italy, and particularly three neighbors living in our apartment block who had watched the daily tragedy unfold. I was close to the breaking point. I felt I had to remove myself from a Maria who seemed to become crazed whenever I was around. Months of trying to find a way to keep our family together. The devastating pain that it must cost a child, now and in his future, to see his parents in such torment. Yet a separation would also be very hurtful.

Her pain, my son's, mine. If we separate, should he stay with his mother or his father? In our situation, the conventional choice, given the child's age, is the mother. Could I hope that he might live with me later on? At very least, that I would see him often, that I would be nearby, or if I were far off, that I would be ready and able to travel often to be with him, take him on trips as he grew older, to find adventures together? These unresolved inner conflicts finally led me to realize that I needed help, that my obsessions had led us into prolonged pain wherever I turned. Yes, I needed help.

While working on *The Joshua Tree* in California, I had found myself in the midst of the counterculture. The Esalen Institute was much in evidence as a seedbed for many of its aspects, including group therapy as an alternative to the psychiatrist's couch. I learned of an Esalen-inspired residential program in southern Spain. I enrolled. Leaving Maria with an investment account in her name in a Swiss bank, a monthly allowance, and detailed household instructions, I headed for southern Spain.

～ 20 ～

The Funny Farm

A DOZEN OF US—English, Americans, Spanish, Germans, Dutch, Canadians, Portuguese—would be living together closely for two months, seeking to understand ourselves, to confront personal difficulties, to find our paths ahead. For me, it was an opening of worlds that I had largely only guessed at, read about. In February 1975, I celebrated my fifty-first birthday at the Finca la Follenca sitting stark naked in a circle, men and women—I was by a wide margin the oldest—holding hands, chanting Auuuoomm. Then each of us, in turn, would stand before the others, being told one by one around the circle what our bodies told about our personalities and problems. Most of the others seemed comfortable with this. For me, it was. . . well, just the casual exposing of genitals, let alone psyches, was new territory—embarrassing, difficult, exciting.

The Finca's two or three resident group leaders and the five or six visiting leaders used many different techniques to help us understand ourselves, to learn how better to deal with others, to help us find our way. Group therapy, under different names too, has a long history, but it became particularly popular in the "New Age" emerging from the counterculture. Many of the techniques were developed at Esalen on California's spectacular coast. At the Finca, we used a variety—encounter, sleep deprivation, active meditation, three-days in lightless-soundless-foodless isolation, enlightenment intensives, counseling, dance, others I have forgotten.

Three or four of our group were dealing with at least incipient psychoses. Most of us would appear to be representatives of a cross section of young, thoughtful, seeking Western adults. Most were reasonably well-to-do, though some were on scholarships or work-study plans. Yet one of the strongest impressions I got as the weeks went by was the intensity of deep suffering in and around every one of us. Stifled feelings, grievings, loss, rejection, humiliation, parental and spousal cruelties, crippling guilt, low self-esteem, addictions, failure, betrayal. There is no way to compare these sufferings with such horrors as genocide, rape, beheadings, torture, mutilation, starvation, honor killings, lynchings, sexual slavery—but what I observed there at the Finca was profound, damaging pain. My own torments were thoroughly belittled.

What emerged for me about me? The main demon that kept reappearing was my father. At one point, I spent hours in front of my increasingly bored and wandering group pounding a mattress with a tennis racket, yelling at The Old Man till my throat closed. I clocked up more hours than kids almost a third my age. It was a lasting catharsis.

To the group, I was Mr. Nice Guy, which in that setting meant passive-aggressive phony-nice. It took me some time to stand up for my moniker, to conclude that it was my natural way and aspiration to be non-judgmental of people, to be "nice," and that that was quite okay.

The Finca gave me time and human interaction to find my way through my deep aversion to divorce, to taking the hard decisions, to leaving this second little family of mine. I phoned them several times, hoping to speak to Alexis, but Maria's rage made that impossible. I came to more fully understand the degree of my own responsibility for the dissolution of two families. With Charlotte, if I had understood myself better at the time, shared whatever I felt with her and our daughters, we might well have made it through our differences without divorcing. With Maria, my common sense and several of my friends told me that it was a very risky venture from the beginning. Once I had nevertheless moved to her, if I had stuck to the path I thought we had started on and not given in so often to her erasing of my principles, my past, my daughters, even my advanced age—if, if, if…

But those ifs are dangerous, I realized then, and I certainly do now. I would not be where I am now—a place of deep contentment, a wife and dearest companion whom I had been seeking for so long, family all about me, dear friends—if I had not learned and taken myself forward. And what might have been shambles left behind have turned out, I believe, to be better resolutions for all concerned, though I know that recently Alexis has found a deep-seated anger toward me for not having stayed nearer to him after the separation. Yes, all suffered as the relationships deteriorated—divorces, sundered families. Resentments no doubt linger. But Charlotte eventually remarried and is living near our daughters. Maria still lives in Rome nearby Alexis, who has recently married a Sicilian lawyer. I am emotionally close to my daughters in spite of the disruption of their young lives.

֍

It was a short walk from the Finca down to the town of Estepona. Through the old village, its narrow alleys, gera-

niums at every window, still the occasional donkey bringing firewood in from the campo. On down to the largely
rebuilt center. A popular bar was called the Manicomio, the
mad house, and we inmates of the Funny Farm Finca would
often hang out there, chat with nearby sidewalk tables in
whatever common language we might muster. We would
usually manage to avoid the obvious tourists. The old fishing village was disappearing under the flood of sun-seekers.
For them, the dark cloud of fascism was only a slight inconvenience, the peseta was cheap, and was it not Franco who
gave us those comic-opera Guardia Civil hats?

There was a substantial colony of non-Spanish in Estepona—artists, restaurant and bar owners and employees,
writers, retirees, architects, beach bums. One of our group
leaders at the Finca, an American, lived in town. She invited
a couple of us "inmates" to a cocktail party at her home. It
was a mix of maybe twenty or so, largely foreign residents.
Not the usual cocktail party vapidities, eyes wandering on
toward the next empty target. People were lounging, relaxed,
no sign of the usual pecking order.

I found myself at the finger-food table beside an immediately friendly young woman, Penny, Penelope Lintine.
Different, attractive, an unobtrusive British accent. I can still
remember the shirt she was wearing, light green with a scattering of tiny flowers, her hair pulled back smoothly despite
a suspicion of underlying tight curls. There was something
about her—her manner, her dress, her directness—that
spoke of a free spirit, of her own style, of her ability to make
the best of and enjoy whatever came her way. She was ready
to listen and to talk, giving no sense of needing to move
on, to do the usual cocktail party circulating. She knew our
hosts well and had visited their Finca. She spoke amusingly

of the impressions the town had of the "Funny Farm"—the odd comings and goings, the nudity, the screams heard far down the hill, the reports from the Finca's gardener and janitor of unspeakable goings on—he'd proceed to speak of them in detail.

And we talked of our sons, almost of the same age. We were instant friends. Thereafter, we enjoyed many free times together—bars, restaurants, picnics with her son Dominic. She was helping an Irish friend of hers, owner of a small bar and restaurant, as a barista and waitress. In the ten years since leaving school she had had a wide variety of jobs— truck driver, dental assistant, secretary, waitress in up-scale restaurants in London and Estepona—whatever was needed to support her and later her son as a single mother. She obviously took on these jobs gratefully and with relish. Her eclectic employment matched her eclectic friendships, ranging from polo players and sherry heirs to the illiter-ate widow next door—and with no trace of discrimination. Early in our relationship, I came to admire and envy her extraordinary ability to connect with people of whatever color, creed, or status.

Weeks passed, many delightful times together, and fi-nally—twice-burned cautious me, Penny extricating herself from two difficult relationships—finally we became lovers. My time at the Finca came to an end, she invited me to stay on with her and little Dominic in her tiny row house in the old part of the town. She had bought it for very little and made it very livable.

❧

Before leaving Koufonisos for the last time, I had *Aeoli* hauled out by the fishermen in the tight but protected winter harbor a mile or so from the village. They had never hauled a full-keel boat or anything with much of a mast. The largest boat in their fishing fleet was beamier and longer than *Aeoli*, but with the traditional relatively flat, shallow-bilge bottom built around a massive beam running the full length of the boat—a structural keel. The ways were two rails of adzed tree trunks that fortunately extended underwater just deep enough to accommodate *Aeoli*'s five-and-a-half-foot full keel. There are virtually no tides in the Mediterranean that would have made such an operation easier.

They greased the ways with a stinking mix of fish fat, used engine oil, and propeller shaft grease. They got her onto the flat-bottom cradle, which they then had to build up around her much higher narrower hull, working half under water. At the top of the ways was a massive cast-iron winch maybe an arm's span in diameter. They claimed it came off a French warship wrecked by Nelson. Apocryphal—warships used anchor capstans that, unlike this winch, did not store the entire cable on itself. Eight men struggled on the rusty winch bars, and up she came, shuddering, tipping forward dangerously, but she made it, up to her winter resting place to cheers and bottles of ouzo.

My plan, hatched in Estepona, was to drive my car to Florence, leave it with my daughter Sara who was living there with her growing family, then go on by bus and ferry and a fishing-boat hitch-hike to Koufonisos. I'd launch *Aeoli*, sail to a shipyard in Lavrion on the far side of the Attica peninsula from Athens to get her spruced up, and have Penny and Dominic meet me there for a long summer's cruise across the Aegean, along the southern coast of Turkey and Cyprus to Syria, and back.

Penny was game, Dominic elated. It was a delightful cruise. We were joined for a time with two friends from my

Finca group. The Aegean was conveniently swept free of most yachts by the meltémi blasting at us from the north. And in that summer of 1975, the Turkish coast had been largely undiscovered by tourists. Cyprus was tense and tourist-free, Turkey having just annexed the northern half in response to an attempt by the Greek junta of dictators to annex the entire island. The southern half became a separate nation, bolstered by the presence of two British military bases, hold-overs from colonial days, and by a UN peacekeeping force that had already been there for ten years to keep the Greeks and Turks—mortal enemies for millennia—from slaughtering each other. That British base provided Dominic with several jars of British Marmite, his favorite bread spread.

The Taurus mountains, snow-capped with some glaciers, many peaks over eleven thousand feet, seem to drop straight into the Mediterranean along almost that entire southern coast of Turkey, three hundred miles. There are many bays and coves and islands, deserted beaches, palms and umbrella pines, fishing villages and the four or five port towns. We would usually find quiet, deserted anchorages, often stopping in a cove, a bit of beach, for lunch. For one such lunch we—just the three of us by then—had sailed into a rather large protected spot but found no beach. The wind was very light, so we drifted, sails up, along the shore as we picnicked on deck. We'd seen two Turkish soldiers walking along the coast, but took no notice of them until they started yelling at us. One of them dropped into the prone position and took aim on us with a monstrous rifle. We dropped the sails, drifting to a stop, and tried to look as helpless as possible. The soldier who'd done most of the yelling stripped to his underwear and swam out to us. We put out a ladder for him to board, and produced our passports. He studied them carefully but upside down, gestured for us to leave immediately, and swam back to shore. We motored away, no longer an invading force of Cypriot Greeks, but at least a good excuse for a heroic swim while on patrol duty.

Twice we left *Aeoli* in a port town for a week or so, rented a car, and explored the high country and the southern plains beyond. Remote country, small towns providing us primitive hotels, local foods, pita bread picnics on alpine meadows, herds of sheep and goats and ponies.

A ramshackle highland town, a night in a flophouse—Dominic on a rickety cot, an extra narrow single bed for us—heavy stinks, a pair of enormous filthy socks found under the bed the next morning.

Smaller villages, often hidden in the pine forests, maybe a minaret showing through the tree tops. Men with fierce moustaches, fezzes, long knives in their belts, guns slung on

Poised on the bow off Rhodes, Greece, 1975.

their shoulders. The women still dressed in their traditional bright colors—one, resting from her hoeing, takes off her head scarf to wipe her face, balding gray hair, comes up to touch Penny's thick flowing curls in amazement.

High over the sea we climbed through the ruins of Greek temples, sat on the top steps of an amphitheater slicing tomatoes and cucumbers into yogurt cupped in pita bread. Silent ghosts on the stage below us, the sun dancing on far waves. And the camels—no, not on the stage, that would be more likely in Rome—but they'd still surprised us, lumbering by in most unlikely places, much to the delight of Dominic.

We sailed east almost to the Syrian border, Mersin, a big and busy port. We moored near the commercial docks, dinghyed ashore, bought ice cream cones from a barrow street vendor, watched the stevedores loading an enormous freighter flying the red flag with the hammer and sickle of the Soviet Union, two enormous rats jumping from a bollard onto a bow hawser, shinnying up to sniff out Russian fare—caviar, perhaps? Dominic, true to form, was immediately talking, somehow, with a Russian sailor who hoisted him on his shoulders, scrambled up the ladder, and there they were maybe eighty feet above us waving cheerily. So much for the Cold War.

Back into Greek waters, their easternmost island, Kastelorizo. It was a lively island. The harbor was a perfect circle but for its narrow entrance, an omicron Ω. Fishing boats and a couple of yachts bow-anchored, sterns belayed to bollards around the stone quay. As we finished supper, a dozen or so men gathered in a circle linked by handkerchiefs and began the syrtos dance. Dominic was soon bouncing on the knee of a bouzouki player who had to leave the little band when a string broke.

Island after island, each with a bit of adventure for us. Tangled anchors more than once. Sailing together for a couple of island hops with Eric Williams and his wife. They lived on their small sloop where he continued to write sequels to his novel *The Wooden Horse* about his and others' prisoner-of-war escapes from German camps in World War II. And I, of course, told him of my relationship to Pat Reid, author of a similar book, *The Colditz Story*. He had escaped a PW officers camp, crossed into Switzerland where he met and married my Aunt Katy's daughter Jane.

Onward. A solitary cove on Karos where the sole inhabitants were a couple living on the other side of the island—a stone hut, a herd of sheep, a few tomato plants, a row boat to get them to the nearest village on a neighboring island ten miles away. And often we'd be out in an angry meltémi, reefed, naked in the fierce sun, soaked as short steep waves came aboard.

Throughout these adventures, a central theme for me was my growing admiration for and attraction to this woman, this "lovely bird," as I would often call her. Feisty, independent, direct, ready for anything. Not a posturing cell in her lovely body. No neediness, no manipulations. Ever ready to identify the pretentious. And her rambunctious little son was a delight, a free spirit. We were fast becoming a team. I was wary of commitment, yet when I later asked her to join me in a return to America, still without a declaration of commitment, she was ready to say yes, however risky that move might well be for her and Dominic. Decades later she sometimes faults herself for acquiescing to my unpredictable and unorthodox ways, but I am deeply grateful that she did, grateful for her adaptive courage.

~ 21 ~

Talking, Walking?

THE WORLD was out there still during that summer idyll. In conversations with Penny, with fellow travelers, or alone on deck keeping watch under the stars as the self-steerer does the work on an overnight passage, I re-examined my disillusionment with my country. Was it still justified, was there a better alternative, was it Italy again with my son Alexis to be nearby?

The war in Vietnam had finally ended in April of that year, 1975, with the helicopter evacuation of the last Americans from the U.S. Embassy roof. It had exacted a huge human cost, fatalities now estimated at four million Vietnamese from both sides, two million Laotians and Cambodians, and fifty-eight thousand U.S. soldiers. The genocidal killing fields of Cambodia were later to claim a quarter of the country's entire population of eight million.

The economic and material costs of the war were huge. The scars left on America were deep. Much of the counter-culture movement owed its vigor to the massive anti-war protests. And those protests had proven crucial in finally ending the war.

In 1964, President Johnson had announced to the radio audience, in his Texan southern drawl, the passage of the Civil Rights Act. It was a stirring moment, the more so coming from the segregationist South. I had been born in an era when lynchings were commonplace, a photographic sport with folks exchanging snapshots on postcards in the U.S. mail to prove how many lynchings they had personally attended. By 1975, five thousand people had been hanged by vigilantes and the Ku Klux Klan. Hate crimes continue, but the laws and their enforcement have made an exponential difference.

In 1965, Johnson signed into law the Voting Rights Act. During the first half of my life, millions of my fellow citizens had been effectively barred from voting because of the color of their skin. In 1975, it was clear that my country would never have a black president, but at least there was finally substantial progress toward racial equality. My father would by then not have been able to get away with his "Jew-boys" comments.

Betty Friedan's *The Feminine Mystique* had been published in 1963, a major influence in furthering women's rights. In 1965, the last state law prohibiting the use of contraceptives was struck down by the Supreme Court. No-fault divorce law had been adopted by California, Gloria Steinem's *Ms.* magazine was on a roll. In 1973, Roe v. Wade legalized abortion, and it looked as if Nebraska would soon be the first state to criminalize husband-wife rape. Single-gender colleges and universities were on the defensive. Feminism, the women's rights movement were gaining momentum.

More good news. In 1974, President Nixon had been forced to resign in disgrace over his bungled Watergate dirty tricks and his deceitful attempt to cover it up. He, who as a congressman had been the rabid ally of McCarthyism, who as president had expanded the Vietnam War clandestinely into Cambodia and Laos. Yet it was he who had opened relations with communist China and had initiated détente with the Soviets, he who had not succumbed to the urgings of several high level policy wonks to nuke North Vietnam into submission, he, this conservative Republican, who had pushed through many liberal improvements in social, environmental, and financial sector regulation policy.

He had accomplished much in his two terms, but he succumbed to his dark side, committing serious crimes, degrading public service and the office of the presidency, betraying the American people. A dangerous, bitter, unhappy, even pathetic man. It was an enormous relief when he resigned under threat of certain impeachment and conviction. The hearty wave as he stepped into his helicopter, the forced smile, the deus ex machina lifting him forever away—a scene repeated when the crushing weight of Bush the Second was whisked away over the heads of the huge crowds celebrating the inauguration of President Obama.

The Cold War had clearly lost some of its threatening edge. The policy of containment that had justified the Cold War and the wars in Korea and Vietnam faded, being replaced by the realpolitik of détente. The nuclear arms race continued, but there was some talk of agreeing to cap it.

In Greece, fascism under the colonels' Junta had been overthrown in 1974 as a result of their botched attempt to annex Cyprus. The colonels and dozens of their crowd had been tossed into Korydallos Prison, then exiled for life to a barren island prison. Papadopoulos, the head of the Junta, had been employed after World War II by the CIA as a Greek Intelligence anti-communist liaison officer and was supported during the Junta regime by the American ambassador, Henry Tasca, for a time my Marshall Plan boss in Rome. The Junta's torturers had nearly killed my friend Kevin Andrews. When he was released, he wrote several articles and essays about the Junta regime that I, in my trips between Rome and the Aegean, smuggled out of Greece for European publication. Perhaps partly as a result of the torturing, Kevin suffered many grand mal seizures after his release and perhaps died of one. He was a particularly important friend, his story and mine weaving in and out.

⊷

Kevin and I graduated from Harvard together a year and a half after returning from our very different World War Two years in Europe—he a dog-face in several heavy battles, I an intelligence analyst behind the front lines. Kevin got a Classics fellowship and left for Greece. He returned only once, for a short time, and later became a Greek citizen. The reality of a country bled dry by the Nazi occupation, now in a bitter civil war, removed any trace of his college preciosity.

Kevin was a dedicated, disciplined writer. The setting of his writings was Greece—largely modern Greece, but throughout history too. His theme was always the beauty and the bitterness of uncompromising truth. His *Flight of Icarus* is still in print in a Penguin edition. It is the story of his time during the worst years of the civil war, wandering largely on foot throughout the Peloponnesus. He was researching for his classics fellowship study, later published and republished as *The Castles of the Morea*. He dedicated his life to a tormented, violent, yet heartbreakingly beautiful and creative Greece, to its overwhelmingly generous, proud people. He struck out against blind Grecophile romantics, the tyranny and hypocrisy of foreign interventions, Greece's rapacious rulers and bourgeoisie. His last years he spent in despair at the banal modernization of Greece, the hideous,

Kevin Andrews in Athens, 1987.

ubiquitous expressions of bourgeois greed. His death remains an enigma.

During my first years in Washington, Kevin stayed with
me for some weeks of his only return to America. I visited
him several times in Greece. We hiked the Pindus Mountains. We were together for a time in London. There were
strains in our friendship, misconceptions that took years
to reconcile. But over the decades, he remained for me an
important measure of being true to oneself. I differed with
his standards but admired his fidelity to himself.

In a world that operates by compromise and so readily
accepts hypocrisy, deception, superstition, injustice, Kevin's
unwavering dedication to his measure of truth, of right and

wrong, was what for me made our friendship deeply important. The consequences of his holding determinedly to his rigorous standards were often devastating to others. He antagonized family and friends. Some might characterize him as a hair-shirt fanatic. Yet he walked his talk, he was true to himself, he used his brilliance, his extraordinary talents, his charm, his heart to their fullest. I was honored by his friendship. His life and death, heavily fictionalized, is central to my novel, *The Isle of Khería*.

There are always more isms out there to discover and deal with. They are often abuses of originally commendable or at least benign movements. Radical religious fundamentalism was becoming an important political and social force in America. The New Age, an aspect of the counterculture, was developing an array of fringe nonsense and scams which even at my distance were reason for circumspection—crystals, pyramids, auras, tarot readings, occultism, even the Ouija board was back in fashion. The word "socialism" seems to be a bugaboo for many people whenever government may be forced to regulate or even take over flawed institutions and industries or those in distress.

The year before, I had been on my Greek island for my fiftieth birthday, a long respite from family agony at home in Rome. I was alone on that wild north end of Koufonissos.

Long walks under stormy skies, high on limestone cliffs, an angry sea white with spindrift, no one-man fishing boats or even the big shrimper out today. A wild sea, "a sea that has no handles." Back into low hills, the maquis greening from the rains, goats eyeing me as they tear off new leaves.

Long evenings by my smoky fireplace, reading by a

propane lamp. Reading the new historians, the poets, the novelists, the essayists as they uncover the countercultures emerging in the Western world. Kerouac, Gary Snyder, Fritz Perls, Theodore Roszak, William Irwin Thompson, Chomsky. Those who walked their talk—Thoreau, Aldo Leopold, Edward Abbey. I didn't have writings of each of these authors with me, but earlier piecemeal readings began to coalesce for me there, lying on goatskins before the fire, or out under a mastic bush when the sun found an opening in low clouds. It was a host of welcome voices to encourage my wondering and sometimes doubting heart—voices seeking for redemption, for renewal, a turning from obsessive materialism to natural surroundings and life styles, intentional communities, sustainable use of the planet's resources, voluntary simplicity, natural spirituality rather than religion. They spoke to me.

I was particularly interested in the "intentional community" movement. In recent years, it had rapidly become a reinvigoration of the utopian community movement of the nineteenth century, though more populist and widespread, particularly in America and Great Britain. By "intentional" was meant one's deliberate choice to join a residential community of like-minded persons—if they would have you— people sharing a clearly stated goal—a practice, an aim, a purpose. Most of these new communities were manifestations of some aspect of the counterculture. As such, a study of a wide sample of them would be a revealing look at that emerging culture.

❧

Anchored off a bit of beach in the lee of a low island, supper finished, Dominic asleep in the tiny fo'c'sle, we had played a Chopin nocturne on our tape player in the candlelight.

Later, Penny sleeping, I went on deck. A display of dozens of shooting stars had me lying on the deck on pillows under a blanket the better to see them. That nocturne was still sounding in my head, a sublime, ethereal voice. It seemed to draw me on, out into a new dimension. At that moment, I felt impelled to return to my country, to seek its best rather than staying away from its worst. I must leave Rome, my son, discover a new America. I would sail there solo in my *Aeoli*. "Go west, young man, and grow up with the country." I would travel across the continent, visiting intentional communities. I would find a way back into my writing.

I would manage to get back often to see Alexis, or perhaps somehow he could join me. My daughters would be leaving Italy for the States. Kathy and Michael Fitzgerald, their sons Kieran, Brendan, Aidan, for the world of movie producing. Sara and Guli Arshad and their three young children Shergul, Shehime, Yasmin, moving to Massachusetts. I would be nearer them again and released from Maria's painful jealousies.

As was my way, this was an impulse rather than a decision, an impulse to be examined and reexamined before acting. I did not discuss it then with Penny, wanting to think it through carefully, and being uncertain how she and Dominic might fit into that new life, might be ready to join me. Nor was I entirely sure of my own feelings, still scarred from the wounds of two separations. Was I ready to ask them to take what would be a defining step in becoming a family?

We left *Aeoli* at Lavrion's shipyard again, taxied to Athens. We had come to a deeply painful moment for all three of us. Unready to commit to a future, I merely asked for the ambiguous time-to-think-things-out. I stood in a filthy downtown bus station, looking up at two sweet faces pressed against a dusty window, tears on their cheeks, tears on mine. Fading in a blast of black diesel exhaust. They were headed to England to be for a time with Penny's parents and an entirely uncertain future. I returned to the shipyard distraught, angry at my failure of resolve. I was letting my past cloud my future, something that Penny would not do.

That night aboard *Aeoli*, I lay awake for many hours. By morning I had worked out a plan. I would do the solo sail, do it in the late winter hurricane-free season, to the island of Grenada, leave *Aeoli* there, and return to America. I would buy a van and travel the land, visiting intentional communities. I would go now to England, praying that Penny would still be there and would not have given up on me completely. In England, I would order equipment for my ocean passage, wait for it to be readied, then load it on my car. Beyond that, I dared not plan until I had regained or lost dear Penny and her Dominic.

I bussed from Athens to Italy—a long freezing night, pounded by disco music, dense cigarette smoke, empty pot-holed roads, communist Yugoslavia in the dark. In Florence, where I had left my little Citroen, I stayed with daughter Sara and family for a few days, then drove up through Germany, ferried to England, on to London.

I phoned, a crucial moment, she was there, still there, Penny and Dominic still with her parents in Dorset. She would meet me the next day in Gosport, where *Aeoli* was born, where our family was born.

Grazie a Dio!

∽ 22 ∽

Fifty Ways to Leave Your Lover

MY *Aeoli* and I, we will sail the Atlantic alone, we will discover America. Penny and Dominic will fly to Boston, join me in the search. The first leg, from Gibraltar to the Canaries, Penny and I will sail together, Dominic to be left with friends in Estepona. From Tenerife, I will sail on solo to Grenada in the Caribbean.

A strange place, Gibraltar, tacky, military still, Gibraltarians rather unattractive. Even the restaurants seem cobbled together largely for transients who don't need to be enticed to return. The famous apes, waiting for tourists' handouts at the funicular station on the cliffs above the city—nasty, aggressive, flea-infested, smelly.

With *Aeoli*'s bilge filled with Gibraltar's guinea-a-bottle whiskey, provisioned up, it is time to set sail. Westward ho! A bright, windy morning, whitecaps out there. No brass bands to send us off, no signals flown at Victory's maintop—Admiral Nelson Confides That Every Man Will Do His Duty. Up sails and off in the following breeze, a choppy sea with the westerly Atlantic swells rolling in against us as we pass Trafalgar at dusk. Nelson signals, Engage In Close Action—the French fleet is spotted sailing out from Cadiz.

Innocent *Aeoli* engaging rusty freighters and the endless tankers of Arabian oil. We turn sharply south to cross the ship lanes quickly, get on our private way to the Canaries. We reduce sail for the night, dead-reckon our position with cross-bearings from lighthouses. Running lights on, the self-steerer checked. Make up the bunk for Penny.

For her, it's a cockleshell on an endless rolling sea. Ten days without respite, rolling violently in what was left of a major storm off to the northwest. Heavy winds, rain, then no wind at all—still rolling horribly, though—the air turned thick yellow, no horizon, no sun, no sky, the sails streaked with mud. Hundreds of miles off the African coast yet here we were in the results of a Saharan dust storm turned wet. With no chance of getting a shot at the sun with my sextant, I balance on the cabin top taking bearings on radio-direc- tion-finding signals from African airports.

Tenerífe harbor at midnight in a heavy wind. We try to anchor, but it's too deep. We tie up to a commercial dock astern of an enormous freighter, bunk down—and two hours later are tipped out of bed. I stumble on deck, slack off our mooring lines—after years in the tideless Mediter- ranean, I had forgotten about Atlantic tides, and docks don't float, stupid.

It is a sweet time, our few days on Tenerife. Driv- ing around the island, beaches, skinny-dipping—chilly, though we were down to the twenty-eighth parallel, but it was March—up the volcano Teíde, way above the tree line, twelve thousand feet.

Penny flies back to Spain.

⊷

A toast, Rioja red wine from my demijohn, to our vol- cano, its snowy pink tip sinking in the sunset. Here, sliding through these southern seas, swirling, foaming, never silent seas. The song of the wind in *Aeoli*'s rigging, tackle slatting, the slap of a choppy sea, the surge and fall of the bow wave as we're carried on the immense swell of that endless sea. And, lying here below on the open bunk, curled around a book, the insistent murmur of girlish voices, wisps of voices—I can't quite catch what they say.

Fair winds, a tropical rainstorm in the hot morning sun, naked in the cockpit with a bar of soap—naked all the way, why not? Flopping of flying fish on the deck above my head, three dead this morning. Whiskey, the demijohn of wine, pump up the pressure on my Tilly lamp. A can of tuna, clump of bean sprouts—they're growing well—rusks twice baked. To sleep, curled tight in the roll of my cockleshell home.

Fear, always this nagging fear, fear of a tanker steaming blind through the night. I've slept through my staggered oven timers, rush on deck—nothing to be seen. Twenty-four days, that passage, and I never see another ship, an airplane, flotsam—nothing from man's world but the clutter of radio waves.

A struggle, through one long night, on deck in my umbilical harness—halyard frayed loose, both twin sails wrapped around the keel. And one morning, dozing below decks, shaded from a fierce sun, there's a heavy blow on the hull, a lurch. I leap on deck to see a basking shark in our wake—white belly, glowering eye.

A noon sight, every day a noon sight, propped up here in the companionway. I'm getting really good with my sextant. Reach up to the sun, and he'll tell you where you are. But this calm, dead calm, two days of it now, rolling, really rolling in this giant swell, sails, rigging, everything below decks slamming about, boom dipping in the water. Wedged in my bunk, wrapped in my Moroccan cape, Mozart on tape.

Birds now, distant clouds. Must be over the hills of

Barbados. Porpoises playing in our bow wave. Lead us in, my friends. Grenada, sailing into Saint George's, no brass band, nobody noticed, just Paul Simon crooning Fifty Ways to Leave Your Lover, beer and peanuts in the local bar in celebration. A phone booth—Penny's sweetest voice. *Jaws* in a rickety theater that night.

Leaving *Aeoli* at the Georgetown marina, I flew from Grenada to Miami, bought a small van cum motor home, Vanita, backpacked for a few days in the rainy Great Smoky Mountains, attended daughter Kathy's wedding, and was joyfully reunited in Boston with Penny and little Dominic. We set out on our new adventure. Vanita was to be our traveling home for two years, then our largely stationary home for two more years.

~ 23 ~

Hippyish

THIS America I was seeking, was it significant, was it there at all?

Ten years earlier, living in a trailer in San Jose, I was on the fringes of a counterculture. The Flower Children had pretty much taken over San Francisco's Golden Gate Park. To walk through the east end of the park on a sunny day was to walk through clouds of pot smoke, through groups of young people in wildly creative attire, hair let to do what it will, bare breasts, circling dancers, chantings, guitars everywhere, aimless LSD trippers with their fixed smiles. To my bemusement, I was often taken to be Timothy Leary, a graying Guru of the Psychedelic amongst the Children.

And the Vietnam War protesters, the anti-establishment hippies with their banners and peace symbols, free-love-makers under the rhododendrons, Free University sessions impromptu by the duck pond. At night, there'd be Jefferson Airplane bashing out strobic music in the Fillmore Ballroom, Janis Joplin mocking materialists with her pleas shrieking to the Lord for happiness, for a Mercedes Benz.

From what I had read and heard, particularly at the Finca, by 1975 that hugely libertarian aspect of the counterculture had been somewhat eclipsed. Though we still have such derivatives as the Rainbow Gatherings and Burning

Man, a New Age had introduced a swarm of disciplines to
release and realize our "human potential"—a Mecca was Esalen, hanging on the Pacific rim—and to explore spirituality,
often through Eastern practices. "Growth centers," ashrams,
Zen centers were opening across the country. Bookstores
offered shelves of New Age books.

My morphosis was still underway. Though I admired and
envied the activists, the major progress they were making
against the isms of the American culture, I had been largely
an observer. I had taken more private paths of protest. But
there was much that appealed to me of this New Age that I
had set out to explore and perhaps participate in. It seemed
to hold promise of moving beyond angry protest, of finding
alternative ways, attitudes, modes of living, moving from
institutional and structured ways, philosophies, religions,
moving toward humanism, toward living lightly, sustainably
on the planet, toward an embracing of the here-and-now.
From rapacious capitalism to a socialism that respected and
nurtured life. And much of this promise seemed to be the
theme of most of the hundreds of new experiments in the
Western world, particularly North America, in "intentional
community" living.

It is hard for me now to recapture that exploration of
mine without some disbelief, skepticism, even a touch of
embarrassment. But it was very real at the time. There was
hope, there was enormous energy to experiment, to find
better ways. And from the vantage point of a new century,
a changed world, a changed me, however naïve and starry-
eyed those experiments may now seem, some of what they
sought began to spread into the mainstream culture despite
heavy opposition, particularly from the political right.

The excesses of the counterculture and the New Age

were many. They were often damaging, even lethal—scams, snake-oil purveyors, murderous gurus, mind-fucking, mass suicides, junkies, extortionists, practices more structured and corrupted than the derided religions they were replacing. Yet the core remained mellow, thoughtful, progressive. As the terms "counterculture" and "New Age" faded into history, many of the attitudes and practices of those years have become commonplace, a part of the mainstream. Though intentional communities are no longer newsworthy, there are as many of them in America now as during the decades when they were under scrutiny and often ridiculed, the years in which Penny and I explored them and then founded and lived in one for five years.

My curiosity, my quest for alternatives to the culture into which I was born, was always tempered by my skepticism. I tested several of the modes and practices of the New Age—the spiritual, the communal, the local, the small, the appropriate, the sustainable, the common aim, the living lightly, the intuitive. In the end, I believe I have internalized some of their lessons and found a certain peace beyond the embrace of structure. It is an unlikely peace, well beyond the limits that my innate skepticism alone would permit. Is this my substitute for the religious faith that many of us turn to at the end of our lives—if not before? Is this my reward at the end of my private century?

There seems to be little hope that my country, as its century of ascendancy winds down, will assimilate similar lessons. The devastating eight-year spasm of the Bush II administration, followed by the tragic gridlock of our evolving political process with Obama, the predatory destructive steps of the Trump administration toward fascism. The overwhelming influence of money, special interests, hypocrisies, greed, divisiveness, even criminality at the high-est levels. What we are now living bears little promise of a democratic America living with humility, equality, justice, peace, with the will to protect its planet. Shall we recall again Eisenhower's parting words as president, his warning of the dangers of the military-industrial complex, of the rise of misplaced power, of the plundering of our natural resources...?

Wise counsels unheeded.

~24~

Utopia Hunt

Escaped from the Holland Tunnel, tooling down a free-way on a southerly course, the little guy, five now, up on his cab-over bunk watching the New Jersey smokestack wasteland out his own windows—his new dad had cut and glazed them for him, two square eyes in that plastic fore-head. Mom, so pretty and young, in the passenger seat, jeans, a well-worn shirt, checked bandana over her super-curly head, pushing a Moody Blues cassette into the player. Rob—Dom, the little guy, would always call him that—at the wheel. Already unshaven, gray and balding, he's tour-guiding, a preview of Washington's Greek monuments they'd soon be cruising through.

Onward, south into Blue Ridge country, back roads now, rolling country, farms, bugs smearing the windshield. Pull-ing up at a white farmhouse, two figures in flowing robes, turbans, a scraggly red beard, they offer warm greetings to our little traveling family.

John and Ana Koehne, old friends from Washington days. He was a Harvard graduate, a mid-level CIA agent, escaping the establishment in the late 'sixties. Their chil-dren had been saved from drug addiction by Sikhism and its guru, Yogi Bhajan. The whole family became Sikhs in Punjab's Golden Temple. John and Ana went on to become active in the humanistic psychology movement, started an intentional community near Mendocino, California, then moved to Virginia at the Yogi's bidding. By then it had been reduced to themselves, a daughter, her husband, another couple.

A graceful plantation farmhouse looking across rolling hayfields at the Blue Mountains. A farm, vegetables, horse breeding. A pond where everyone proceeded to cool off—naked, turbans off, hair unwound to waist length. A circle, holding hands, chanting the "Auuuuummmm." A vegetarian supper—spread on a grass mat on the porch floor, they sit cross-legged on prayer mats.

Next day a massage workshop, four or five outsiders joining. Naked again, spread out on the floor, massaged and massaging. A reluctant beheading by John of a copperhead that snakes almost under Dom's feet. A turn at the hay bailer, battling the no-see-'ems. Back to the pond to paddle in the bulrushes. Dinner talk about the state of the world. Bedtime in Vanita, a waning moon in the sycamores, a bobwhite with his "bob-bob-white." Thus, their first intentional community. A bit of a shock—thoughtful, sophisticated, once worldly intellectuals, transforming themselves. Their Sikh organization is called the 3HO, Healthy, Happy, Holy—hierarchal, rigorous, and quietly in-your-face with their garb. Lovely, warm folks, friends to return to, but not a fit for us.

Moving on.

A gray beard—eventually it would reach Santa lengths—a filthy crusher hat somewhere between cowboy and backwoods trapper, a heavy black-and-red lumberman's wool jacket. That is our intrepid helmsman, as he will be for most of the next seven years. He even shows up like that when interviewing a pricey lawyer in Rome who would break the

Penny with John Koehne and Yogi Bhajan commune members,
Charlottesville, 1978.

court injunction Maria had out to prevent him from visiting his Alexis.

⌒

The hunt for the communal experience. Is there something new out there, not just extensions of the nineteenth
century's elitist utopias? So far, their visits to the ex-spooks'
Sikh experiment and to a couple of other communes—one
churchy, another intent on raising buffalo for beef—showed
no signs of a populist movement. Strike out westward, into
the rolling farmlands of Tennessee.

To The Farm. Local folks, inscrutable, point the way
through a maze of back roads to this most famous of the
hundreds of communes springing up in North America. A
closed entrance gate, a brick guardhouse. Resident hippies
in pickups are waved through, our little family is shunted
into the guardhouse, interviewed. No reservation? I'll
phone the office. Our guest roster's full, but y'all seem okay,

and they say if you live in your van you're welcome to a week's look-see, work details every day, though. Eat with us, Sundays a gathering with Stephen—a talk and ironing out personal kinks. And here's a map—that way, maybe a mile, don't really know, you'll see.

They're greeted at the office, shown where to park, when to hear the introductory rap for visitors. There's a mimeographed handout listing work options, schedules, community rules. No animal products, no tobacco, no alcohol, no manmade psychedelics. No sex without commitment, no overt anger, no lying. For Farm members, no private money, no large pieces of private property, savings and earnings into a collective pot, accept Stephen as your teacher. And a tacit rule that Mary Jane will be a helping hand on the path to enlightenment.

Swarms of Farmies, more than a thousand—women with their long skirts and eclectic hats, hairy men mostly stripped to the waist, hordes of children—everyone hard at it, the myriad chores of a massive communal farming enterprise. Heat, dust, sweat, curses, laughter, song, sweet smoke of the weed. Rusting buses scattered through the woods, leftovers of the Caravan.

Stephen Gaskin, their beatnik-hippy guru—Marine vet, charismatic philosopher—had led his following of hippies in a caravan of sixty old buses in 1970. From San Francisco's North Beach, weaving across the country, seven months of counterculture antics and sermonizing before settling into the Tennessee farmlands, next door to Amish communities and the birthplace of the Ku Klux Klan.

Many of the buses, though seemingly derelict, are lived in, had been added-on to, decorated. There's a variety of buildings. A hodgepodge of homes jammed with families and singles, a school, workshops, sheds, barns, a midwifery hospital run by Stephen's wife Ina May, the Farm Store, a brick house built secretly for the Gaskins while they were in Guatemala. A scattering of structures for their many enterprises—assembling and selling the CB radios popular with truckers and motorists, handheld devices for detecting radiation which became a big seller, processing food products of soy and preserves, the Farm Band's hangout when not on tour, a publishing project for their CB cartoon book and Ina May's natural-birth handbooks, the office of their philanthropic outreach arm, Plenty, which is planning to build more than three thousand homes in Guatemala for destitute refugees.

The central enterprise is farming, hundreds of acres—hay, alfalfa, soy, potatoes, peppers, tomatoes, marijuana hiding in the woods. Horses and tractors plowing, hauling trailers loaded with produce. Planting, praying for the weather's clemency, weeding, harvesting, sorting, preserving, trucking surpluses to markets. It's a grueling, poverty-level life, yet there is high energy, ingenuity, dedication to hard work, determination to counter the prevailing culture. It's an impressive undertaking by a mix of star-struck kids, flower children turned serious, college grads usually of the English-major type, professionals—accountants, physicists, lawyers—but no silver spoon is in evidence. Any freeloaders are soon winnowed out. Do our travelers sneak a glass or two of whiskey in their motorized refuge? Oh yes. Do they high tail it out of there after a quick not-for-us look-see? No, they'll give it few days more here, give it a good try.

What do the Farmies ask of their visitors? There's one day in the summer sun sorting and washing potatoes—long troughs and tubs and burlap sacks. Another harvesting acres

Steven Gaskin holding forth at The Farm in Tennessee, 1976.

of green peppers. An all-night, crash effort to preserve tons and tons of tomatoes, everyone turning out—a rambling barn, the Farm Band keeping all awake with homemade rock, steaming barrels on wood fires, peeling, boiling, granny's glass preserving jars by the thousands. Finally sneaking out for little Dominic's sake—thanks, kiddo.

Sunday, they gather at a grassy amphitheater on the edge of the woods, Farmies en masse, attentive to Stephen's rap but with a friendly, joshing familiarity that takes some of the edginess off guru-worship. Stephen's charisma is appropriately homespun. He's approachable, intelligent, hairy, fun—and definitely in charge. He rambles through a forgettable rap, then invites exchanges with and between members. A fellow with a mass of black hair, name of Wolf, stands up, brushes off the hay seeds and ants, and launches into a complaint, though humorously, that the Farm Store refused him a comb. Laughter, joshing from Stephen, and a lent comb to settle it.

⤖

On westward. Always there is the adventure of new places, new sites to park for the night. They eschew the commercial RV parks. In the more populated areas, they might end up in a shopping center or hospital parking lot, a cemetery. As the country opens into its vastness, it might be a back road, a farmer's yard, a mountainside, a wilderness river, a perilous logging road in a National Forest.

In Arkansas, they rent a canoe for three days, drift down a river, camping on the willow banks, Dominic in his own wee tent. In Nevada, they backpack from the desert to a tree-lined lake on the eleven thousand foot Ruby Mountains, camp for three days, hike up to picnic by an ice arch over a waterfall, the high desert stretching out into the blue five thousand feet below.

In Colorado, they backpack into the Rockies for ten days, lakes, alpine meadows, acres of wildflowers, a herd of elk they sneak up on. They pack out the immense antlers of a bull elk that had died on the edge of a snowfield. Those antlers are bolted proudly to Vanita's forehead. Later another single antler goes on the rear with a sign SHED, NOT SHOT, and later still under the rear window they bolt on a flower box, plant it with herbs, carve on its face GREEN PEACE.

He the middle-aged hippy wannabe, making up for lost time? She the amazed, bemused, game but sometimes doubtful Brit—did she bargain for this? The little guy five years old and game for anything.

As they go, they tick off communes from their list. Some are no more than dreams, some with only one or two couples, some have quite vanished. Most have a significant spiritual element as an objective, a few have a heavy dose of religiosity, some are determinedly democratic, some hierarchical.

Ananda, in the western foothills of the Sierra Nevadas, they roll up to it in Vanita, are assigned a place to park, and are signed in for the Visitors' Introduction. It has the appearance of a well-to-do suburbia transplant, neat new homes, cars, lawns. Several hundred folks live and work here, sitting at the feet of Kriyananda—an American, Donald Walters. He is a disciple of Yogananda, a Hindu Yoga guru from India who, in the 1920s, was one of the first importers of an Eastern religion to America. On the tour they're taken to the nearby meditation center, the guide proudly dropping the names of Gary Snyder and Alan Watts—poet of a New Age, philosopher of Zen—as one-time-some-time neighbors. The economy of Ananda has evolved into many private enterprises carried out independently by members but with some sort of tithing to the community. Families living separately, but with group practice. It seems a viable place, but rather boring, and there are murmurs of dissent and rumors of their guru's sleeping-around hanky-panky.

Move on.

To the slopes of Mount Tamalpais looking over San Francisco Bay; our little family attends a wedding in a suburban back yard, friends who'd been group leaders at the Finca—he of the fasting, three-day, sleep-deprived Enlightenment Intensive, she of the sometimes brutal Encounter Groups. They're in white robes, sitting full-lotus on oriental rugs. Buddhist monks, a Sikh, Haight-Ashbury flower-children grads, an Afro big-hair, a Jewish Rastafarian. Garlands of orchids, incense, gongs, bells, chants, a mellow haze of pot. A multi-cultural enchilada, though with no sign of the Cross.

And on. To Carlin, Nevada. Carlin was once a busy railroad stop in steam-locomotive days. The water towers are collapsing now, the roundhouse is derelict, most of the multiple tracks unused. A benumbed population, a struggling town, lonely in the rolling sagebrush country, the Ruby Mountains far to the southeast. It's mid-winter in this high desert, deep drifting snow, blizzards hurling tumbleweeds against Vanita. This time she's parked in an empty-lot trailer park, needing electricity to keep pipes from freezing. Expecting to stay for several weeks, Dominic is enrolled in a preschool.

In a decaying frame house by the railroad tracks they find Rolling Thunder—Shoshone shaman, founder of his Native American community Meta Tantay, Walk in Peace. An imposing man, larger than life, displaying his charisma, his shaman status, his Shoshone origins—the black Stetson, the beaded vest, the braided hair, the eagle feathers, the to-bacco pipe in its prominent place. His bread-and-butter job is as a brakeman on Union Pacific freight-train cabooses.

Rolling Thunder—John Pope on the records—friend of the Grateful Dead, Buckminster Fuller, Tibetan monks, Bob Dylan with his Rolling Thunder Revue concerts. The protagonist and performer in the three Billy Jack movies. Healer of all ills with his shaman's hands, his meditations, his trance inducing, his Indian rituals. He takes his visitors to Meta Tantay in wind-swept country east of town. It's a collection of platformed tents, sheds, pickups and jalopies. A dozen or so folks, most seem to be Indians, go about their chores. One tent houses exiled menstruating women. The foundations for a truck garage are being staked out. Rolling Thunder officiates in a tobacco ceremony to the four direc-tions asking permission to clear the site of sagebrush.

It's bleak, yes, maybe slightly hokey, the whole feel of the place and the man. Yet may he walk in peace. "Rolling Thun-der" was the code name for the sustained U.S. bombing of

North Vietnam—does he know? After a sunrise tobacco ceremony with a circle of a ten or so on the abandoned tracks back of his house, Vanita is untethered. They roll on.

Back to California, to Occidental north of San Francisco, to the Farallones Institute. Not a commune, not exactly, but the staff—architects, engineers, gardeners, the many-skilled—is largely self-selected and self-governed. They share a vision of an ecologically self-sustaining, small-bore, lovingly crafted lifestyle. They work with resident students, trainees, in developing technologies and practices consistent with that vision. Gardening, solar ovens, energy-conscious home construction, composting toilets, recycling, largely vegetarian. Penny enrolls—veggie gardening, welding, carpentry—pitches in on whatever is presented with her ever-

Vanita, our camper van home for four years for Penny, Dominic, and me,

willing energy, on her way to becoming a first-rate gardener. Dominic signs up in a country school. Vanita continues as home, hidden in the woods, wastewaters piped illegally into a covered pit. The propane tank for cooking is refilled, the batteries for their reading lights are recharged by frequent hippy-loaded drives to the local movies.

It's a good life for them—grateful for daily rewards, for learning, for energy, for love—but it's more than time that they be married. Twice burned by divorce, cautious, with a residual of a counterculture resistance to established legalities—his wary fondness is wholeheartedly replaced with a deep, lasting love. She, almost having given up on him, has a ready, *Yes*.

They'd go east soon, already planned. Visits to her parents in England, to be with Alexis in Rome, to his daughters living now in New England. And to their Sikh friends in Virginia—could they officiate, did he not once say that he had the authority, that he had married others at their former community in California? They'll ask, they'll write.

But first a foray deep into Canada, two or three more communities to tick off the list. A thousand-mile side trip.

Up through the volcanoes of northern California, the immense wetlands teeming with migratory birds. Into Oregon's Coastal Range, they pull up at a small intentional community, name forgotten. Seems to be doing well, a growing membership, their economy based on specialty food products and doubtless the deeper pockets of one or two members.

Near Eugene, they stay for a time with another community, Approvecho. It's leader a gnome of a man, Ianto Evans, a Welsh botanist and appropriate-technologist who helped support his fair-sized agricultural community with his government-sponsored trips in underdeveloped countries to demonstrate and promote such simple technologies as mud ovens which drastically reduce the use of ever scarcer firewood. It's an unusually pragmatic community with no strong spiritual component. There will be more contact with Ianto in the next years, his brilliance and charisma drawing people to him, his rigid judgmental leadership style driving many away—until he himself leaves Approvecho in other hands.

Over the Columbia into Washington. To Neah Bay on the tip of the Olympic Peninsula for a visit with a girl they'd met at Rolling Thunder's, now living in a tree house with a Makah Indian, pregnant, too stoned for much connection. Gorgeous beaches, Indian mounds, the tribe on the reservation keeping a tenuous hold on their traditional whale hunt.

Vancouver, on up the Fraser River to Hope. The Texas Lake Community runs a youth hostel there in a rented rickety riverside collection of cabins. They seem to be thriving under the leadership of a bear of a man, Thyson—he'd changed his name, and given it this odd spelling at the direction of his faithful numerology and perhaps with support from his secretive Rosicrucian practice. He appears to be a laid-back benign leader, though we will see a different side of him in the next years. When our little family arrives, the community is coming in, still mostly naked, from an evening skinny dip in their pond. They gather around a barbeque pit for roasted corn, tofu, rose-hip tea, and an out-loud reading of Tolkien. By now, nothing much surprises.

On into the heartland of British Columbia, another six hundred miles to go for their goal, Bella Coola. Through ranch country, the Coastal Range to the west, the Rockies to the east. A quick looksee at an intentional community near 100 Mile House. Onward, dirt roads now, hundreds of miles, climbing through the wild mountains of Tweedsmuir Park and down into the Bella Coola Valley.

They hike up a trail along the river, seeking the last community on the list. Grizzly bear tracks in the sand, water still seeping into them. Enormous salmon, some holding out against the gentle current, some dead, one with a huge bite just taken out of his belly. The first sign of the community is of two bear-proof beehives on the tops of slender fifteen-foot poles. A comfortable house, two small families hoping to eschew money through barter and self-sufficiency—a veggie garden, a homesteader's apple orchard, the coffee they served up was roasted dandelions and burdock roots with honey. They are uncertain, though, whether they can handle many more of the brutal winters.

Then down the valley to the river's mouth, to Bella Coola village at the head of a spectacular fjord—mountainsides of fir and hemlock rain forest, snowfields, glaciered peaks. Population three or four hundred—mostly Nuxalt natives and Norwegian transplants, though they'd all acquired touches of the lilting Canadian brogue. Fishermen, loggers, one or two resident hippies. A fish cannery, a small pulp mill. That's it.

Trips back to Europe. Rome to see Alexis. Florence, staying with daughter Sara and family. Spain to visit Penny's father and sister. England to be with Penny's mother and stepfather. Visits to intentional communities while in Britain. An appropriate technology center in Wales similar to Farallones, a very primitive subsistence-farming community in England, and the best known of the spiritual intentional communities, Findhorn in Scotland. Founded in 1962 by

Rosicrucians and a small group of New Age spiritual practitioners, Findhorn is a large and prosperous community, self-supporting with various enterprises, governed through a practice of finding decisions through group meditation, closing out egos, finding inner truths—the voice of God to some.

A rather random sampling of our search in the realm of intentional communities. Penny would, I think, put a disclaimer on the word "our," describing her role as that of a bemused and passive participant in what was my search. True, it originated with me, but she was at the forefront in every encounter.

With Alexis in Rome.

~ 25 ~

Turtle Island

A FTER Bella Coola, we had continued our contact with
the Texas Lake Community, visiting them again at
Hope, and joining with some of them on a trip to the Kettle
River valley in the largely wild country of south central
British Columbia. They were interested in buying a vacated
homesteaded farm there, a large riverside property rising
from alfalfa fields into conifer forests bordering on Crown
Land. They intended to put it under the ownership of a land
trust organization. We hiked over the fields and forests, up
into the low mountains on the Crown Land, we swam in
the river, we tented near the ever-swaying suspension foot-
bridge from the nearest dirt road across to the property.
Some of the community's couple of dozen young people
hoped to move there as a sister community to Texas Lake.
Over the years, they had squirreled away considerable
funds from their lucrative but brutally strenuous summer
tree-planting stints. It was not enough for the purchase.
Could we help?

⇔

The notion that land, that discrete pieces of the globe's
surface, could become private property was not an idea
shared by all peoples and cultures. Even those cultures
that accepted the idea of land ownership traditionally kept

some land communal or public—commons, city parks, national forests, national parks, tidewaters, highways, substantial rivers and bodies of water, and so forth. My father, certainly a convinced capitalist and believer in private property, had done much, both privately and through governments, to create and foster land trusts, conservation land, conservation easements, multi-use public lands. He had put much of his accumulated wealth into public land projects.

And a very small part of his wealth had come my way. It was finally time to put that to use. What with four years in the army, subsidized education for veterans, and my years as a well-paid employee of various governmental agencies, the government had supported me for much of my adult life. After I had resigned, my life style had been relatively modest, supported by only a small part of the income from the capital I had received from my grandfather and father and had let accumulate over the years. It was time to steward this capital in an active way, find areas of philanthropy which Penny and I would like to support.

The United States leads the world in per-capita charitable giving—about $1000 each year for every man, woman, and child. The government incentive to this is the deduction of charitable donations from taxed income, though the majority of Americans at least claim that the removal of the incentive would not change their giving. And in proportion to income, giving is lowest in the highest income brackets. Individual giving is by far the largest proportion of total giving, in spite of the massive donations from foundations and corporations. We are also at the forefront in charitable volunteer work, donations of time that are not deductible. It's been estimated that about 80 million adult Americans volunteer a substantial part of their time per year, a giving worth perhaps 250 billion dollars.

We are a nation of givers.

⟶

We said Yes to the Texas Lake folks. They already had Canadian charitable status. With our contribution added to their savings, The Kettle was bought. It was understood that ownership would be transferred to a land trust organization, and that use of the land would be under the stewardship of an intentional community. The land trust would monitor the land use. If the stewards failed to abide by strict use covenants, the land trust would replace them. This became the model for a number of small land trusts that we helped create. Some of the difficulties in fulfilling the stewardship aspect of this pattern were to be exemplified by the case of The Kettle during the next six or eight years.

While acquiring The Kettle, the Texas Lake community was losing its lease on the Hope hostel. They began to disband. Penny and Dominic and I had visited Cortes Island, one of the North Islands between the British Columbia mainland and Vancouver Island. It is a large island, hilly, lakes and ponds, many bays, inlets, harbors, surrounded by many small islands. It was two ferry trips away from Campbell River on Vancouver Island. In those days its population was perhaps seven hundred—subsistence-farming homesteaders, fishermen, loggers, a small Indian reserve, a few back-to-the-land hippies, an Esalen-type growth center, Cold Mountain, later to become Hollyhock, and one or two summer residents had discovered Cortes, too. Four or five of the Texas Lake folks still wanted to continue with communal living, but were not ready to take on The Kettle. We, or largely I with Penny game to give it a try, had seen enough of the intentional community movement to conclude that however difficult, it could be the best way to organize human society. We were ready to find a place, put it into a land trust, invite the Texas Lakers and perhaps others to join us.

On Cortes, we were told of a half-section, 320 acres, homesteaded by Ken and Hazel Hansen, which was perhaps for sale. They were rightly bemused by our plans for their farm but agreed to sell if and when we put together the money and the land trust ownership details. The farm fronted on a small lake, had thirty or forty acres of hay fields, two vegetable gardens, orchards. A stream running down to the lake, a spring. It backed against conifer forests, climbing up to high, balding Easter Bluff. We would be taking on a herd of forty small horses they'd used for a summer camp, a dairy herd of about twenty including Monty the bull, a raw milk business for islanders, chickens, bees, canoes and a pier out into the lake. Two ancient tractors, a tedder, a bailer, a harrow, and a large accumulation of dead or dying equipment. A farmhouse, three big barns, several outhouses, and a large Quonset hut they had used as a dorm for the summer-camp kids.

Thyson, his new partner Mooey, and three or four other Texas Lakers were ready to join us. The financial, legal, and bureaucratic work to make it all happen was intense. The idea was that I would make a charitable donation for a bit more than the negotiated price of the property to a charitable land trust organization which would then, by tacit but unenforceable agreement, buy the property, put stringent enforceable land-use covenants on it, install the bunch of us as stewards, and agree to a back-up charitable organization which could take over if both the stewards and they, the land trust owners, failed.

Nature Conservancy of Canada was ready to take it on, with the likely back-up to be a local private or governmental conservation organization. They pulled out at the last minute. We turned to the Trust for Public Land in San Francisco. They hesitated because of the possibly onerous policing and enforcement problems they would face if they ended up holding title. They were intrigued, though, by our innovative concept of stewardship, and eventually agreed to take it on. The newly formed Tides Foundation in San Francisco assumed the role of financial conduit, providing convenience and anonymity. They would grow later into a large conduit, handling the charitable giving of hundreds.

We wrote up the covenants to be part of the package. No private ownership, construction limited to a small area back from the lake, Easter Bluff and one steep forested area at the end of the lake to be untouchable wilderness areas, logging in other areas under strict selective-cutting rules.

Everything fell into place by the early winter of 1978. Penny, Dominic, and I got landed-immigrant status, similar to the American green card. All would be ready for our little band to move in by spring.

Now to be married.

⟿

Back to Virginia with our Sikh friends, midwinter. We sit on a grass mat around a circular brass tray, a chocolate cake in the center. Our hosts' turbans in place, hair tucked in, their untrimmed beards knotted discretely under the chin and held there with cotton cords. Flowing white robes, scattered roses—a blizzard of snow stinging the windows. Our friends, he the ex-CIA officer, were to have married us, he having been accredited in California where they had first launched an intentional community. But Virginia refused his credentials. So we had been married that afternoon in Charlottesville, at the colonial courthouse. We'd found a silver and gold ring in an antique store. With Dominic—munching corn curls—and the court secretary as witnesses, the sheriff in his on-duty uniform—holster emptied, I think—reading a Khalil Gibran poem, we were finally husband and wife. The chocolate cake our Sikh friends baked for us was the culmination of a lavish wedding dinner.

↬

Leaving Vanita there, we flew down to Grenada, greeting *Aeoli*, preparing for more voyaging, destination Cortes Island. Brother Tommy and his wife Mary happened to be there—good times together. Daughter Kathy and her husband Michael joined us for a bit of Windward and Leeward Islands cruising before Penny and Dominic and I sailed for Panama.

With light winds and heavy freighter traffic to be avoided, that westward sail of the length of the Caribbean took us ten hot, slow days. A reward was landfall on the islands and coast of Panama south of the canal. A swim over the side drifting off a coral beach, then we poked our way carefully up a jungle river a mile or two, anchoring off a village. A few huts on stilts leaning over the muddy river, two canoes came out to look us over, to invite us for a supper with their family. Naked children, adults in undershirts, shorts or wrap-around skirts, flip-flops. Eggs, rice, beer, tortillas, Penny managing well enough with their peculiar mix of Spanish and what was probably Kuna. To sleep on board deep in the chattering jungle.

Our original idea was to leave *Aeoli* in Panama, for we needed to get back to Cortes soon to begin our community. We would then come back the next winter to sail her to Cortes. Bad idea. Humidity there hovered around one hundred percent, vandalism was rampant, and pirates were always on the look for vessels to sell into the drug trade.

The yacht harbor in Colon at the Caribbean end of the canal was a staging point for yachts heading out on ocean passages. At any time of year, a group of young people would be hanging around hoping to sign on as crew. We found a Canadian hockey player and a Danish musician, signed them on to provide the required crew of four plus the pilot to handle us through the locks. I undertook to teach the two of them celestial navigation, for they had agreed to sail *Aeoli* to us in Canada by midsummer. No money either way.

Little *Aeoli* squeezed into the first lock behind an enormous freighter which was evidently without cargo, a third of her propeller out of water. That propeller threw a tsunami at us when she pulled out of the lock, ripping off one of our cleats. We sailed through the lake in the middle of the canal, a good breeze off our quarter, though the pilot half-heartedly told us that it was against the rules, that we should stay under power only.

Aeoli made it to the Pacific. She headed for Victoria, British Columbia. We headed for Cortes Island.

⊱

Linnaea, the twinflower, ground-clinging, evergreen with tiny pale pink double blossoms, grows in the temperate zones around the globe. Linnaeus—the prince and poet of botanists, who had undertaken the enormous task of botanical classification in the eighteenth century—Linnaeus chose the twinflower as his favorite. It was his personal symbol when he was raised to the Swedish nobility. We named our lovely place, our little community, Linnaea.

Hard, heavy work, new to most of us. Milking, bot-

Penny and Amiel, Linnaea Farm, Cortes Island, BC,
with a truckload of seaweed for fertilizer, 1982.

tling, milk deliveries all over the island, veggie gardening, orchards of fruit trees, haying, bailing, never-ending fencing, chickens and bees to tend. Forty horses, most of which we eventually trucked to auctions. Twenty cows, they were mellow enough, but Monty the bull was fierce and over-sexed, frequently breaking out of his ever higher and more rugged enclosure.

A sod-covered root cellar to build for our apples, potatoes, and onions. Firewood to get in, deep snows, hard freezes. Rebuilding living quarters in the farmhouse, the Quonset, a loggers' cabin on skids. We moved that cabin with our tractors up near the front gate. Penny and I did much of the carpentry and plumbing and wiring to make it our home—a loft for us, a bunk-bedroom for Dominic, a new dormer bedroom for the imminent arrival of baby Amiel.

Endless hours of meetings every few days. The Findhorn way to decision-making largely did work for us, but unanimity was tough. Who does what, how, when, how much. But the key recurring problem was membership. We vacillated between strict and lenient. When lenient, we got some lulus.

The Blue Meanie, a would-be guru who, it turned out, was on the ten-most-wanted list in the States for counterfeiting dollars to finance an armed vigilante group on the far left. A band of latter-day, vandalizing Luddites. With the Royal Mounties hot on their tracks, he and his wife and little daughter escaped into the woods. Months later he was seen by us strolling the streets of Vancouver. In our state of shock, it never occurred to us to try to turn him in.

Rain in the Face, a wannabe Indian from Brooklyn, a draft dodger on a stolen ID.

And there was a guy on welfare whose brain hardly functioned, living for a time in a squalid shack with a rabid born-again until they managed to burn the shack down and were finally—the consensus process again—asked to leave.

We found some time for fun and celebration, too. Canoeing, riding, skinny-dipping in the lake and the sea, group picnics high on our hill, Easter Bluff. One or two sails on languishing *Aeoli*, beach bonfires, music making, heartfelt Christmases, skating on our Gunflint Lake. A funeral to the music of a French horn on Easter Bluff, spreading the ashes of one of our members killed in an airplane accident.

With our demonstrated dedication to the farm, our supplying the island with raw milk and cream, our offerings of vegetables and of plots of garden to islanders to cultivate themselves, we were soon accepted by each element of the ex-

traordinarily varied societal mix. The Twinflower children—
there were three of school age at Linnaea—quickly integrated
into the local school. Some of our members began to serve in
the island's administration, to help in island projects.

Most of us were determined to make communal living
work, were hard workers and fast learners. It was by and
large a successful enterprise and still is. Linnaea gradually
morphed toward education. For two or three years we took
on groups of Canadian youths just out of high school who
had signed up for a year in a government program rather
like AmeriCorps. They were with us for three-month periods, pitching in to help on the farm, to work on appropriate
technology projects, to learn something about conservation
and the ecology. A largely hands-on learning process in a
communal setting. In recent years, Linnaea has run annual
nine-month residential programs of gardening apprentice-
ships. For many years, they had a successful K-8 school, only
closing it in 2010 when the local public school morphed
into acceptability.

Penny and I also continued our growing involvement
in mini-philanthropy and stewarded land trusts. Working
with a San Francisco tax attorney, I rearranged my modest
capital so that most of it was irrevocably committed over
the long run to charitable giving. Lead trusts, charitable re-
mainder trusts, a descendant-operated mini-foundation in
my will, donor-advised funds at the Tides Foundation for
their expertise, administrative convenience, and anonymity
for Penny and me.

Penny was a wise partner. Her empathy in dealing with
the myriad human problems at Linnaea was invaluable
also in making difficult judgments in our use of charitable
funds. Over the years, she took charge of an ever-greater

proportion of the charitable giving required or encouraged by the trusts I had set up. Yet, though we effectively have an entirely shared bank account, it remains a reality that the origins of our resources came largely from my side. Even now, there are still some differences in our spending and giving attitudes and in our priorities. I believe, however, that by now this difference makes neither of us uncomfortable.

Not long after we had all settled into our new lives at Linnaea, a small group of us became informal trustees of a project we called the Turtle Island Fund. We set out to find potential candidates for intentional-community-stewarded land trusts. Several of us, in ones or twos, would visit communities, largely in the Pacific Northwest, who were trying to acquire and conserve the lands where they had begun their communities. Channeled through our donor-advised fund at the Tides Foundation, in the course of three or four years we were able, with carefully crafted conditions and donations of from twenty to ninety thousand dollars, to help in the land acquisition as stewarded land trusts for eight communities. Seven are still intact thirty-five years later. Approvecho, Linnaea, Chinook/Whidbey Institute, Findhorn, Caravan Farm Theatre, Summerfield Waldorf School and Farm, Hague Lake Island. Only The Kettle finally failed to survive. The goal was that these trusts be not just land-use restrictions, covenants put on the private owners of land, but that they put carefully covenanted ownership in the hands of charitable land trusts, backed up with a second tier of trusts to hopefully ensure something approaching perpetuity, with the occupants of the land being stewards, not owners. Compromises sometimes had to be made, but the goal was in each case at least largely achieved.

There were essentially four of us who were the committed founders of Linnaea—Thyson, of Texas Lake, his new wife Mooey, Penny, and me. Thyson and Mooey were both, in their very different ways, charismatic. We shared goals— the validity of community living, the urgency that we all live lightly and sustainably on the land. Thyson and Mooey were particularly the leaders of the government programs of youth training at Linnaea. They eventually were drawn away from Linnaea to lead Canadian groups in Peace-Corps-type work in Pakistan. They soon separated as his infidelities were revealed. Mooie turned inward to her family and friends. We continued to visit often—Canada, the States, England. She had become our three sons' godmother. A deeply intuitive person, a wise counselor, a dearest friend.

Thyson moved to south central British Columbia. He continued, I believe, to be dedicated to the promotion of land trusts. He needed capital to help in their creation. Unbelievably, he undertook to sell Linnaea, and when that failed, the ownership being clearly far beyond his control, he turned to The Kettle, setting in motion its prospective sale. By then, that land was under the stewardship of a severely physically handicapped man, Tim, and a handful of colleagues. They were using the land as a camp for handicapped youths who could be helped through horse therapy. Tim was getting help from government programs and private donations and was in the final steps of the process of getting a local charitable society and a quasi-governmental agency to take on the first and second tiers of land trust ownership.

The lines were drawn, the battle was on. Thyson's determination to create land-trust projects in his new area outweighed his legal commitments to Linnaea, his moral commitments to The Kettle, and to what we thought were still our shared principles. After months of dealing with attorneys, twenty of us communitarians from or associated with Linnaea came hundreds of miles to the interior to a trumped up annual meeting of the charitable society of which we had all been members. As the meeting got underway, Thyson enrolled local teenagers as members of the society. We lost the crucial vote. The outcome was bitter. Thyson's "concession" was to sell half of the Kettle, taking the proceeds, leaving the other half to Tim—who proceeded to complete its land trusting. And they passed a resolution taking away our memberships. Greed and ego outbid morality. To recall those confrontations with Thyson is still dismaying.

For the remaining half of The Kettle, the outcome too was sad. It turned out that the land trust had never quite been formalized, and those of us who continued to support Tim and the land trust idea acceded to sale of the land. Tim had become desperately ill, destitute, and almost immobile. Communal lands became private.

~26~

Doughnuts

ONE EVENING in 1981, half way through a communal supper in Linnaea's Quonset hut, the phone rang. Penny answered it, talked for some time, and came back to say it was for me. She took me aside to say quietly that it was a man who seemed to be after my money.

As a result, a month later I was sitting on the grass outside a barracks of a Boy Scouts camp in Estes Park, Colorado, high in the Rockies, sitting as part of a circle of a dozen relatively wealthy men and women, largely baby boomers. After several days of often violent disagreement, of each of us blatantly trying to talk the others into throwing money at our own favorite charitable project, we decided that we should meet again, organize ourselves into some sort of philanthropic group, and that we needed a name. Holding hands, meditating, maybe an "aaauuummm" or two, we came up with nothing. Then, looking up into a clear blue sky, there was one cloud, only one, right overhead. It was in the shape of a doughnut. Our name, at least among ourselves, was henceforth Doughnuts. That was thirty plus years ago. The Doughnuts today number several hundred, and the total past and present membership would, I'd suspect, be hundreds more.

One joint project did, in fact, prevail out of that first

meeting. Two of our group persuaded six or eight of us to gather the next day in Boulder to further discuss the project they had flogged in the meeting, and to talk with its founder, Dr. Robert Fuller. It was called the Mo Tzu Project after an ancient Chinese peacemaker. It was one of the early steps toward what later became a quite substantial and effective movement, particularly during the height of the cold war—"citizen diplomacy" or "track-two diplomacy"—a search by private citizens, individuals and groups, to go to the hot spots in global, international, and intranational tensions, to seek their origins and to help find common interests between the contending sides that could lead to peaceful, even win-win solutions. Formal contacts between governments, spokesmen for contending sides, and corporate interests are often locked into failure. Fuller—he formerly taught higher mathematics and quantum physics at Columbia and became president of Oberlin College at the age of thirty-three—had upended his professional life in the pursuit of alternatives to the paralyzing attitudes and factors in world and local affairs. He was persuasive in getting financial support for the Mo Tzu Project from our small group of Doughnuts. Within a few years, I had taken on most of this project support, support over a span of about two decades until his pension kicked in. This became effectively unconditional support for whatever he chose to do with his talents and vision.

Over the next fifteen years, I was to take several trips with him to the Soviet Union, Afghanistan, Pakistan, and China in the interests of citizen diplomacy, writing articles jointly with him, radio interviews, live presentations. He has become a close friend. I can imagine no better person to be at the receiving end of this rather unique form of personal philanthropy.

Perhaps it's an odd pairing. An eminent scientist, educator, writer, activist, thinker, a man who keeps his emotions well in check—and me. His rational, inquisitive, analytic mind is extraordinary. He has a rare talent for listening carefully, asking penetrating questions, eliciting surprising answers. He has a manner that harbors no nonsense, yet is non-judgmental, profoundly democratic. He is forever probing, curious, learning. And it is for me alarming to see that though he has always been optimistic that technology can solve the world's more material problems such as climate change, his longstanding optimism about the solution of social, political, and economic problems is sorely tested. There are too many situations now in the world that are clearly deteriorating.

↭

The Doughnuts, meeting two or three times a year, soon had formed a foundation, Threshold, to take in member donations and receive, appraise, and support appropriate proposals sponsored and submitted by, and only by, members. Penny joined the Doughnuts in our second meeting, our baby son Amiel in her arms. For many years, she was an active participant, particularly in social justice and indigenous people projects. We are now emerita and emeritus.

↭

In our second year at Linnaea, our son Amiel is born. Dominic, enrolled in the local elementary school, his usual cheery, energetic self a joy to the entire community, becomes a devoted brother. A family within a family, it seems an ideal way of organizing society. It does work, but there are tensions. Between our home-making instincts and our larger community, loyalties and obligations are stretched. By the time our third child is well on his way to being born, these tensions are abruptly uncovered. Emerging from a group meditation, one of our closest friends declares that it quite suddenly was revealed to her that we are not the leaderless community we so proudly had advertised ourselves as being. That Penny and I were crypto leaders, and that this felt very uncomfortable.

Do we, Penny and I, publicly accept the roles of leadership, and expect that as a result several of our members will leave? Do we leave? I spend two days alone on Easter Bluff, fasting, meditating, sorting out feelings and options and priorities. Penny is relieved when I concede that we'd best go. To leave Linnaea largely intact, to be more completely available to our growing family, to relocate to somewhere on the American west coast closer to a city from which we could travel more readily to our families in England, Italy, Spain, Colorado, and New England, and to travel for our widening interests in social justice and environmental projects. To move quickly and be settled for the imminent birth. And neither of us felt we would be comfortable and effective in assuming a dominant leadership role. Many good reasons to go, yet a sad and wrenching departure.

We move to Whidbey Island near Seattle. Our son Arian is born on the Fourth of July, 1983. A new life for us begins.

∼27∼

Tree Huggers v. Libertarians

IN THE second half of the twentieth century, the particular new global preoccupations were the fear of nuclear annihilation, and the consequences of the population explosion coupled with the sacrosanct doctrine of growth—consumerism, degradation of the planet, climate disaster. They had joined the panoply of historic concerns such as hunger, injustice, plagues, war, brutality, the human capacity for evil. The twenty-first century quickly added to the list—terrorism, global warming, and the struggle for depleted resources.

The population of the world quadrupled in the twentieth century, my century, as did the population of the United States. Global gross domestic product increased forty-fold, and a large part of that must have been the market cost of non-renewable resources. The true cost of those resources is immeasurable, resources that are for practical purposes largely lost forever.

Much research and writing were done in that second half of the century on population growth and its likely Malthusian consequences—Ehrlich, Commoner, Brown, Meadows, the Club of Rome. In 1951-52, The President's Materials Policy Commission—where I'd served on the staff—was a sincere attempt to measure the consequences of population growth for the supply of finite resources. It is an example of the concern but also of the difficulties of projecting the future. It was way way off the mark when the twenty-five years of its projections had passed, understating both the population and the reserves of resources by wide margins.

⌒

When I resigned from government service, moving to Italy, my life was upended. My work became that of reading and writing about these concerns on a personal level, both in non-fiction and fiction.

For me, the 'sixties and early 'seventies were years of frequent despair. The world seemed finally to have become super-saturated. Like a solution that crystallizes when you add one more grain, we had arrived at a place where any additional consumer caused consequences that the planet could no longer absorb. My non-fiction writing, largely in letters, one or two articles, urged what by my measure was simple sanity. Better red than dead. Bomb shelters require murdering your neighbors. Nuclear war would not only shatter the globe, it would incinerate it through firestorms, or maybe deep-freeze it in a nuclear winter when dense dust clouds shut off the warmth of the sun. My fiction was to a large extent pessimistic, elegiac, with only shreds of hope emerging in a devastated world. If you looked for it, and I often did, doom was everywhere.

⌒

During the 1980s and 90s, my father acquired the Bar NI Ranch in the Sangre de Cristo mountains in southern Colorado—and simultaneously land trusted it to Nature Conservancy of Colorado. His company had been leasing it as a vacation spot for its employees and customers since the late 'forties. The arrangement he made with Nature Conservancy effectively leaves its use, however, virtually exclusively in the hands of his descendants, though subject to use restrictions and monitoring by Nature Conservancy. Eight thousand to fourteen thousand feet in elevation, thirty-six thousand acres. Gorgeous high country, lakes, streams, pastures at lower elevations. Land stolen from the Indians, then from the Mexicans. Sheep ranching, cattle ranching, logging for a hundred years. By the time the family and Nature Conservancy took it over, human activity on the land, except for one failed attempt to drill for oil, was largely only hunting and exploring by horseback and vehicle. On the lower pastured area, a lodge, cabins, outbuildings, corrals, irrigation, fishponds. A family fiefdom, untaxed by careful financial planning.

My father and mother, 1987, Sangre de Cristo mountains.

For a few of us in the family, this was a unique opportunity to preserve the land completely. One small gift back to the planet and the wildlife of the area, one example of what a wealthy family can do to set aside an area of wilderness, to ban guns completely, to stop the sports-hunting of its wildlife, the destructions of its forests, to stop motorized access. Even perhaps an example of the benefits to the planet and the individual of forgoing the eating of meat. A place where family, friends, the public can appreciate, enjoy, learn from a glorious piece of untrammeled land. Could not such a goal be the very foundation of family solidarity, our special pride, our gift?

It was not to be. The libertarians of my vast family, the descendants of my parents, largely won out. One mountainous corner of the property was ultimately preserved as a no-hunting, no-motorized-vehicle zone. Otherwise, guns are still there, hunting continues, more building, a comfortable cabin half-way up the mountains, jeeps, four-by-fours, and snowmobiles.

My East Coast family is quite used to my own dissent about that ranch, but it is a divisive issue. Less divisive is a small family foundation endowed by my parents that is very actively and largely harmoniously administered by a revolving board of family members, making between one and two million dollars of grants each year. There is something of an issue between those who lean toward favoring a few large grants to big established institutions, and those who hope and work for many lesser grants to small, often new charitable projects where small infusions of help can make huge differences. The family leaders give priority to family participation whatever the mix of recipients. Some of us would prefer more focus on strategic giving that would make a difference. We end up making a wide variety of grants.

These family affairs, this family of mine. I don't know much about the other branches of the family stemming from my Cabot grandfather, let alone the many other Cabot family trees rooted in Boston. As for our vast branch stemming from my parents—my father still to some degree the paterfamilias though he died in 1995—it does maintain a varying degree of cohesiveness given its Puritanical, hardheaded, competitive, and intolerant origins. That Colorado ranch, the family-run foundation, and a family-run financial office in Boston make up much of the glue. Most of us live comfortably but not ostentatiously on the wealth largely created by my father and my oldest brother. Most of us have moved away from knee-jerk Republicanism, and many of us are convinced Democrats. Many of us have seized opportunities that some wealth makes possible, others may not have, though the judging of that must be largely subjective. My own sub-branch, twenty-four at last count, seems to be like-minded with regards to public and family-wide issues. Given the distances separating most of us, we do connect.

~28~

Branson Dunks Sir Jimmy

THAT MOVE from Cortes Island to Whidbey Island led us into a very different life. The demands of community living, of the dairy, of farming, the isolation of Cortes, those limits were no longer there. They had been good years, hopeful years, years of direct engagement with the earth, with the truer aspects of the counterculture, with rewarding aspects of our own beings. That community, Linnaea, which we had fostered, still flourishes, its principles of land stewardship rather than land ownership are intact. I miss it, I knew I would, and it is deeply gratifying to know it is there, a living example of a sustainable way of life.

Yet it was time for us to move on. No regrets. Other challenges and rewards awaited. And other jobs, other projects. Three sons with us now, a house to make into our home. A new school, a Waldorf school, a schoolhouse to build. New friends, new community, new gardens to grow. New opportunities.

Penny was particularly drawn to working with indigenous peoples—Native Americans and peoples in Central America and South America. That she could help with small donations was an entrée, but her ability to connect with people was of special value in helping along the grassroots movements she was involved in. Many lasting friendships were formed, connections made in her hands-on work in these projects.

The five most substantial donations that we have made were also to projects in which we are still involved or were for years. The first was a donation that enabled The Trust for Public Land to buy and put into trust the homestead land in Canada that became Linnaea.

The second was a series of donations to the Turtle Island Fund for helping in the establishment of land trusts to be stewarded, not owned, by residents and monitored and owned by a structure of non-profit conservation entities.

The third was to finance the Whidbey Island Waldorf School's schoolhouse construction, the land trust where it is situated, and some of its early working capital. Our two youngest sons were students there for several years. We served on the board and in many volunteer capacities. A successful undertaking that has by now drawn many families to Whidbey Island.

The fourth was donations to the citizen diplomacy projects of Bob Fuller, support which soon evolved into an open-ended support for twenty years of whatever Bob chose to put his extraordinary talents to work on. Citizen diplomacy, then many articles and books on "rankism" and the Dignity Movement, with many hundreds of lectures and public appearances around the world, a dozen books.

The fifth was to put to work in our Seattle region an assignment from my mother's estate of $750,000, a like sum going into the control of each of my siblings. Each portion was required to go to charitable purposes. With particular guidance from Penny, we formed a local foundation, the Seattle Peoples Fund, to help local ethnic minorities, most of them recent immigrants, to find their voice, their identity, their role in the melting pot that is Seattle. Friends joined us in forming an active board, finding many good small projects, and we later found a program manager who has been invaluable. One of the board's directors in early years was Pramila Jayapal. She had to withdraw when she was elected to the House of Representatives in 2016. She has become an effective, high profile, progressive member of the U.S. Congress.

The SPF has been making small grants—no more than $3000—at an annual rate of about $40,000 for several years now. Small projects, small grants, making big differences.

We also for many years continued to be involved in the Doughnuts' Threshold Foundation, gradually withdrawing as we focused more on our own undertakings. We frequently submit grant proposals to my family's VWC Foundation and rotate in and out of its board.

An amusing footnote to our roles in small-scale philanthropy. When I was living part-time in an old farmhouse in Tuscany, a next-door neighbor—next-door being a half-mile through an oak forest on the other side of a "wild" boar farm—was Teddy Goldsmith, editor and publisher of the British "Ecology" magazine and a charismatic figure in the green movement. His brother was Sir James "Jimmy" Goldsmith, one of the richest men in Britain. Years later, Teddy called me and invited me to join a small group of philanthropists and environmental activists at Jimmy's estate in Mexico. Jimmy was ready to put some of his wealth to work and turned to his brother to organize an appropriate meeting to advise him. With a vastly, in fact hilariously overblown idea of my role, he invited me to join the group. He rattled off a bunch of names—Jerry Mander, Norman Lear, Jeremy Rifkin, Doug Tompkins, Richard Branson, others I've forgotten. I demurred, then, out of a consuming curiosity—and a familiar, *Ha! Maybe I can snag some of the billions for my pet projects*—I let my arm be twisted. I'm to fly to Los Angeles, be met as I get off the plane, and they'll take care of me from there on.

My flight is late. A long black limo is waiting for me. We drive across several runways to the other side of LAX. I climb into a private jet, the others of the eight or so of us coming from that part of the world are already on board waiting for me. Introduced around, familiar names but not faces. We settle into luxury—a steward brings us champagne and lobster and whatever else we might want. Teddy tells me that Jimmy has three of these jets and a couple of large propeller craft, each with its own crew.

There's very little small talk, Teddy keeping us on subject—what can we offer Jimmy, what ideas, advice, projects. I watch the monitor, a toy airplane headed south along Mexico's Pacific coast. I had no idea where we were going until our target destination's name starts flashing on the screen—Manzanillo.

Though Manzanillo turns out to be merely our port of entry. We are treated like heads of state—no police, no customs, no paperwork whatsoever. We transfer to a propeller craft, Jimmy's runway up the coast being too short to handle jets. A short hop and we're landing on a well-groomed grass strip. We taxi up to a line of vans, jeeps, and pickups headed by a huge man wearing an enormous plain sombrero, Sir Jimmy himself.

By twos and threes, we are directed to vehicles to take us to whichever one of several villas we will be sleeping in. Jeremy Rifkin and I are to be roommates. The convoy sets out, led by a pickup in the bed of which is mounted a machine gun manned by three heavily armed men in uniforms—Jimmy has a private army of fifty or so. We wind through a wild animal park, border a lagoon, climb up to the bluff where Jimmy's palace sits overlooking miles of Pacific beach, and are then taken to our various villas. Each one seems to house one of Jimmy's many wives and offspring, and a special one for brother Teddy. Many swimming pools, exotic plantings, thousands of acres of this kingdom. He has built two villages, complete with schools, churches, shops for his huge staff and army.

That afternoon I wander down to the lagoon. Norman Lear invites me to join him on a boat tour to check out the

Sir James Goldsmith's mansion above the pool where
Richard Branson pushed him in.

Norman Lear and Richard Branson and friends on a lagoon of a "wildlife preserve" on Goldsmith's Mexican estate, 1992.

alligators, the exotic birds, the gazelles, giraffes. Richard Branson and family have just arrived in one of his own jets from his own private Caribbean Island. He joins us. Later Branson and I walk and chat.

The first evening was an elaborate poolside dinner, many tables on one side, each hosted by a wife or other family member. Across the pool was a marimba band in full regalia outlined against huge bonfires on the beach. Branson arrives late, goes up to Jimmy, who is jollying up table after table. I happen to be watching them as they meet. Casually, Branson pushes Jimmy into the pool, linen suit, sombrero, cigar and all, then jumps in after him. Up floats the sombrero, then the cigar still clamped in his teeth.

Our host is furious, gestures to the marimba band, to Teddy, and stalks out. Teddy tells Branson to leave, and quickly. The next morning Teddy calls a rump meeting of our group in his villa, announcing that there was no changing of his brother's mind. Branson has been told to leave immediately. He had come within a hair of being shot down by the marimba band, each member doubling as security guards, weapons hidden under their serapes.

We meet as a group, minus Branson, in one of the circular wings that surround the immense central room under a Moroccan dome, a room with benches and hundreds of exotic cushions circling the space

It soon turns out that Jimmy was already well decided on how he would set up and direct a new foundation and what its emphases would be. We seemed to be there largely to gratify his ego. Days later, over brandy and cigars after the final dinner, I find myself sitting on a terrace beside Jimmy. Though I by then had realized that there was no way to shoehorn one of my pet projects into his essentially conservative agenda, I decide to bite the bullet and, with the hope of upping his relatively small allotment of his wealth to his foundation, tell him in a few words my own experience in the little leagues. I tell him that, to a large extent under the constraints of the charitable trusts I had deliberately set up, I had been giving for several years at an annual rate of from a half to two thirds of my unearned income. His response is silence.

~ 29 ~

Cracks in the Curtain

THE SORTIES I took with Bob Fuller into citizen diplo-macy led to interesting situations and adventures. At the height of the Cold War the world was appalled by the race between the Soviet Union and the United States toward MAD—mutual assured destruction—with enough nuclear weapons to many times over wipe out maybe all life on our planet. In that Cold War, governments seemed incapable of rational action. The Reagan-Gorbachev meeting in Reyk-javik showed a flash of sanity when they appeared to be seriously considering total nuclear disarmament, but insan-ity took over within a few minutes. Back to the race, each superpower stonewalling.

⊕

In the hills behind San Bernardino, California, 250,000 young Americans are dancing on the grass in front of an enor-mous television screen showing crowds of dancing young So-viets. On a similar screen, dozens of young people are dancing to the same identical music in a TV studio in Moscow, their screen crowded with the American dancers. September 1982, the first time American and Soviet TV are linked in a "space bridge", an interactive TV rock concert courtesy of Steve Wozniak of Apple. Three months earlier, President Reagan had declared the Soviet Union to be an "evil empire."

Common lives, joys, concerns, fears—could we not start there, build a mutuality of interests across the Iron Curtain which might tip the balance away from our race toward destruction, away from distrust, from our knee-jerk patterns of hate and fear, the ever escalating Cold War rhetoric from our leaders and official representatives? Tip the balance toward sanity by opening citizen-to-citizen contact on a massive scale?

The use of this new spacebridge technology was a part of what was to become a significant non-governmental element in the defusing of the Cold War. Many thousands of visitors from the Western bloc began to flow into the Soviet Union, travel and contact restrictions were slowly eased. The U.S. State Department was predictably bemused if not openly derisive of this citizen diplomacy. They often advised strongly against particular privately organized trips, but the movement continued to gain momentum. And the Soviet leadership increasingly tolerated some reverse flow.

⊷

Red Square, the Hammer-and-Sickle flying from the Kremlin battlements over Lenin's tomb, Stalin's ghost lingers, impassive on his balcony, the center piece in the Party's latest pecking order, reviewing the endless parades of nuclear missiles, of drab ranks, of rumbling tanks and artillery. Now it's Ground Zero, the target of hundreds of American warheads, their clocks ticking in their silo lairs, the target of the multi-warheads on missiles stacked in Trident submarines circling the enemy. And the Puget Sound base for those submarines, near Seattle, near where our protagonist lives, that's a Ground Zero where the Soviets might start their assured planetary destruction. Weird, makes one look cautiously over one's shoulder to see if the nukes are flying in. Over one's shoulder, and there's the huge and largely empty GUM department store, a Victorian-train-station of a building staring glumly across Red Square at the mile-long queue of Lenin worshippers. Somewhere behind the medieval brick walls of that Kremlin, maybe in a bunker, there's a finger poised on a button. Somewhere—the White House, Air Force One, a bunker in nearby hills...

I simply walk though the massive gates in that Kremlin wall, flashing a pseudo press card, miraculously rid of the hovering Intourist spy-guide. Wandering, ignored, here in the enemy's citadel. Marble corridors fading to vanishing points, acres for the coat checking, a Men's with a hundred urinals. I find my way to the vast austerely modernized assembly hall for the rubber-stamping Party sycophants.

On a large screen behind the podium, a space bridge program is being broadcast in Moscow and New York to tens of millions of Soviet and American viewers. My job is to keep an eye on the TV reception and watch the response of the audience. News anchors—Peter Jennings for the U.S. network—are moderating a discussion between Soviet and American generals and scientists on the subject of nuclear winter. Will a nuclear war throw up so much dust into the atmosphere that it will blanket out the sun and bring on an ice age? This is to be a the first time that Soviet viewers will hear some of the likely consequences of a nuclear war from their leaders. Another first for the Soviet viewers is to be subjected to American commercials—the usual dog foods, deodorants, cars, vacation cruises, bras. Shocking, dangerous glimpses through cracks in the Iron Curtain.

To report back to New York during the broadcast, I step out to the broadcast vans lined up in a Kremlin-style back alley, phone in on the open line while watching the program on a monitor. No problems, routine. Chuckles, heads gesturing in disbelief at the commercials. Back to the assembly hall, pick up the earphones at a vacant legislator's desk.

⊷

Other visits to cold, dreary Moscow. Its endless thousands of hideous apartment blocks, its towering Stalin-era structures, architectural monstrosities. Its ragged potholed boulevards, billboards to the glories of the Soviet empire, queues everywhere for everything. Its lurking black market, an undercurrent everywhere of scrounging, of petty deals, of envy and curiosity and hate. Of bitter caution. And too, a deep sense of innate generosity, warmth, spontaneity, humanity. A love and a longing for good times, family times, friendships. Making much from little.

A visit with an endangered dissident in his cramped apartment, hoping to find a way to get him onto a space bridge program, the notoriety from which hopefully would serve as some degree of protection. Meetings with policymakers in the quasi-governmental Academies, discussing the Soviet occupation of Afghanistan and its comparison with the American experience in Vietnam. A lunch with a contact at the Writers Union in the faint hope of finding interest in and a translator for his first novel.

An early morning jog with colleague Fuller in an empty stadium near our foreigners-only hotel. Meals in shabby restaurants, tattered remnants of tsarist glory. Dreadful slabs of salted meat and fish, cabbage, potatoes, slimy sweets. Bread and cheese and beer seemed the only reliable fallbacks.

A hire-car trip to Peredelkino to visit Pasternak's dacha and grave. A hillside cemetery in a copse of birch, a simple stone in the snow. A train trip to Georgia, to Tbilisi, thirty hours of soot and stink and wooden benches. The filthy dining car offers only an ever-thinner borscht, though fortunately at frequent stops in the towns, hawkers offer bread rolls, bits of wizened sausage. A thousand miles through drab, often ravaged countryside. Hundreds of rusting, dilapidated factories, warehouses. Neglected farms. The politically precarious Orthodox churches give the only grace and color and signs of care in countless dingy towns and villages. No storied country estates and dachas to be seen.

No signs of that rich land of evil power set to conquer the world, not on this route. So much of the vitality of the land seems to have been sucked away. Twenty million lives lost in defeating the German war machine, lost in the brutal enforcing of Party loyalty, in the hordes disappearing into the gulags and the insane asylums. Wealth drained into that endless march of power through Red Square, into the arms race, into cosmonauts circling the planet, into world hegemony. Are they on the edge of collapse?

And there's Leningrad, a city in the Baltic marshlands where no city should be. Saint Petersburg, the crazed creation of the opulence of tsardom built on the backs of serfdom by an Italian architect. Half demolished in the thirty-month siege by the German armies, a million dead. Yet reconstructed by Stalin to that same opulence on those same backs. Acres of new gold leaf hammered out by hundreds of goldsmiths, a whole silk industry recreated—the worms, the mulberries, the weavers, the artists—to reproduce the tapestries for the dozens of palaces and monuments rebuilt from rubble. Masons, painters, sculptors, historians, architects, engineers, the armies of workers forced into this labor to recapture the glory of tsarist Russia. Go figure.

↤↦

And then Afghanistan. The Soviets are in trouble. Their occupation is under constant attack by the mujahedeen guerillas. The costs in life and treasure and reputation, both international and internal, are crushing. Their dreams of expanding on through Pakistan to the Indian Ocean are thwarted. Can there be a role there for citizen diplomacy? What form might it take? What objectives might best serve the interests of peace? The two of us set out, Fuller and Cabot. Most likely a quixotic venture, and admittedly also driven by a degree of curiosity about this hottest of hot spots, but what the hell.

A stopover in Athens for what will prove to be the last visit with Kevin Andrews before he drowns. Then Rawalpindi. They're hosted by a Pakistani army general in his megahome. The whiskey flows despite Muslim prohibitions, but conversation gets little beyond a what-can-be-done toss of the hands, a lift of the eyebrows, a cynical smirk. We taxi to government offices in Islamabad. We interview a Western-educated woman in a key policy-making government position, impressed by her intelligence. But still, what can be done?

To Peshawar, teeming with a million Afghan refugees. A colorful city with its busy bazaars, juice and snack barrows, wild mixes of ethnic garb, the gaudy decorations of the over-crowded buses and trucks, the beggars, street-corner musicians, rifles as de rigueur accessories. We stay in a modest hotel, screened verandas, a bar teeming with journalists—worthy of Graham Greene. Free-flowing gin-and-lime, whiskey, wine, but restaurant meals seem limited to variations of dhal and rice and fruit.

{282}

We contact the U.S. Consulate and have long conversations with a young man who shows every sign of being the CIA station chief. We show him an article in the *International Herald Tribune* we had picked up at the Athens airport which speaks of leaked information that the Americans are now supplying Stinger missiles to the mujahedeen, the heat-seeking shoulder-launched weapon which can finally challenge the Soviet Air Force. Is this true? But the only answer we get is to the effect that the U.S. supports the Pakistan military, not the muj. As consolation, we are offered a contact with the commander of a muj military training camp.

In bleak sandy scrublands outside Peshawar, the well-camouflaged training camp seems impressively disciplined and equipped, though no Stingers are to be seen. Fuller can't resist a few shots with a Kalashnikov. The commander offers to arrange to have us escorted in convoy through the Khyber Pass into the war zone. We decline, not wanting to deflect any of the muj from their mission. Nearby is an enormous refugee camp, thousands of families in acres of orderly tents, no men to be seen, women and children busying about, dogs scrounging, water trucks circulating, a lone camel complaining loudly.

No role for citizen diplomacy thus far. Perhaps the best we can do is to report our observations to whomever will listen or read or look at their photos.

On with the adventure. North through Pakistan's Northwest Frontier Province, up into the Karakoram Mountains, the Himalayas and K2 in the distance. Lush valleys, immense mountains, towns brilliant with flowers, with mosaicked mosques, monasteries backed against the cliffs, fortresses. A palace for *The Man Who Would Be King*. We are on the last bus out of Gilgit, a rust-bucket van, rattling

Near the Kunjerab Pass between Pakistan and China, 1989.

up the valley. The Karakoram highway, built by the Chinese and Pakistani armies, was completed only a couple of years earlier and is about to close for the winter. Twenty years to build, a thousand lives lost to landslides. Winding up for hours to the Khunjerab Pass, almost 16,000 feet, we struggle for breath to merely stand for a photo by the border maker. On into China—yaks and yurts, camels, herders on horseback. Vast barren spaces, snow fields, frozen rivers, gorges through these glaciered mountains of the snow leopard, the ibex, the mad mountaineer. A few miles further we come to the cinderblock Chinese border station. The end of the road for the bus, it hurries back up the road.

Hours of waiting, finally a police van takes our adventurers on, deep into the vast high barren land, on to Tashkurgan. A treeless, grassless plateau, windblown, red-caked earth and sand, patches of drifted snow. A small town, adobe fortress, scattered homes and sheds mostly made of mud, camels in their compounds, one miserable hotel—no toilets, no heating, no water. An austere barn of a communal dining hall where much of the town eats dhal in glum silence. And there will be no transportation either back to Pakistan or on into China's northwest desert and the first town, Kashgar, hundreds of miles on, no transportation until spring—six months on.

Well. Telephones have not found their way to Tashkurgan. We find the town's telegraph station in a freezing shed. Telegrams are written, paid for—thirty years later they have still not arrived. So. Days of whining, pleading with the few vehicle owners in evidence. Reports that the Chinese Army has closed the highway ahead, major repairs, serious accidents, etc.

Days of reflection.

We're sitting at a table in the communal eatery, after moving the table as near as possible to the warmth coming from the kitchen door, working our way through a kind of samovar of very hot tea. Somehow, we have managed to

Himalayan highway, 1989.

achieve for the moment a state of predicament denial, fueled, though, by a slightly positive development—the arrival
from Pakistan, in spite of the official highway closure, of a
new Toyota SUV with five well-dressed men.

A middle-aged, overweight man in an expensive-look-
ing woolen cloak, evidently the senior member of the newly
arrived group, has taken a seat at the far end of the Americans' table, silently lighting up a cheroot, pulling a magazine
out of his pocket. We continue talking.

Is this adventure giving any useful insights other than
that of our own folly? Why are we here? What were we
thinking, what are they thinking? What are we learning?

Here in Tashkurgan, where we are sitting, China, Ta-
jikistan, Afghanistan, and Pakistan almost meet. They
come within a hundred and fifty miles of each other. This
is the center of one of the great geopolitical vortexes.
These passes, particularly the Khyber, were the thirteenth
and fourteenth century invasion routes of the Mongols
through these most formidable of mountain ranges south
and east into the subcontinent. The road ahead leads to
Kashgar, a hub of the Silk Road, a principal commercial
link for hundreds of years between the Orient and Europe.
This region lies at the center of the Great Game, the long
rivalry between the British, the Russian, and the Chinese
empires. It now is not far from the heart of Cold War
military conflict. Here, this godforsaken outpost where the
only reliable means of transport is the camel, where there
appears to be no contact at all with the rest of the world.
Trapped, sucked into the vacuum of a historic vortex.

The silent figure at the end of the table sets down his
magazine, takes a silver case from his breast pocket, reaches
over to offer us Americans his cheroots. We decline, offer

him tea, he moves his chair to sit near. In adequate English, he apologizes for having overheard us and joins in the conversation.

A bit of his life's story unfolds. He was born in Kashgar, an oasis city in northwest China's enormous Taklamakan Desert, a high sand desert of extreme temperatures with a few oasis towns that sustained the Silk Route caravans through the ages. He was of a Uighur Muslim family, prosperous, owners of a clothing factory.

This region of China has been in ethnic, religious, and political turmoil throughout history. In modern times, it has been pulled repeatedly back and forth between the Russian-Soviet empires, Chinese dynasties, the People's Republic of China, and intermittent short-lived periods of quasi-nationhood. Only in 1949 did the People's Liberation Army "liberate" it from its latest attempt at self-determination. In 1960, Mao's Great Leap Forward caused thousands of Kashgaris to flee. He, a boy of ten, escaped with his family in a brutal march over the Himalayas into Pakistan. Settling in Gilgit, they started again as tailors. With Beijing currently more conciliatory, he and his companions are on their way to Kashgar hoping to reclaim properties that the Han Chinese had taken from them.

He invites these two travelers to ride with them. They will be joining a convoy of Chinese Army trucks that is readying to leave the next morning to relieve a road construction crew. The Gilgit group intends to go on through to Kashgar.

More mountains, more frozen wastes, yaks and camels and shaggy ponies. Hundreds of miles, a rudimentary road, landslides, a company of army engineers clearing boulders to let us through. One or two farmhouses—mud construction, metal roofs, half buried in drifts of sand and dust and snow. A face in a barred window. Miles from anywhere, a lone herder, heavy woolen cloak, goat-hair hat rolled down over his ears. He's screaming curses at his goats, a wrecked bicycle hangs on his shoulder.

Late afternoon, a pale sun dying, the three trucks and the SUV pull into the first settlement—three mud houses, a salt-and-tobacco shop, and a very basic restaurant. Dirt floor, dark with one kerosene lantern, one long table with mud benches. An enormous cauldron of water steaming on a wood-fire grate. A cook's table covered with flour, large balls of dough at one end. The cook takes a ball, pulls it out into a rope between his outstretched fists, rolls it in the flour, doubles it, pulls out again. Doubling, ever doubling, flour in clouds, tossing, looping, laughing, singing to his many-stranded rope. Finally, a boy cuts it free from the blobs in each fist, the spaghetti drops into the cauldron. A contribution via Marco Polo to Italy and the West. Soon they're devouring it in thick gravy on tin plates.

To Kashgar in the night. We Americans are escorted to a shabby hotel hiding in a small garden of mistreated palms and flowers. There's a heavy stench from the open ditches of sewage, but there are beds and sheets and water and one electric light and most welcome of all, a toilet that, with some coaxing, flushes.

The next morning it's Sunday, the day of the famous market. On a vast open space, maybe forty acres of packed earth and sand only a few minutes from the center of town on their rented bicycles. An immense crush of people, a wide mix of costumes and colors and tongues. Hundreds of booths and barrows selling everything. Dozens of the spaghetti makers vying for the most spectacular whirlings and twistings of the ever doubling and doubling ropes. Many booths selling snow-leopard skins, powdered tiger testicles. Rows of barbers doing creative things with beards and braids and razors. A track in the midst of the crowd, maybe two or three hundred feet, where gorgeous white stallions are charging back and forth, a line of buyers watching carefully, the riders robes streaming in clouds of dust. A corral with a dozen or so camels being led in circles, some decorated with colorful harnesses. Mats and baskets and carpets and tools. Mountains of grains and fruits and nuts and root vegetables. Meat is sold live by the thousands on the hoof and paw and foot and belly and feather.

Kashgar, in the heart of Xinjiang, an immense oasis at the northwestern end of the Taklamakan Desert, the Go-In-And-You-Won't-Come-Out Desert, with the great barriers of the Pamir mountain ranges to the north and west, the Karakorams and the Himalayas to the south. The Kashgaris are largely Muslim Uighurs and Tajiks, in stark contrast physically, culturally, and religiously to the Han Chinese who are rapidly colonizing the province. The political tensions and distress are similar to the much more widely known situation in Tibet.

A city of mosques, bazaars, forts, and an enormous statue of Mao. Of teeming alleys and wide boulevards, of beggars and the wealthy, of modern encroachment on thousands of years of tradition, of architecture, of culture.

Except for the noodles, they find the Uighur restaurant offerings also unrelated to Han Chinese food. Bread-like little bagels, chickpea salads, dumplings of greens and herbs, pumpkin dumplings with roasted red pepper and yogurt sauce, and pomegranate juice and amazing nougats of honey and nuts and spices at every street corner. Goat-meat

Eating melon in Kashgar, 1989.

kebabs, but we avoid the lung-and-intestine sausage and the goat-head soup. And one of us is vegetarian.

Around the corner from their hotel, we come upon a modern little coffee shop advertising pizza in blue neon. As Fuller travels the world, he always asks for the local equivalent of apple pie-dumpling-tart-etc. That's also on the posted menu. They step in.

Mediocre fare, but at a nearby table we overhear an American voice. A burly young guy with a handsome Chinese companion. They join us. The Chinese is a rock star from Beijing who apparently is allowed much freer travel privileges than most Chinese in those days. For several years, the American has been crewing on commercial fishing boats in Alaskan waters, making something like $15,000 in a short season. He then travels the world. It unfolds that on a recent fishing stint when the season had ended, and they were headed back to port, he'd heard a radio interview of Fuller discussing citizen diplomacy, and he had read through my novel, *The Joshua Tree*. He's the first and only American we were to see in Kashgar.

Stopovers in Urumqui, Beijing, Bangkok. Then several days in Katmandu, particularly to arrange a sister school connection between the Waldorf School on Whidbey Island and an elementary school for the children of the Tibetan refugees there. This was to lead to many exchanges of letters and drawings and photos over the next years.

We write articles about this Asian Vortex, visualized while trapped in Tashkurgan, in several modest-circulation magazines, and op-eds, radio interviews, slide show presentations. There is enough public exposure that in 1988 we are asked to join a private Washington think-tank group to meet up with a quasi-official Soviet delegation and fly in to Kabul to discuss with Afghan leaders how a post-Soviet Afghanistan might evolve.

High-profile Soviets, headed by Primakov, ex-academic, ex-KGB chief, later to become Foreign Minister, special envoy to Saddam—in 2003 he advised Saddam to turn his weapons of mass destruction over to the U.N. and by gesture was told that there weren't any—then was for a short time Prime Minister of Russia until Yeltsin fired him. Low-profile Americans—except perhaps for the head honcho, Robert White, ambassador to El Salvador until Reagan fired him for criticizing U.S. support, legal and illegal, of brutal Central American dictatorships.

Munching smoked fish sandwiches, balancing bottles of beer, an Ilyushin jet entering Afghan airspace. Over Kabul now, still very high, two Soviet MiGs circle them, waggle their wings. Explosions, flares puffing nearby. Assurances that they are friendly, merely precautions, decoys to fool American heat-seeking Stinger missiles now abundant in the hands of the muj. A tight spiraling descent, keeping as clear as possible of the hostile units surrounding the city with their one-man portable missiles. Very steep approach, pulling out at the last second onto a pitted airstrip lined by Soviet tanks.

The Soviet occupation is failing. Twenty thousand Soviet soldiers have been killed, the countryside is everywhere dangerous, Kabul is being shelled by mortars. Much of the impressive infrastructure the Soviets have provided is destroyed. This conference, hosted by Afghan officials, is supposed to be planning for the future when the Soviets have withdrawn.

The Americans caucus in the hotel dining room, the Soviets caucus in the lounge, the Afghans arrive each morning in chauffeured limos, solemn, largely silent, some women in their delegation, none in Primakov's or ours. Talk about development—agriculture, roads, schools, maybe U N help, World Bank, private investors. Maybe this, maybe that. No specific offers. Mostly polite, though Primakov takes a shot at Cabot when, in a short statement on behalf of the American caucus, Cabot fails to address the Afghans as hosts rather than the Soviets. Ow! Well, he had not spoken on behalf of the entire American caucus either, for the think-tank's executive director, who'd had to miss the caucus, outspokenly disagrees with Cabot's therefore unapproved and far too conciliatory tone. Ow! Again.

Afgan/Soviet/U.S. conference as Soviets prepare to leave. On right is Yevgeny Primakov, who later became Soviet prime minister.

There's a meeting of the Soviets and the Americans in the Soviet embassy, a vast fortified compound. Mostly a courtesy, nothing much achieved except an invitation to visit a Red Army camp in the heart of Kabul. We are introduced to a tank commander, look silly climbing up on a tank, watch muscular soldiers in combat fatigues play volleyball. We're offered lemonade in the mess hall, off-duty soldiers stripped to the waist playing chess. And later we are driven a few miles out of the city to see the countryside, but retreat quickly to the sound of nearby small-arms fire. There's a farewell visit to the Afghan Presidential Palace, a reception hosted by President Najibullah, installed by the Soviets in recognition of his brutal leadership of the Afghan secret police.

The last detachments of the Red Army left Afghanistan the next year, 1989. After tumultuous years with various warlords asserting power, in 1996, the Taliban took control of the country, arrested Najibullah, tortured him, castrated him, and executed him.

Robert Fuller engaging with a Soviet general. Kabul, 1988.

❧

It was becoming clear that the Soviet Union was in a deteriorating state. The economy could not sustain an already low standard of living under the burden of the Cold War arms race, their space program, their aid to many other countries and movements where they hoped there could be a tipping of the balance in favor of world-wide communism, and the heavy drain of their failing Afghan adventure. The Soviet response to the ever-clearer signs that they were losing the Cold War struggle was a reluctant pulling back from Afghanistan. In 1989, the Berlin Wall came down, and soon Germany was reunited.

A side-note: Margaret Thatcher, prime minister of Great Britain, was joined by Mitterand, the president of France, in strongly urging Gorbachev, by then president of the Soviet

Union, not to let the Wall come down. She made a special trip to Moscow to make the point. They were terrified of the thought that a united, resurgent Germany would again set out to conquer the world.

The growing power of the West, the growing separatist movements in the eastern European countries that the Soviets had grabbed, the severely overstretched economy, the dissident movements throughout the Soviet Union in spite of the history of brutal repression of dissent, the defeat of the Red Army in Afghanistan—change was inevitable.

In August 1991, Fuller and Cabot are back in Moscow, invited by a friendly member of the Soviet delegation to that 1988 Kabul conference, to join a group of largely Russian friends in an adventure. Together with Sir Edmund Hillary of Everest fame, the plan is to go in a convoy of jeeps from Kyrgyzstan on very rudimentary roads over a pass in the Pamir Mountains and into China. Apparently, it is to be an arduous expedition, and a first gesture—if by no measure other than political—of reconciliation with China. The announced objective is to publicize and help protect that mountain region, as well as to ease lingering tensions between the two empires.

Perhaps it's not much to do with citizen diplomacy, but still, it sounds interesting, and maybe we can renew contacts in Moscow. The Berlin Wall is down, The Red Army is out of Afghanistan. Under the leadership of Gorbachev, there is an easing of tensions, repressions, and Cold War rhetoric—perestroika and glasnost are the catchwords for this radical trend. Hopeful developments.

Early morning, we pull on jogging clothes while watching a news broadcast on the antique TV in our Moscow hotel room—clips of Gorbachev in swim shorts on a Black Sea holiday beach. Off for a run in the park across the street from the fifteen-room family hotel on the outskirts of the city. A peaceful summer morning, Cabot holding Fuller down to an easy jog on the footpaths, alone among the birches and firs. We are soon drawn back to the hotel by the thought of the breakfast we'd been offered. The concierge, a heavy-set babushka—warm smile, kerchief, bare arms—is listening to the radio, martial music. She hands us our key but stops us. She tips her head back, runs an index finger slowly, dramatically across her throat—Gorbachev!

A young Russian entrepreneur friend, already a millionaire in this new economy, had offered to meet us for a meal. We phone him, are told that there's been a coup by a conservative group in the power structure. By the time he arrives in his expensive car, we have decided that rather than be a distraction for friends dealing with the dangerous uncertainties, we had best get out to the airport and hope to get out of the country. Our friend reluctantly agrees to take us to the airport but offers to drive us around Moscow first to see what was going on while keeping in touch with the news on the car radio. The streets and boulevards are largely empty. One or two convoys of Red Army trucks full of solders go by, now and then a tank, but no shots are fired, no commotion until… There is a small crowd in front of the White House, the parliament building of the Russian Republic of the Soviet Union on the banks of the Moscow River, and a seemingly unmanned Red Army tank.

The airport too is unusually quiet. We leave by noon. That afternoon Boris Yeltsin, an often out-of-favor member of the Soviet power structure and elected president of the Russian Federation the preceding month, climbs up on that tank in front of the White House and defiantly urges a general strike in protest of the unconstitutional coup. Two days later Gorbachev is back, the coup leaders arrested, some suicides. Within four months the Soviet Union is dissolved, Gorby retires, Yeltsin becomes the president of the reborn Russian nation.

∽ 30 ∽

History Ends?

WAS THE world at a tipping point? Were we at Fuku-
yama's *The End of History*? Now that the Cold War
had ended, nothing more of concern, peace and dotcom
prosperity for all? At the time, there was much said and
written in the affirmative, even predicting that life would be
bland and boring from now on. Much of the world seemed
to breathe a sigh of relief, to get on with self-indulgent consumerism, get on with enjoying the soap operas of the day
such as the peccadillos of Bill Clinton—Nixon's Watergate
soap twenty years earlier had been diverting too, but harsh
and heavy, while Bill's was sudsy and salacious, quite fitting
for the current mood.

As psychologist Steven Pinker has pointed out, a study
of global statistics regarding such things as poverty, health,
pollution, homicide, and even terrorism fatalities, shows
that we are doing better now when compared with thirty
years ago.

America had been dragged into two world wars during
our century of ascendancy. Those wars reflected a norm for
our species. Throughout history tribalism and greed have
led us into conflict. Great powers clashed, and most people
lived in misery, fear, and hate. Democracy was an exceedingly rare form of government. But since World War II we

have lived in great-power peace, seventy years of global prosperity, and an extraordinary blossoming of democracy.

Think of the transformation of Japan and Germany from brutal expansionist dictatorships to pacifist, successful, thriving democracies. Think of treaties, alliances such as NATO, of the European Union. Of the World Trade Organization. Of the effectiveness, for all its failings, of the United Nations. Think of the peaceful results of threats of nuclear war.

And think of the economic, democratic, and military power that America used to maintain that seventy years of largely peaceful prosperity. We were a successful superpower, however much we were fueled by self-interest, however much that American hegemony was deeply distasteful to many, was inequitable, was driven by the extremes of capitalism, was cynically selective. However, clearly the seeds of disaster were germinating.

Those seeds. The paranoia of McCarthyism, of socialism. The lies and hypocrisies of our foreign policies, of our failed regional wars. Of mankind's degradation in a cyber world. Of our cynical so-called tax reforms. Of racism, white supremacy. Of the denial of global warming. Of the tipping point of Bush v. Gore.

⊷

In the second year of the twenty-first century we are living in Seattle to be near our sons' schools. September, the first days of high school. Amiel, Arian, and Eliza—a school friend boarding with us—are busying about upstairs, readying for breakfast and school. I'm keeping an eye on the morning TV news. There's a sudden jump from humdrum reportage to a view of downtown New York, the Twin Towers, an airplane has crashed into one tower.

Penny, everyone, quick, TV news, crash, come, come!

A second plane is heading in, crashes the other tower. The explosion, the falling bodies, the dust, long seconds, the tower, both towers, they crumble slow-motion into rubble.

America's century in the sun ends. Mankind's history ends when our suicidal actions and inactions succeed.

~31~

Elegies

IN THE LAST decade of the twentieth century I was closing in on old age. The domain of the octogenarian and nonagenerian was just around the corner. I continued with Threshold and some citizen diplomacy, but I was moving inward. My life style was becoming less assertive, less a statement of opposition, of dissent, of unease with privilege. Though I have never let go of my concern for the ever more precarious future of mankind, I was ready to accept the here and now. Family, friends. Beauty, fun, ease. Good health. Reading, writing.

With three novels written, one published and to gratifying reviews, I had a growing urge to re-engage in that inner world of writing fiction.

I spent considerable time working on an earlier manuscript I called *Flotsam*, a look at a world that had suffered the massive destruction of a World War III. I reworked bits of *Nima*, and started yet another novel.

I reread *The Cell* and pondered giving it a new try. I showed it to a friend, Jascha Kessler. He suggested redoing it into a triology of three novellas, leaving out the opening section describing the protagonist and his extreme conditions in a subterranean cell to which he had been driven. The three novellas became substantial rewritings of the three escapes from the cell through elegiac ancestral memories. Kessler recommended the result to his publisher at the time, McPherson & Co. They snapped it up and published it in 1999 as *That Sweetest Wine.*

Thereafter, for several years I did most of my winters writing in a mountain town in Sonora, Mexico, and in recent years in a mountain town in southeast Arizona. In 2012 McPherson & Co. issued my novel, *The Isle of Khería.* I owe special thanks to Bruce McPherson who guided a manuscript entitled *Blue-Eyed Boys* into a very different book. It fictionalizes the often tormented relationship between a somewhat autobiographical me and an epileptic friend modelled to some extent after Kevin Andrews.

At the MacDowell Colony, where I began *The Isle of Khería* in 2001.

~32~

May God Bless America Real Good!

A BIT of a review of where we were, where we are, where we seem to be headed.

Like the president in the early years of America's ascendancy, Teddy Roosevelt, my country was arrogant, ruthless, determined, bent on becoming a colonial power. From the first years of its occupation by Europeans, America was a hypocritically self-righteous country of brutal, even genocidal conquest. It was following the pattern of emerging powers throughout recorded history.

America went on in her century to be engaged in dozens of small-scale military engagements and four more major multi-national wars. World Wars I and II were successes, and for us, those wars were perhaps as just as you can get. The Korean War was at best a draw. The Vietnam War was a massive disaster, Goliath defeated by the insurgent David. In the first decades of the twenty-first century, we are again engaged in bitter wars with insurgencies, wars that may never be clearly won.

Though conspiracy theories abound, with the exception of that century-opener in Cuba and the Philippines, the immediate motivations for our hundred years of wars were not in the territory-grabbing tradition of empire building. At play were and are ideologies, economic self-interests, preemptive defense against terrorists, some degree of humanitarianism, the cynical need of politicians to look good whatever the cost, and arguably our species's lust for war.

That America, after the dissolution of the Soviet Union, was the sole and essential superpower policeman for the world, a world that desperately needed ever more policing, was and is a much-debated motivation. The argument is that, given the frequent paralysis of the United Nations, if the U.S. were not around, ready and able to step in, the world would be a far worse, chaotic, suffering mess. Perhaps. But where none of the other motivations seem compelling, we are often off-duty policemen, or at best reluctant, inadequate—Rwanda, Sudan, the Iraq-Iran war, Ireland, Georgia, Chechnya, Tibet, Ecuador-Peru, Eritrea, Syria, Pakistan-India, Egypt, Libya, on and on, many dozens of insurrections, genocides, brutal injustices, with only the United Nations and occasionally regional forces sometimes able to keep the peace while America sits on the sidelines, or intervenes recklessly, often disastrously, rarely achieving the promised results.

Though the United Nations is often unable to intervene in situations where there are conflicting major-power interests, there are dozens of cases in recent years where the U.N. peacekeepers have sent in coalitions of military forces and controlled threatening conflicts. The U.S. contributes about 30% of the budget for these interventions and provides considerable amounts of technical support and expertise, but without significant numbers of combat troops. It is encouraging to see that the U.N can be an effective policeman. It is discouraging to see that it is largely helpless when the stakes are highest. There are probably as many wars as ever going on today, though the total casualties as a percentage of population are historically much less.

⊕

Measured by gross domestic production, China's economy was the world's largest in the nineteenth century, the American economy was the largest during the twentieth century. By the middle of the twenty-first century, the Chinese economy may be twice that of the American.

America has fallen far behind in health care and education. Even in entrepreneurship and inventiveness, other countries may be moving ahead of us. The better education in sciences and technical skills, as well as lower wages offered by many other countries, is drawing production away from the U.S.

The crass materialism, the destructive, unneeded consumerism that is epitomized in the American culture has spread around the planet. A long and familiar litany. The largely unexamined assumption that economic growth is essential for human wellbeing and happiness. The insatiable demand for fossil fuel energy with its consequences for climate change. The draining of the planet's supplies of fresh water, metal ores, many irreplaceable resources. The ruthless power of multi-national corporations, of monoculture agribusiness. Pollution and the poisoning of our air, our water, our food. The failure to deal with climate change. The abuses of medicines, particularly in animal husbandry, that lead to uncontrollable mutant viruses and bacteria. The list goes on, and the epicenter is so often America.

⊕

There are, of course, other perspectives, other trends, other outcomes. The intellectual flowering of America has its roots in the late eighteenth century with the development of an elite ruling class. It was made up of the descendants of largely upper-class English colonials, men and women of contentious, dissident, freethinking, and often agnostic or atheistic leanings. They were mostly of some wealth, professionals, politicians, well educated—and many were slave owners. They shaped the new country. Several of these founding fathers and mothers were as close as we got to an aristocracy, though many of their class were Loyalists during the Revolution and moved to England. Not until well into the nineteenth century was room found for populism, for those of more humble origins.

I suspect that most of us look to the nineteenth century for the greatest of America's philosophers, essayists, artists, writers. This may be at least partly due to a maturing of opinions, the test of time, but America's intellectual ascendancy in the twentieth century we do largely assign to supremacy in the sciences, applied sciences, technologies, and entrepreneurial and manufacturing abilities. The foundation for that supremacy was public and private education and the general American readiness to take risks, to experiment, to break out of the mold. In the 1880s, my grandfather went to Zürich and England to study engineering. Many of his contemporaries went to Europe to study medicine. In the twentieth century, my father and one brother stayed at Harvard for their engineering degrees, another brother for his medical degree. I never considered going to an English university to study law rather than to an American law school.

Ironically and unjustly, we also benefited enormously, I believe, from our many wars. Their urgency, their call for nationwide sacrifice stimulated innovative, creative thinking and the productive capacity of the people and the economy. Contrary to much of the world, this country suffered no substantial non-military physical damage from war since the Civil War. Our wars were soon paid for with higher taxes and economic growth.

Our economic and military power gave leverage to American zeal in attempting to spread democracy, self-determination, social justice, the rule of law everywhere. Yet our own domestic record was far from perfect. Our idealistic zeal was often naïve, blind, hypocritical, or had to be tempered by pragmatism. But still, there were remarkable advances here in the twentieth century.

America was close to the forefront in extending the vote to women. Some of the barriers to voting for reasons of race and indigence have been removed. Many discriminatory laws, mores, and prejudices have been modified, reflecting a culture of greater tolerance and respect. Support for the rights of gays and for gay marriage is finally emerging. Resistance and backlash to these trends, however, are very much with us as well.

We were also at the forefront in enacting social welfare legislation, particularly during the Great Depression and the middle years of the century—social security, some medical insurance for the elderly and for at least some of the indigent, workmen's compensation, labor laws, and many regulatory laws concerning safety in such areas as transportation, work environment, food and drugs, finance, banking, pollution, sanitation, and many others. Again, though, there is resistance.

Universal medical insurance has still not been achieved, and a backlash was building up which reflected a philosophy spreading among conservatives that government has no business providing safety nets for the needy.

Regulations are eroding under attacks from conservatives and lobbies. The Republican administration during

Reagan's presidency was particularly effective in this attack, and in the Democratic Clinton administration in the 1990s, the erosion worsened. With the Trump administration, the erosion has become a landslide.

With regard to religious tolerance, and the heavy influence of religion on policy in America, there was no great improvement over the century. The 1920s gave us the hypocrisy of the Bible thumpers, chronicled in Sinclair Lewis's *Elmer Gantry*, the moralistic excesses of Prohibition, the blind ignorance of the Scopes trial. True, these were tempered in the 1930s when Roosevelt spearheaded the repeal of Prohibition and creationism was pushed to the fringe. But Americans who felt betrayed by the Great Depression took to cheering gangsters such as Dillinger, turned to the populism of Huey Long, to right wing and anti-Semitic demagogues like Father Coughlin, or to the Communist Party. The Bible bigots continued, moving into the political sphere with often extreme positions. By the 1970s, creationism reemerged, and the white supremacists, the fascists, religious far right loomed ever larger in shaping politics.

There are now polls that reveal a large, growing, but very silent minority of atheists and agnostics. It is not likely, though, that any national politician can successfully emerge from an unbeliever's closet for the foreseeable future. Virtually every major political speech will continue to end with the obligatory, God bless America!

❧

The planet, or much of it, came close to annihilation in the Kennedy administration. The Cold War was at its hottest, the arms race was in full swing, otherwise sane citizens were digging bomb shelters. Our invasion of Castro's Cuba through surrogates failed. The Soviets started building nuclear weapon missile sites there. The Khrushchev-Kennedy game of chicken was a very close call. Yet thirty years later that Cold War was "won," the Soviet Union was no more. The madness of the arms race broke its back. The determination of the Western World, with American leadership, to stand up to the Soviet Union prevailed, whatever the risk and the cost.

⊹

America's century ended with the Clinton administration—for liberals a frustrating and disappointing eight years, his brilliance and charm and his vision were trumped by his penchant for wanting to please whomever he was listening to, by his messy private life, and by his slippery evasions. But he left the country prosperous, with a budget surplus, and at peace.

Will historians tell future generations that in the year 2000, by one vote in its Supreme Court, America, and the world with it, was driven into disaster? That vote gave us Bush instead of Gore. In a very few years, we seemed faced with endless wars, bitter distrust and disillusion, a withdrawal to a do-nothing stance on doomful global warming, the bursting of economic bubbles, devastating recession, a Constitution in tatters, deep budget deficits, legislative paralysis, the domination of the Republican party by deeply retrograde conservatism, the enormous power of wealth in the hands of few. Obama's eight years were largely marking time as the Republicans took over Congress. Isolationist fascism seems the path that we are on with Trump as president. Major shifts in geo-politics and geo-economics are under way, the balance tipping decisively away from America. Her time in the sun seems spectacularly on its way out.

Epilogue

W<small>E</small>—my friends, my colleagues, my generation, my country—have left to our successors a planet in a dreadful, entangled mess, in perhaps fatal danger. A new century, new generations—it is theirs now. Our children are acutely aware of the dubious future, of the risks of hope and of hopelessness, of the imperative to seize each moment. And many are increasingly vocal, determined, liberated from convention and hypocrisy. In them must rest hope.

To have lived through America's century, a bit player, an uncertain voice in the upstage chorus of millions as the glory and the tragedy played out, to have watched what was happening among the lead players downstage, listened to the directors in action. It has been an exhilarating though often deeply depressing, sometimes despairing experience. The entry into the twenty-first century did prove to be a tipping point for both America and me. The downstage lead actor was headed upstage, if not for the wings. I too shall soon leave that stage. One voice in the multitudinous chorus line—the whisper of a few words.

My deepest concern is death—death of our home, our species, our planet, ourselves. The degree of catastrophe from the global warming that we have set in motion. Extinction, immolation in the fires of our glory and greed. The many tipping points in the intricate mechanisms of the planet, of life—are they irreversible, beyond all hope of human control? If the answer is yes, is there an end to the tipping, a balance regained, and when? What will be the condition of our planet? Will our species have survived? How? Where?

I carry a tangle of attitudes, of often conflicting answers to these questions. The evidence keeps pouring in that there are many accelerating factors pointing to irreversible disaster. Unexpected acceleration of ice sheet melt, loss of albedo, enormous quantities of methane predicted from permafrost and clathrate deterioration, acid oceans destroying aquatic life, rising sea levels, drastic implications for agriculture from drought and floods and scorching temperatures, human population increases of several billion in the next three decades, extinction of thousands of species. On and on.

So, both my rational mind and my intuition tell me that the likelihood is very high that catastrophes are imminent, that we are already experiencing some of them, and that at least some of them are, or soon will be, out of the control of mankind. Yet I find it strangely calming, optimistic, to see where my minds have led me. An attitude of appreciation for whatever beauty and love life has given us.

In 2015, my life-long dearest friend, Larry Lunt, died. He had lived for many years in an extraordinarily beautiful high desert home against the Santa Catalina Mountains in Arizona. Debilitated by failing eyesight, deaf, his sense of balance gone, he told me that he had lost all sense of beauty, even in memory. With the beauty that had surrounded him now gone, his life must end. Two weeks later, peacefully, gently, with his deaf and failing dog beside him, he ended their lives.

⟜

Here, an island village on the Pacific edge of my country, and there, a winter home in the high mountains and deserts of Arizona. A richness of family, friends, surrounded by flowers, by love and beauty. By the greatest privilege, my memories.

With Penny in 2010.

Acknowledgements

A Memoir of the American Century—with Bush v. Gore and 9/11/2001 that century has ended. I have chosen to end this memoir here, too. My life's responses to the ever-changing story of that century has been a theme of this memoir. I have selected events in my life that may best reflect these responses. A memoir, not an autobiography. Much of my personal life, particularly in the last three decades, has been largely left out.

Yet there has been a special intimate sweetness to those years, years with a loving family, with a bounty of friends, with joyful adventures, with beauty. I owe so much to so many.

⊸

A special thanks to Penny for her love and support, forty-three years, the second half of my life. Her wisdom, her courage in joining me and my wildly changing lives, her guidance to our children, to the quiet solitudes in nature that enrich us so.

⊸

My children.

Arian, Amiel, Dominic, Sara, Kathy (Alexis absent) in 2014.

Two daughters—boomer babies.

Kathy and Sara making castles in their sand box under the fig trees by our home off the Appia Antica outside Rome. Playing house in Casa Tua, a piano crate I converted for them. Their mother painted and decorated it. They've lived through the second half of my century, through much of the disillusionment of that century, the erosion, yet the lasting beauty of their native lands, Italy and America, of their worlds. They are children of the doomful Nuclear Age, the Cold War with its mutual assured destruction, the catastrophe of global warming. They've felt the brunt of remorseful actions, cruel decisions, mine and others'. And as women, they've found their very different ways to move on through life, on into this new century. With love, with pain, with searing illness, with courage, with caring forgiveness—determined wives, devoted mothers, precious daughters.

Four sons—generation X.

Dominic, at four years old in Spain with his English mother, is presented with an enigmatic new father. He is flown from his natal England and Spain to endless adventures. Bouncing in stormy Mediterranean waves. Watching through the window in his cab-over cubbyhole home-on-wheels, watching this endless country, this America, unroll. Hiking forever in the snowy-top mountains and elks and campfires and very-own tent 'cause I'm five years old now. On and on. Hippy America, back-to-the-earth, Canada. Cows, tractors, parents so busy. Then bad times, good times. A wife, three children, a divorce. Their mother absent, he with the children start a new life in California. A devoted, caring single dad.

Alexis married to the beautiful Pierangela. I watch the video over and over again. The stately ceremony in Rome's City Hall on the Campidoglio, the gorgeous reception on the Appia Antica. Friends, family, so many hugs, kisses. The wedding gown, the party dresses, the lavish dining, the cake. Alexis happy, smiling, laughing, a can-this-be-true? look. And memories of our separation, and of our times together. Climbing New Hampshire's Mount Washington, he skips on ahead. Sailing in *Aeoli*—the Aegean, Patras, Sicilia, Sardegna, Spain. Vesuvius, Amalfi. Moscow, Leningrad. Ibiza for a visit with Mike and Linda, once our neighbors in Rome. Mulinaccio in Tuscany, Whidbey Island, the mountains of southern Arizona. His brilliant mind, his ever seeking for truth. And those Roman pizzas!

And our two youngest sons.

Amiel. As a ten-year-old, he gets that honorable mention award—hanging there in the bathroom window, a wreath of gaudy junk—for the Junk Machine he cobbled together, the Soupbox Race down our hill, tin cans and pots and rattling junk and the brakes just avoid a crash. Hippy days hung on to still. But now is now, and the worst is out there, the Bush disasters, Obama's frustrations, Trump's destructive turmoil. The planet, the wars, earthquakes, hunger, talk of the end. Yes, the worst is there, but the immune systems still do work. Thankfully, the niches are found, Maui, a delightful partner. Photography art, a garden of flowers and veggies and fruit and bees, caring, a looking ahead, a determination to be true to the inner voice whatever the static out there may be.

Arian. The last, the tallest of all in that platoon of sibs. Okay. But wait. It's Fourth of July, your birthday time, you're maybe four? Parade time along the beach, hippy time with the funny floats and silly girls with bunny ears and that Uncle Sam on stilts, and big bro' the clown with a curly red wig, and you this little guy with grandpa's tall gray opera hat—it crushes flat and pops up again good as ever. Events seem kind of muddled there, compressed maybe, but never mind. Jump ahead, way ahead, over those dreadful teachers, over that aborted college start, to many loving friends, to movie grunt work, to reading-reading-reading and writing and writing and music and knowing lots of what ails this world. And to its beauties. Traveling the world to know the world. To settle, for now, a green life of friends and thoughts, creating a growing mini-eco-retreat on a jungled hillside high above a Pacific beach in Nicaragua.

We four survivors in 2012.

My brothers Louis and Tommy, my sister Linda. Though separated by geography for most of our lives, we have remained close friends.

Louis with his remarkable successes as entrepreneur, as CEO, as leader of the Brookings Institution, as leader of our enormous family when our parents died. Tommy with his spectacular grasp of financial planning—mysteries to most of us—his warmth, the traits from our mother that are so strong in him. Linda, her determined self, her unswerving dedication to opera, to her own path.

I have written of several friends in earlier chapters. Kevin Andrews, Luba Radoyce, Manlio and Ana Guberti, Larry Lunt, Mooey, Bob Fuller.

So many others as memories flash by.

Revisiting Paolo, an Italian Communist journalist, and his German wife Ulla—they were central to my life in Rome.

An Australian violinist who became the world's authority on the history of typewriters, a collector of antique clocks, a voluminous writer, too acerbic to be published. Living now on Ibiza.

An American sculptor in Rome, a sculptor's sculptor, as his many fellow sculptors characterized him, who several times moved in with me to deal with his bipolar depressions. Another sculptor, a master of the lost-wax process, and his tough-minded wife—they eventually abandoned the oppression of crowded, noisy Rome to live in the half-abandoned countryside, creating an extraordinary oasis around their home and studio.

A Greek theoretical physicist, Stanford professor, often manic in his Greek exuberance, who moved to Athens to head the government's nuclear research center in Athens—he killed himself in a siege of depression.

A fellow Marshall Planner who became a professor of international law, a peripatetic conciliator, author of such handbooks as *Getting to Yes*.

An aeronautical engineer, escaped to a Buddhist monastery in Japan, who became a successful financial adviser to a wealthy family in Tokyo and eventually moved to Whidbey Island and founded a Zen center.

A lovely naturopath, her ex-hippy entrepreneur husband.

Another Whidbey Islander, a playwright, screenwriter, movie director and producer—a wise and gentle friend.

An accomplished, delightful novelist and her photographer husband.

A host of newfound friends in our winter home in this mountain town in southeast Arizona.

And from earlier years the unforgettable ninety-five-year-old Bill Keys, inspiration for the character of Will Spear in *The Joshua Tree*, who invited me into his life briefly a year before he died. We spent many long evening hours together over cans of Mountain Dew, looking through his scrapbooks, starting with his origins in Russia. Many hours in the desert sun poking about in his lifetime collections as a prospector, miner, rancher, murderer, as a husband and father—his artifacts, tools, photos, albums.

The list can go on, as it could for anyone, and many friends are gone now—living on in memory, in their life's work. One special loss, my brother Ned. Devoted to his family, to his career as a doctor. Lost at sea, sailing off the coast of Newfoundland, a storming sea, a rogue wave, thrown overboard, his beloved sail boat *Cielita* helpless, disappearing into the twilight. A picture that replays endlessly in my mind.

And again, thanks to the remarkable Bruce McPherson for his patience and skills, for his contributions to the art of words.

⌁

Dear friends. Dear family. Dear planet. Beauty abounds—in us, about us. To hold it, to live it, to be it. May it carry us through to whatever will be the end.

Patagonia, Arizona
April 2018
www.robertcabot.com